The Alien Presence

Andrew Parry

Published by Andrew Parry, 2024.

THE ALIEN PRESENCE

First edition. October 9, 2024.

ISBN: 979-8227007575

Written by Andrew Parry.

Table of Contents

Foreword: The Growing Awareness of Alien Phenomena

In recent years, the awareness and interest in UFOs (Unidentified Flying Objects) and UAPs (Unidentified Aerial Phenomena) have surged dramatically. What was once a topic relegated to the fringes of popular culture has now entered mainstream discourse, fueled by an increasing number of personal accounts, video evidence, and even governmental acknowledgment. This rise in visibility has led to a global conversation about the possibility of extraterrestrial life and its implications for humanity. I have personally encountered individuals who have witnessed these phenomena firsthand—people who have seen what are traditionally known as "flying saucers," but are now more commonly referred to as UAPs. These witnesses, once hesitant to speak out due to fear of ridicule or disbelief, are now finding the courage to share their experiences. This shift is part of a broader cultural change, where discussions about UFOs and potential extraterrestrial encounters are no longer dismissed as the domain of conspiracy theorists, but are instead treated with a newfound respect and curiosity.

The evidence supporting these phenomena has grown exponentially. Today, there are countless personal accounts, supported by video recordings and other forms of documentation, that suggest something unexplained is happening in our skies. From military pilots to everyday citizens, people across the globe are reporting encounters with objects that defy conventional explanations. These reports have become so numerous and credible that even governments are beginning to take notice, as evidenced by recent declassified documents and official reports on UAPs.

This book is a reflection of the information that has emerged from this growing body of evidence and public discourse. It is important to clarify that I am not an expert in this field; I have no special access to classified information, nor do I claim to have insider knowledge. The content of this book has been meticulously sourced from publicly available information on the internet. None of the material presented here is new or fictionalized; it is all based on existing reports, studies, and firsthand accounts that have been shared by those who have experienced these phenomena.

The purpose of this book is to compile and present this information in a way that is accessible and informative, allowing readers to explore the many facets of the UFO and UAP phenomena. By bringing together these accounts and sources, I hope to provide a comprehensive overview of what is known—and what remains unknown—about these mysterious occurrences. As you delve into the chapters ahead, you will encounter a wide range of perspectives, from sceptics to believers, from government officials to ordinary people who have had extraordinary experiences. This book is not intended to persuade or dissuade you from any particular viewpoint, but rather to offer you the opportunity to explore the evidence and form your own conclusions about the phenomena that have captivated humanity for generations.

The increase in awareness of UFOs and UAPs signals a shift in how we approach the unknown. As more people come forward and more evidence is analyzed, we are beginning to move beyond fear and skepticism, toward a more open and inquisitive exploration of these phenomena. Whether these encounters represent visitors from other worlds, misunderstood natural phenomena, or something else entirely, the growing awareness and ongoing discussions are leading us to rethink our understanding of the universe and our place within it. In the end, this book is a journey into the unknown—a journey that many of us are already on, whether we realize it or not. As we continue to explore these mysteries, let us do so with an open mind, a critical eye, and a sense of wonder at the possibilities that lie beyond the horizon.

Introduction to the Extraterrestrial Phenomenon

When we consider the vastness of the universe, it's almost inevitable to wonder if we are alone. For centuries, humanity has looked to the stars with a mix of awe, curiosity, and trepidation, pondering the possibility of extraterrestrial life. The idea that we might not be the sole inhabitants of this cosmos has intrigued philosophers, scientists, and dreamers alike. But it's only in recent decades that the concept of extraterrestrial beings visiting Earth has gained significant traction, not just as a matter of science fiction, but as a subject of serious investigation and speculation.

The extraterrestrial phenomenon, as we understand it today, is a complex and multifaceted topic that spans across scientific inquiry, folklore, conspiracy theories, and personal experiences. It is a subject that has captivated millions worldwide, driven by countless reports of unidentified flying objects (UFOs), mysterious encounters, and even alleged abductions by non-human entities. The phenomenon challenges our understanding of reality, pushing the boundaries of what we consider possible and urging us to re-examine our place in the universe.

At the core of this phenomenon is the question: Are we being visited by intelligent beings from other worlds? This question, once relegated to the realms of science fiction, has gained a new level of legitimacy with the increasing number of credible reports and the involvement of respected figures in the scientific community. The topic of UFOs, for instance, has evolved from being a subject of ridicule to one of serious consideration, especially with recent acknowledgments from government agencies, including the U.S. Department of Defense, that these unidentified aerial phenomena (UAPs) do indeed exist and remain unexplained.

Witnesses and researchers have reported a variety of experiences that suggest interactions with beings not of this Earth. These range from fleeting sightings of strange craft in the sky to detailed accounts of abductions where individuals claim to have been taken aboard extraterrestrial vessels. While many of these accounts are met with skepticism, the sheer volume and consistency of reports across different cultures and time periods suggest that something extraordinary might be happening.

Throughout history, different civilizations have recorded their encounters with beings from the skies. Ancient texts, cave paintings, and religious scriptures often describe gods or celestial beings descending from the heavens, sometimes in what could be interpreted as advanced technological craft. The Vedas of ancient India, for example, speak of flying machines called "Vimanas," while the Bible recounts the prophet Ezekiel's vision of a "wheel within a wheel," which some modern theorists interpret as a UFO sighting.

In modern times, the phenomenon has become more defined, with specific alien races being identified by witnesses and researchers. These races, including the Greys, the Reptilians, and the Nordics, among others, have become central to the discourse on extraterrestrial life. Each of these alleged species comes with its own set of characteristics, behaviors, and intentions towards humanity, as described by those who claim to have encountered them.

The Greys, perhaps the most well-known of these races, are often described as small beings with large heads and almond-shaped black eyes. They are frequently associated with abduction scenarios, where individuals report being taken aboard their craft for medical examinations. The Reptilians, on the other hand, are depicted as tall, humanoid beings with reptilian features, often believed to be malevolent and involved in a secret agenda to control humanity. The Nordics, in contrast, are described as tall, blonde, and human-like, often seen as benevolent and concerned with the spiritual evolution of mankind.

These accounts, while fascinating, also raise many questions. Are these beings truly extraterrestrial in nature, or could they be interdimensional entities, visitors from parallel realities, or even manifestations of our collective unconscious? The truth remains elusive, shrouded in mystery and speculation.

Adding to the complexity of the phenomenon is the role of government secrecy. Numerous accounts suggest that governments, particularly that of the United States, have been aware of extraterrestrial presence for decades but have actively suppressed this information. The infamous Roswell incident of 1947, where an alleged UFO crashed in New Mexico, is often cited as the beginning of this cover-up. Despite official statements dismissing the event as a weather balloon crash, many believe that the government recovered alien technology and even bodies, sparking a massive disinformation campaign to keep the truth hidden.

This alleged cover-up extends to various secret programs and facilities, such as Area 51, where it's believed that recovered alien technology is being reverse-engineered. Whistle-blowers like Bob Lazar have come forward with claims of having worked on extraterrestrial technology within these secret bases, further fueling the belief that the government knows far more than it is willing to disclose.

In recent years, the push for disclosure has gained momentum, with activists, former military personnel, and even politicians calling for the release of classified information on UFOs and extraterrestrial life. Organizations like Dr. Steven Greer's Disclosure Project have been at the forefront of this movement, gathering testimonies from credible witnesses who allege that humanity has been in contact with extraterrestrial civilizations for decades.

Despite these efforts, the mainstream scientific community remains largely skeptical, often citing the lack of empirical evidence and the challenges of studying a phenomenon that is elusive and often anecdotal. However, the growing body of credible reports and the increasing number of serious investigations into the phenomenon suggest that the question of extraterrestrial life may eventually move from the fringes of science to its forefront.

As we embark on this exploration of alien races and the extraterrestrial phenomenon, it is important to keep an open mind while remaining critical of the sources and the information we encounter. The subject is rife with speculation, hoaxes, and disinformation, but it also holds the potential to expand our understanding of the universe and our place within it.

In this book, we will delve into the different types of alien races that have been reported, examining their characteristics, motivations, and the evidence that supports their existence. We will explore the testimonies of witnesses, the research of ufologists, and the theories that have emerged over the years. By the end of this journey, you may find yourself rethinking what you know about the universe, and perhaps even questioning the very nature of reality itself.

The Greys: Humanity's Most Frequent Visitors

The Greys have become one of the most iconic representations of extraterrestrial beings in popular culture and ufology. Their image is instantly recognizable: small, slender bodies, disproportionately large heads, and those haunting, almond-shaped black eyes. But beyond their visual depiction, the Greys are often cited as the most frequent visitors to our planet, involved in a multitude of encounters, abductions, and mysterious interactions with humans. This chapter will delve into the origins of the Greys, their alleged activities, and the evidence that has led many to believe they are real.

The origin of the Greys as a concept in ufology can be traced back to the 20th century, particularly with the rise of reported alien abductions. One of the most famous cases that brought the Greys into public awareness was the 1961 abduction of Betty and Barney Hill. The Hills, an ordinary couple from New Hampshire, claimed to have been taken aboard a spacecraft by small, gray-skinned beings with large heads and eyes. Their detailed account, under hypnosis, described these beings conducting medical examinations on them, an element that would become a recurring theme in many abduction stories to follow.

The Greys are often associated with this type of invasive medical procedure, which some abductees describe as cold, clinical, and devoid of empathy. This has led to the perception of the Greys as emotionally detached, highly intelligent beings, more interested in scientific study than in establishing a relationship with humanity. Many of those who claim to have encountered the Greys report feelings of helplessness and fear, as if they were mere subjects in an experiment beyond their control.

One of the most intriguing aspects of the Greys is the consistency with which they are described across different cultures and time periods. Reports of encounters with beings that resemble the Greys come not just from modern-day America, but from all over the world, including Europe, South America, and Asia. Even ancient cultures have left behind artifacts and writings that some interpret as depicting similar beings. For example, some point to the ancient Sumerian carvings of the Anunnaki, or the depictions of the "gods" in ancient Egyptian hieroglyphs, as evidence that encounters with the Greys—or beings like them—are not a recent phenomenon.

The question of where the Greys come from has been the subject of much speculation. Some ufologists believe they originate from the Zeta Reticuli star system, a binary star system located approximately 39 light-years from Earth. This belief is partly based on the testimony of Betty Hill, who, under hypnosis, recalled seeing a "star map" shown to her by one of the beings. Later, amateur astronomer Marjorie Fish created a model that matched Betty's recollection to the Zeta Reticuli system, further fueling this theory.

Theories about the Greys' intentions vary widely. Some believe they are here to study us, perhaps as part of a long-term research project to understand human biology, behavior, and evolution. This would explain the numerous reports of abductions where subjects are examined, and in some cases, even impregnated with hybrid embryos—a topic that opens up a whole new avenue of speculation about the Greys' genetic agenda.

Others propose a more sinister motive, suggesting that the Greys are part of a larger plan to control or manipulate humanity. Some conspiracy theories suggest that the Greys are working with, or even controlling, certain government bodies, providing advanced technology in exchange for the freedom to conduct their experiments unhindered. The infamous "Majestic 12" documents, though widely regarded as a hoax by mainstream historians, suggest that such a relationship might exist, with secret government factions collaborating with extraterrestrial entities.

Sceptics argue that the consistency in descriptions of the Greys is more likely due to cultural diffusion and the influence of media. As the image of the Greys has become more ingrained in popular culture—through films, books, and television—people might be more likely to report seeing what they have already been exposed to. This could explain why so many alien abduction stories involve beings that look like the Greys, even if they are simply figments of the imagination or sleep-induced hallucinations.

However, those who have experienced encounters with the Greys often vehemently deny that their experiences were mere dreams or fantasies. The physical and psychological effects reported by abductees—ranging from unexplained scars and implants to post-traumatic stress disorder—suggest that something very real is happening to these individuals. In some cases, abductees report "missing time," where they lose hours or even days of their lives with no memory of what occurred, only to later recall their experiences through hypnosis or spontaneous recollection.

One of the most perplexing aspects of the Grey phenomenon is the alleged involvement of hybridization programs. Numerous abductees have claimed that the Greys are engaged in a systematic effort to create a hybrid race, blending human and Grey DNA. These hybrids are often described as being more human-like in appearance but retaining the large eyes and heads characteristic of the Greys. Some abductees even claim to have been shown their hybrid offspring during their encounters, adding a deeply personal and emotional layer to the experience.

This notion of a hybridization program has led some researchers to speculate that the Greys are a dying race, seeking to rejuvenate their gene pool by integrating human genetic material. Others suggest that the hybrids are being created as a bridge between our species, possibly to prepare humanity for eventual contact or integration into a broader cosmic community.

The idea that the Greys are involved in genetic experimentation raises profound ethical and existential questions. If true, it implies that humanity is not the sole proprietor of its genetic destiny, and that our evolution might be influenced—or even controlled—by extraterrestrial forces. This would have staggering implications for our understanding of free will, sovereignty, and the nature of our existence.

In conclusion, the Greys remain one of the most enduring and enigmatic elements of the extraterrestrial phenomenon. Whether they are benevolent scientists, malevolent manipulators, or something else entirely, their presence in the narratives of countless abductees and witnesses cannot be easily dismissed. As we continue to explore the mysteries of the universe and our place within it, the Greys will undoubtedly remain a focal point of both fascination and fear. Whether they are real or a product of our collective imagination, the Greys challenge us to confront the unknown and to question what it means to be human in a universe that may be far more complex and inhabited than we ever imagined.

The Reptilians: Theories of Control and Domination

The Reptilians, also known as Reptoids, are one of the most controversial and sinister figures in the landscape of extraterrestrial lore. Described as tall, humanoid beings with reptilian features, the Reptilians are often portrayed as malevolent entities with a deep-seated desire for control and domination over humanity. This chapter delves into the origins, characteristics, and theories surrounding the Reptilians, exploring why they have become such a focal point in discussions of alien influence and conspiracy theories.

The image of the Reptilian is one that taps into some of humanity's oldest fears. Reptiles, with their cold-blooded nature and predatory instincts, have long been symbols of danger and evil in various mythologies and religions. The Reptilians, as they are described in modern UFO and conspiracy theories, embody these attributes but on a far grander scale, often portrayed as the masterminds behind global power structures, manipulating events from the shadows.

The concept of Reptilians gained significant traction in the late 20th century, largely thanks to the work of individuals like David Icke, a British conspiracy theorist who popularized the idea that these beings are not only real but deeply embedded in our society. Icke's theories propose that the Reptilians are shape-shifters, capable of assuming human form, and that they have infiltrated positions of power across the world, from political leaders to members of royal families. According to Icke, these Reptilian entities are responsible for much of the suffering and corruption in the world, using their influence to steer humanity toward a dystopian future where they can maintain control.

While Icke's theories are often dismissed by the mainstream as outlandish, the idea of Reptilian influence has persisted, fueled by reports from individuals who claim to have encountered these beings. These encounters are usually described as deeply unsettling, with the Reptilians exuding an aura of coldness and superiority. Witnesses often report seeing these beings in positions of authority or in military settings, further feeding into the idea that they are involved in global governance.

The Reptilians are typically depicted as tall, muscular beings, often standing between 6 to 8 feet tall, with green, scaly skin, sharp claws, and snake-like eyes. Some accounts describe them as having wings or tails, while others focus on their ability to shape-shift or project an illusion of human appearance. This shape-shifting ability is a crucial aspect of the Reptilian narrative, as it allows them to blend in with human society and manipulate events without detection.

One of the most prominent theories about the Reptilians is that they are an ancient race, possibly originating from the constellation Draco, which has been associated with dragons and serpents in various mythologies. According to this theory, the Reptilians came to Earth thousands of years ago and have been influencing human civilization ever since. Some proponents of this theory suggest that the Reptilians were worshipped as gods in ancient times, with their likenesses appearing in various cultures' depictions of serpentine deities, such as the serpent in the Garden of Eden or the feathered serpent god Quetzalcoatl in Mesoamerican lore.

The idea that the Reptilians are interdimensional beings, rather than extraterrestrial, has also been proposed. In this view, the Reptilians exist in a dimension parallel to ours and have found ways to cross over into our reality. This theory is often linked to accounts of people experiencing encounters with Reptilians during altered states of consciousness, such as through meditation, near-death experiences, or the use of psychedelics. These encounters suggest that the Reptilians might have the ability to manipulate consciousness and reality itself, further enhancing their perceived power and influence.

Another aspect of the Reptilian narrative is their supposed involvement in human genetics. Some theories suggest that the Reptilians have been experimenting on humans for centuries, possibly even manipulating our DNA to create a hybrid species that they can control. This idea is closely tied to the concept of the "Illuminati," a shadowy group believed by some to be composed of Reptilian hybrids who hold positions of power and use their influence to push humanity toward a one-world government—a New World Order under Reptilian control.

Sceptics argue that the Reptilian theory is a modern reinterpretation of age-old fears and myths, projected onto the unknown. They suggest that the Reptilian narrative may be a psychological response to the alienation and distrust many people feel toward those in power, symbolizing the perceived inhumanity of the ruling elite. The Reptilian archetype, with its cold-blooded nature and deceptive appearance, serves as a metaphor for the perceived lack of empathy and transparency in global leadership.

Despite the skepticism, the Reptilian theory continues to captivate the imagination of many. The idea that an ancient, malevolent race could be orchestrating world events from behind the scenes resonates with those who feel powerless in the face of global crises and corruption. For these believers, the Reptilians provide a convenient explanation for the world's ills, offering a narrative that aligns with their perceptions of reality.

One of the more disturbing aspects of the Reptilian theory is the alleged human sacrifices and rituals that some claim are performed by Reptilians or their human allies. These rituals are said to involve the consumption of human flesh or blood, which supposedly sustains the Reptilians' physical form or gives them the energy they need to maintain their human guise. While these claims are often dismissed as the stuff of horror fiction, they have nevertheless become an integral part of the Reptilian lore, further contributing to their fearsome reputation.

The Reptilian narrative is also tied to various secret societies, such as the Freemasons and the aforementioned Illuminati. Proponents of the theory suggest that these societies are fronts for Reptilian activity, serving as networks through which they can exert their influence and control over human affairs. Symbols associated with these societies, such as the all-seeing eye or the serpent, are often interpreted as evidence of Reptilian involvement.

In conclusion, the Reptilians represent one of the most complex and controversial elements of the extraterrestrial phenomenon. Whether seen as literal beings, metaphorical representations, or psychological projections, the Reptilians embody deep-seated fears of deception, control, and the loss of human sovereignty. As we continue to explore the mysteries of our world and the possibility of extraterrestrial life, the Reptilians will likely remain a compelling, if unsettling, aspect of the conversation. Their narrative challenges us to question who—or what—might truly be pulling the strings behind the scenes, and to what end.

Nordics and the Pleiadians: Guardians of Humanity?

The Nordics and the Pleiadians represent a stark contrast to the sinister reputation of the Greys and Reptilians in the landscape of extraterrestrial lore. Often described as benevolent, spiritually advanced beings, these entities are said to have a deep connection with humanity, acting as protectors, guides, and even distant relatives. This chapter explores the origins, characteristics, and roles attributed to the Nordics and Pleiadians, examining why they are often seen as the guardians of humanity.

The Nordics, as their name suggests, are typically described as tall, fair-skinned, and blonde-haired, with blue or light-coloured eyes. Their appearance is strikingly similar to the idealized image of a Scandinavian or Nordic person, which has led some to question whether these beings are truly extraterrestrial or if they are a projection of cultural ideals. Regardless of their origins, those who claim to have encountered Nordics often describe them as peaceful, wise, and deeply concerned with the well-being of humanity and the planet.

The Pleiadians are closely related to the Nordics in both description and reputation. They are said to originate from the Pleiades star cluster, a group of stars visible to the naked eye and often associated with mythology and folklore. The Pleiadians are believed to be a highly advanced race, both technologically and spiritually, and are often depicted as the teachers and guides of humanity, helping us evolve and ascend to higher levels of consciousness.

One of the key figures who popularized the concept of the Pleiadians is Billy Meier, a Swiss farmer who claimed to have had contact with beings from the Pleiades since the 1940s. According to Meier, the Pleiadians, or Plejarens as they prefer to be called, are here to help humanity navigate the challenges of the modern world and to prepare us for our eventual integration into a broader galactic community. Meier's accounts, though controversial and often disputed, have played a significant role in shaping the modern perception of the Pleiadians.

The message of the Pleiadians, as conveyed through Meier and other contactees, often revolves around themes of peace, love, and spiritual awakening. They are said to emphasize the importance of living in harmony with the Earth and with each other, advocating for a shift away from materialism and toward a more spiritually oriented society. This message has resonated with many people, particularly those involved in New Age and spiritual movements, where the Pleiadians are often revered as enlightened beings who have come to guide humanity toward a brighter future.

Encounters with Nordics and Pleiadians are often described as deeply positive and transformative experiences. Those who claim to have been contacted by these beings report feelings of immense love, peace, and understanding, as if they were in the presence of a higher, more evolved consciousness. These encounters are often seen as a wake-up call, urging the individual to embark on a path of spiritual growth and self-discovery.

One of the most intriguing aspects of the Nordics and Pleiadians is the belief that they are somehow related to humanity, either as distant ancestors or as a parallel branch of human evolution. Some theories suggest that the Nordics are an ancient race that seeded life on Earth, which would make them our creators or at least our genetic cousins. This idea is often linked to the concept of "Ancient Astronauts," which posits that advanced extraterrestrial beings visited Earth in the distant past and played a key role in the development of human civilization.

This theory is supported by various myths and legends from around the world that speak of gods or celestial beings who descended from the heavens to teach and guide humanity. The Pleiadians, in particular, are often associated with the idea of a lost golden age when humanity lived in harmony with these advanced beings. According to some accounts, the Pleiadians withdrew from direct contact with humanity as we became more warlike and materialistic, but they continue to watch over us, waiting for the right time to return and help us reclaim our lost potential.

In modern times, the Pleiadians and Nordics are often portrayed as part of a larger galactic federation, a coalition of advanced civilizations working together to promote peace and stability in the universe. This federation is said to be involved in a cosmic struggle against darker forces, such as the Reptilians, who seek to dominate and enslave less advanced races. In this narrative, the Pleiadians and Nordics are seen as our allies, working behind the scenes to protect humanity from these malevolent forces and to prepare us for eventual contact with the broader galactic community.

However, not all accounts of the Nordics are purely benevolent. Some researchers and abductees have reported encounters where the Nordics appeared to be working alongside the Greys or even the Reptilians, suggesting a more complex relationship between these different alien races. In these accounts, the Nordics are often portrayed as cold and detached, more interested in their own agendas than in helping humanity. This has led to speculation that the Nordics, like the Reptilians, may be involved in genetic experimentation or other activities that are not entirely altruistic.

Despite these darker accounts, the overwhelming majority of reports involving Nordics and Pleiadians depict them as positive, benevolent beings who genuinely care about the future of humanity. Their message of peace, love, and spiritual growth continues to inspire many people, offering hope in a world that often seems dominated by conflict and materialism.

The idea that advanced, benevolent beings are watching over humanity, guiding us through our challenges and helping us evolve, is a comforting one. It suggests that we are not alone in the universe and that there are forces out there that genuinely care about our well-being. Whether or not the Nordics and Pleiadians are real, their presence in the collective consciousness reflects our deep-seated desire for guidance, protection, and a connection to something greater than ourselves.

In conclusion, the Nordics and Pleiadians represent a fascinating and uplifting aspect of the extraterrestrial phenomenon. Whether viewed as literal beings or as symbolic representations of humanity's potential for growth and enlightenment, they offer a vision of the future where we are not only part of a vast and interconnected universe but also destined for a higher purpose. As we continue to explore the mysteries of the cosmos, the Nordics and Pleiadians will undoubtedly remain central figures in our quest for understanding and our hope for a brighter future.

Insectoids: The Mysterious Mantid Beings

In the diverse and often bizarre world of reported extraterrestrial encounters, few beings are as enigmatic and unsettling as the Insectoids, particularly the Mantid beings. These creatures, resembling oversized praying mantises, have been described by numerous witnesses and abductees as being highly intelligent, emotionally detached, and sometimes even compassionate, despite their frightening appearance. This chapter delves into the characteristics, roles, and theories surrounding the Mantid beings, exploring why these Insectoids occupy such a unique place in the pantheon of alien species.

The Mantid beings are typically described as tall, insect-like creatures, standing between 6 to 9 feet tall, with long, slender limbs, a triangular head, and large, wraparound eyes. Their appearance is often compared to that of a praying mantis, with a similar structure and demeanor. Witnesses frequently describe these beings as having a green or brownish exoskeleton, adding to their insect-like qualities. Despite their fearsome appearance, many who have encountered Mantids report that these beings radiate a sense of calm intelligence, and some even describe their interactions as strangely comforting.

Encounters with Mantid beings are often reported in the context of abductions, where the Mantids appear to play a supervisory or managerial role. In these scenarios, the Mantids are often seen overseeing the actions of the Greys or other beings, directing them in their activities. This has led some researchers to speculate that the Mantids are higher up in the hierarchy of extraterrestrial races, possibly acting as leaders or commanders within a broader extraterrestrial network.

One of the most striking aspects of the Mantid beings is their reported ability to communicate telepathically. Witnesses often describe receiving complex thoughts, images, or emotions directly from the Mantids, bypassing the need for spoken language. This telepathic communication is usually described as clear and precise, with the Mantids conveying their intentions and instructions with remarkable clarity. Some abductees have reported that the Mantids can also induce a state of calm or even euphoria during these encounters, which may help to explain why some individuals feel less fear in the presence of these otherwise terrifying beings.

The purpose of the Mantids' involvement in human affairs is a subject of much speculation. Some believe that they are deeply involved in genetic experiments, possibly related to hybridization programs. In this view, the Mantids may be responsible for overseeing the creation and development of human-alien hybrids, ensuring that the process proceeds according to plan. This would align with the reports of their supervisory role during abductions, where they are often seen directing the actions of other beings.

Others suggest that the Mantids are more interested in the evolution of consciousness and may be playing a role in guiding humanity toward a higher state of awareness. This theory posits that the Mantids, despite their insect-like appearance, are highly evolved spiritual beings who are concerned with the spiritual development of humanity. Some abductees have reported receiving profound insights or spiritual awakenings following their encounters with Mantids, which supports the idea that these beings may be involved in more than just physical or genetic experimentation.

There are also darker interpretations of the Mantid phenomenon. Some researchers believe that the Mantids may be part of a larger, more sinister agenda, using their advanced intelligence and abilities to manipulate or control humanity. In this view, the Mantids could be seen as cold, calculating entities who view humans as mere subjects in a grand experiment, with little regard for individual autonomy or well-being. The reports of their involvement in abductions, where individuals are often taken against their will and subjected to invasive procedures, lend some weight to this more disturbing interpretation.

The appearance of the Mantids in various cultures and mythologies is another intriguing aspect of their presence in the UFO phenomenon. In some traditions, insect-like beings are seen as messengers or intermediaries between the human world and the divine. For example, in Native American folklore, the praying mantis is often regarded as a symbol of patience and stillness, and in some African traditions, it is seen as a guide or protector. These cultural associations suggest that the Mantids, if they exist, may have been interacting with humanity for a very long time, possibly even shaping some of our ancient beliefs and symbols.

The psychological impact of encounters with Mantid beings cannot be understated. The juxtaposition of their alien, insect-like appearance with their apparent intelligence and sometimes even benevolence creates a cognitive dissonance that can be deeply unsettling. Many who have encountered Mantids describe feeling a mix of awe, fear, and fascination, as if they are in the presence of something truly otherworldly. This emotional and psychological impact is a common theme in abduction experiences, where the sheer strangeness of the encounter challenges the individual's sense of reality and self.

Sceptics of the Mantid phenomenon argue that these beings are likely a projection of the human subconscious, perhaps arising from deep-seated fears or archetypes related to insects. The praying mantis, with its predatory nature and alien-like appearance, is a creature that has long evoked a sense of unease in humans. It is possible that the Mantid beings are a manifestation of this unease, brought to life in the context of abduction experiences or altered states of consciousness. This interpretation aligns with psychological theories that suggest many aspects of the UFO phenomenon are the result of internal psychological processes rather than external reality.

However, for those who have encountered Mantid beings, the experience often feels as real as any other event in their lives. The consistency of these reports, across different cultures and individuals who have no prior knowledge of each other's experiences, suggests that there may be more to the Mantid phenomenon than simple psychology. The telepathic communication, the detailed descriptions of their appearance and behavior, and the profound impact these encounters have on the witnesses all point to something that is, at the very least, worthy of serious investigation.

In conclusion, the Mantid beings represent one of the most mysterious and unsettling aspects of the extraterrestrial phenomenon. Whether they are benevolent guides, cold-hearted experimenters, or something in between, their presence in the narratives of countless abductees and witnesses cannot be easily dismissed. The Mantids challenge our understanding of life, intelligence, and the possible connections between the physical and spiritual realms. As we continue to explore the depths of the UFO phenomenon, the Mantids will undoubtedly remain a subject of fascination, fear, and intense scrutiny. Their story is a reminder that the universe may be far stranger and more complex than we can currently comprehend, with beings that defy our expectations of what life beyond Earth might look like.

The Annunaki: Ancient Gods or Alien Overlords?

The Anunnaki are one of the most intriguing and controversial figures in the study of ancient civilizations and extraterrestrial theories. Often depicted as powerful deities in ancient Sumerian texts, the Anunnaki have been reinterpreted by modern theorists as potential extraterrestrial beings who played a significant role in the development of human civilization. This chapter explores the origins of the Anunnaki, their depiction in ancient mythology, and the theories that suggest they may

have been alien overlords rather than mere gods.

The story of the Anunnaki begins in ancient Mesopotamia, specifically within the Sumerian civilization, one of the earliest known civilizations in human history. The Anunnaki were considered a group of deities associated with the creation of mankind and the governance of the world. The name "Anunnaki" is often translated as "those who from the heavens came to Earth," which has fueled much speculation about their possible extraterrestrial origins.

According to Sumerian mythology, the Anunnaki were the offspring of Anu, the sky god, and Ki, the Earth goddess. They were said to dwell in the heavens but frequently descended to Earth to oversee human affairs. The Anunnaki played a central role in the creation myth known as the Enuma Elish, where they are depicted as powerful beings who shaped the world and brought order to chaos. Among the most well-known Anunnaki figures are Enlil, the god of air and storms, and Enki, the god of water, knowledge, and creation.

In these ancient texts, the Anunnaki are often portrayed as both benevolent and malevolent, capable of great kindness and wrath. They were deeply involved in the lives of humans, sometimes aiding them and other times punishing them for their transgressions. The Sumerians believed that the Anunnaki were responsible for the creation of mankind, fashioned from clay and imbued with the breath of life to serve the gods.

This narrative of the Anunnaki as creators and rulers of humanity has been reinterpreted by modern theorists, particularly by those who subscribe to the ancient astronaut theory. This theory, popularized by authors such as Zecharia Sitchin, suggests that the Anunnaki were not mythological gods but rather advanced extraterrestrial beings who visited Earth in the distant past. According to Sitchin's interpretation of Sumerian texts, the Anunnaki came from a planet called Nibiru, a mysterious celestial body that allegedly orbits the sun in a long, elliptical path, making its approach to Earth every 3,600 years.

Sitchin's theories propose that the Anunnaki came to Earth in search of gold, a metal they needed to repair their planet's atmosphere. To facilitate their mining operations, the Anunnaki supposedly created humans as a slave species, genetically engineering them from primitive hominids. This idea has captured the imagination of many, offering an alternative explanation for the sudden rise of advanced civilizations in Mesopotamia and the unexplained leaps in human development.

Critics of Sitchin's work argue that his translations and interpretations of Sumerian texts are flawed and that there is no credible evidence to support the existence of Nibiru or the idea that the Anunnaki were extraterrestrial beings. Mainstream scholars maintain that the Anunnaki were purely mythological figures, symbolic of the natural forces and aspects of life that the Sumerians sought to understand and appease.

Despite these criticisms, the idea of the Anunnaki as alien overlords has persisted, largely due to the enigmatic nature of Sumerian civilization and the tantalizing similarities between their myths and the stories found in other ancient cultures. For example, the biblical story of the Nephilim, a race of giants born from the union of "the sons of God" and human women, bears a resemblance to the Anunnaki narrative. Some theorists suggest that the Nephilim were, in fact, the offspring of the Anunnaki, further blurring the lines between mythology and potential extraterrestrial influence.

Another aspect of the Anunnaki story that has intrigued researchers is the advanced knowledge and technology attributed to the Sumerians. The Sumerians are credited with numerous innovations, including the development of writing, the construction of ziggurats (massive terraced structures), and the creation of sophisticated astronomical charts. Some proponents of the ancient astronaut theory argue that such knowledge could not have been developed independently by a primitive society and must have been imparted by the Anunnaki.

The construction of the ziggurats, in particular, is often cited as evidence of the Anunnaki's presence on Earth. These massive structures, which served as temples and places of worship, were built with remarkable precision and alignment to celestial bodies. Some theorists believe that the ziggurats were not just temples but also landing platforms for the Anunnaki's spacecraft, further supporting the idea of their extraterrestrial origins.

The concept of the Anunnaki as ancient gods or alien overlords has also found its way into various conspiracy theories, particularly those involving the idea of a secret, ruling elite. Some believe that the descendants of the Anunnaki still walk among us today, hidden in plain sight as powerful individuals who control global affairs from behind the scenes. This theory is often linked to the idea of the Illuminati or other secret societies, suggesting that these groups are carrying out the Anunnaki's original agenda of controlling and manipulating humanity.

The psychological impact of the Anunnaki narrative cannot be ignored. The idea that humanity was created not by divine intervention but by extraterrestrial manipulation challenges many deeply held beliefs about our origins and purpose. For some, the Anunnaki story offers an alternative understanding of human history, one that explains the sudden rise of advanced civilizations and the inexplicable knowledge possessed by ancient cultures. For others, it raises uncomfortable questions about free will, sovereignty, and the true nature of our existence.

Whether viewed as ancient gods, alien overlords, or simply mythological figures, the Anunnaki continue to captivate the imagination of those who seek to understand the mysteries of our past. Their story serves as a reminder of the enduring power of mythology and its ability to shape our perceptions of reality. As we continue to explore the boundaries between history, mythology, and science fiction, the Anunnaki will undoubtedly remain a central figure in the ongoing quest to uncover the truth about humanity's origins.

In conclusion, the Anunnaki represent one of the most compelling intersections of ancient mythology and modern extraterrestrial theories. Whether they were gods, aliens, or purely symbolic figures, their influence on human culture and history is undeniable. As we delve deeper into the mysteries of the past, the Anunnaki challenge us to reconsider what we know about the origins of civilization and the possibility that we may not be alone in the universe. Their story invites us to explore the boundaries of our understanding and to remain open to the idea that the truth, whatever it may be, is far stranger than we can imagine.

The Tall Whites: Cooperation or Coercion?

The Tall Whites are among the more enigmatic figures in the complex tapestry of extraterrestrial encounters. Unlike the Greys or the Reptilians, who are often depicted as either neutral or malevolent, the Tall Whites occupy a more ambiguous space, with their motives and interactions with humanity being the subject of much debate. Some accounts describe the Tall Whites as cooperative and even benevolent, while others suggest a more coercive relationship with humans, particularly with certain government entities. This chapter delves into the origins, characteristics, and theories surrounding the Tall Whites, exploring the dual narratives of cooperation and coercion that have emerged in relation to this mysterious race.

The Tall Whites, as their name suggests, are characterized by their impressive height, often described as being between 6 to 7 feet tall, though some reports suggest they can be even taller. They are said to have a slender, graceful build, with very pale, almost translucent skin, and large, almond-shaped eyes that are often blue or pinkish in hue. Their hair is typically described as white or platinum blonde, adding to their ethereal, almost otherworldly appearance. Unlike the Greys, who are often depicted as emotionless, the Tall Whites are sometimes described as possessing a more human-like range of emotions, although they are also frequently portrayed as aloof and distant.

One of the most well-known sources of information about the Tall Whites comes from Charles Hall, a former United States Air Force weather observer, who claims to have encountered these beings while stationed at Nellis Air Force Base in Nevada during the 1960s. According to Hall, the Tall Whites had established a base of operations in the Nevada desert, where they maintained a complex underground facility. Hall's accounts describe the Tall Whites as being technologically advanced and capable of interacting with humans in a variety of ways, from simple observation to more direct communication.

Hall's interactions with the Tall Whites, as detailed in his books and interviews, suggest a relationship that is both cooperative and cautious. He describes the Tall Whites as being highly protective of their privacy and territory, often reacting defensively if they felt threatened. At the same time, Hall recounts instances where the Tall Whites demonstrated a willingness to cooperate with humans, sharing limited technology and information, particularly with military personnel. However, this cooperation was always on their terms, with strict boundaries and an underlying sense of tension.

The narrative of cooperation is further supported by accounts that suggest the Tall Whites have engaged in agreements with certain government entities, particularly within the United States. These agreements, if they exist, are believed to involve the exchange of advanced technology for access to Earth's resources or for the freedom to conduct their activities with minimal interference. Some theorists argue that the Tall Whites have been instrumental in the development of certain military technologies, particularly in the fields of aerospace and weaponry. However, due to the secretive nature of these alleged agreements, hard evidence is difficult to come by, and much of what is known comes from whistle-blowers and anecdotal accounts.

On the other hand, the idea of coercion in the relationship between the Tall Whites and humans is a theme that appears in several accounts. Some witnesses and researchers suggest that the Tall Whites, while not overtly hostile, exert a subtle form of control over those they interact with, particularly within the military. This control could be psychological, using fear or intimidation to ensure compliance, or it could be more direct, involving the manipulation of events to serve their interests.

The potential for coercion is evident in the way the Tall Whites are said to enforce their boundaries. According to Hall and others, the Tall Whites have strict protocols for human interaction, and any breach of these protocols is met with swift and sometimes severe consequences. For instance, Hall recounts instances where soldiers or personnel who inadvertently wandered too close to the Tall Whites' territory were subjected to terrifying encounters, including being chased or physically harmed. These actions suggest that while the Tall Whites may cooperate with humans, they do so from a position of power and control, making it clear that they are not to be trifled with.

The duality of cooperation and coercion raises important questions about the true nature of the Tall Whites' presence on Earth. Are they genuinely interested in fostering a beneficial relationship with humanity, or are they simply using humans as a means to an end, ensuring their own safety and goals while keeping us at arm's length? The answer is not clear, and the lack of concrete evidence only adds to the mystery.

Another intriguing aspect of the Tall Whites is their apparent interest in Earth's resources, particularly its natural and mineral wealth. Some theories suggest that the Tall Whites, like the Anunnaki in other narratives, may be here to exploit these resources, possibly for their own technological needs. This would align with the idea that their cooperation with human governments is motivated by access to these resources, rather than any altruistic desire to assist humanity. If true, this would cast their interactions with us in a more self-serving light, where cooperation is merely a facade for a more pragmatic and possibly exploitative agenda.

The psychological and emotional impact of encounters with the Tall Whites is another important factor to consider. Witnesses often describe a mix of awe, fear, and curiosity during their interactions with these beings. The Tall Whites' advanced technology and seemingly superior intellect can be both fascinating and intimidating, leading to a sense of powerlessness in those who encounter them. This dynamic can create a situation where cooperation is not entirely voluntary, but rather a necessity for survival or avoidance of conflict.

Skeptics of the Tall Whites phenomenon argue that these beings, like many other figures in UFO lore, may be a product of the human imagination, influenced by cultural archetypes and psychological factors. The consistent descriptions of the Tall Whites across different accounts could be explained by the influence of popular media, shared cultural myths, or even hallucinations brought on by stress or environmental factors in remote areas like the Nevada desert.

However, for those who have encountered the Tall Whites, the experiences are undeniably real and often life-changing. The consistency of the descriptions, the detailed accounts of their behavior and technology, and the profound impact these encounters have on witnesses all suggest that there is something more at play than mere fantasy. Whether the Tall Whites are extraterrestrial visitors, interdimensional beings, or something else entirely, their presence in the narrative of extraterrestrial contact cannot be ignored. The Tall Whites represent one of the most intriguing and ambiguous aspects of the extraterrestrial phenomenon. Their interactions with humanity, whether cooperative or coercive, challenge our understanding of power dynamics, trust, and the nature of extraterrestrial intelligence. As we continue to explore the complexities of our relationship with these beings, the Tall Whites serve as a reminder that the universe is vast and full of mysteries, some of which may defy our current understanding of reality. Their story invites us to consider the possibility that cooperation and coercion may not be mutually exclusive, and that our place in the cosmic order may be far more precarious than we realize.

Arcturians: Beacons of Spiritual Enlightenment

The Arcturians hold a special place in the pantheon of alleged extraterrestrial beings, often depicted as highly evolved, benevolent entities who are deeply concerned with the spiritual development and enlightenment of humanity. Unlike many other alien races that are described with a mix of fear and uncertainty, the Arcturians are almost universally regarded as positive influences, guiding humanity toward higher levels of consciousness and spiritual awareness. This chapter explores the origins, characteristics, and teachings attributed to the Arcturians, examining why they are often seen as beacons of spiritual enlightenment.

The Arcturians are said to originate from the star system Arcturus, one of the brightest stars in the night sky, located approximately 37 light-years from Earth. Arcturus has been a subject of fascination for astronomers and spiritual seekers alike, and in various esoteric traditions, it is considered a gateway to higher dimensions of consciousness. The beings from this star system, known as Arcturians, are described as highly advanced both technologically and spiritually, embodying a level of wisdom and compassion that surpasses human understanding.

In terms of physical appearance, Arcturians are often depicted as tall, slender beings with blue or green skin and large, almond-shaped eyes that exude a sense of deep knowledge and understanding. Their heads are typically described as elongated, and their features are somewhat androgynous, reflecting a state of being that transcends gender. However, physical descriptions of Arcturians are less emphasized in accounts compared to their spiritual and intellectual qualities, which are considered their defining characteristics.

One of the key figures who has contributed to the understanding of Arcturians is Edgar Cayce, a renowned American psychic who spoke of Arcturus as a high-vibrational star and a center for advanced spiritual beings. Cayce suggested that Arcturus was a portal through which souls pass during their journey between lives, and that the beings from this star system are guardians of this cosmic gateway. Although Cayce's teachings were not explicitly about extraterrestrial beings, his descriptions of Arcturus as a beacon of light and wisdom have influenced later interpretations of the Arcturians as spiritually enlightened entities.

The Arcturians are often portrayed as teachers and guides, working to assist humanity in its spiritual evolution. They are said to communicate telepathically with individuals on Earth, offering guidance, healing, and wisdom to those who are open to receiving it. This communication is typically described as clear, loving, and uplifting, with the Arcturians encouraging humans to transcend the limitations of the physical world and embrace their true spiritual nature.

One of the core teachings attributed to the Arcturians is the importance of raising one's vibrational frequency to align with higher states of consciousness. They emphasize the need for humanity to move beyond fear, anger, and other lower vibrational emotions, and to cultivate love, compassion, and forgiveness as the foundation for a new way of being. This shift in consciousness is seen as essential for both individual growth and the collective evolution of humanity.

Arcturians are also associated with advanced healing techniques, particularly in the realm of energy healing. They are said to possess a deep understanding of the human energy field, or aura, and can work with it to clear blockages, balance energies, and promote physical, emotional, and spiritual well-being. Some people claim to have received healing from the Arcturians during meditation, dreams, or other altered states of consciousness, experiencing profound shifts in their health and awareness as a result.

In addition to their focus on individual spiritual development, the Arcturians are often described as having a broader mission to assist humanity in its transition to a higher state of collective consciousness. This is sometimes referred to as the ascension process, where humanity as a whole moves from a third-dimensional (physical) reality to a higher-dimensional (spiritual) existence. The Arcturians are seen as key players in this process, providing the guidance and support needed to navigate this profound transformation. One of the most intriguing aspects of the Arcturians is their purported role in protecting Earth from negative extraterrestrial influences. According to some sources, the Arcturians are part of a Galactic Federation or Alliance, a group of advanced civilizations that work together to maintain peace and harmony in the universe. The Arcturians are said to be particularly concerned with shielding Earth from the interference of lower-vibrational beings, such as the Reptilians or certain factions of the Greys, who are believed to have more self-serving agendas.

This protective role is often described as being carried out through the use of advanced technology, including energy shields and frequency barriers that prevent negative entities from influencing Earth's inhabitants. The Arcturians are also believed to work closely with other benevolent extraterrestrial races, such as the Pleiadians, to ensure that humanity's spiritual evolution proceeds according to divine plan.

The idea of the Arcturians as guardians and guides has resonated strongly with those involved in the New Age and spiritual movements. Many people who feel a connection to the Arcturians describe them as loving, wise beings who are always available to offer support and guidance, particularly during times of personal or planetary upheaval. This sense of connection is often experienced during meditation, where individuals report receiving messages, visions, or feelings of profound peace and understanding from the Arcturians. Sceptics, however, argue that the Arcturian phenomenon is largely a product of human imagination, shaped by cultural archetypes and psychological needs. The idea of benevolent, enlightened beings guiding humanity is a common theme in many spiritual traditions, and it is possible that the Arcturians are a modern expression of this timeless archetype. The lack of concrete evidence for the existence of Arcturians, coupled with the subjective nature of most encounters, makes it difficult to definitively prove or disprove their reality.

Regardless of whether the Arcturians are real or symbolic, their presence in the narrative of extraterrestrial contact serves as a powerful reminder of the human desire for connection, guidance, and spiritual growth. The teachings attributed to the Arcturians—emphasizing love, compassion, and the importance of raising one's vibrational frequency—offer a path toward greater understanding and fulfillment, regardless of one's beliefs about their origins. The Arcturians represent a beacon of spiritual enlightenment in the broader context of the extraterrestrial phenomenon. Whether seen as real beings or as symbols of humanity's potential, they inspire us to look beyond the material world and to cultivate a deeper connection with our true spiritual nature. Their message of love, healing, and ascension resonates with those who are seeking to transcend the limitations of the physical world and embrace a higher state of consciousness. As we continue to explore the mysteries of the universe and our place within it, the Arcturians remind us that the journey toward enlightenment is as important as the destination, and that we are never alone on this path.

The Sirians: Masters of Technology and Wisdom

The Sirians are another prominent race in the realm of extraterrestrial lore, often described as advanced beings who possess a deep mastery of technology and a profound understanding of the mysteries of the universe. Originating from the Sirius star system, these beings are frequently associated with both ancient human civilizations and modern-day spiritual teachings. The Sirians are depicted as both technologically and spiritually evolved, embodying a unique blend of wisdom and scientific prowess. This chapter delves into the origins, characteristics, and influence of the Sirians, exploring their role as masters of technology and wisdom. Sirius, often referred to as the "Dog Star," is the brightest star in the night sky and has held a place of great significance in various cultures throughout history. Located approximately 8.6 light-years from Earth, Sirius is part of the constellation Canis Major. The star's prominence and visibility have made it a focal point for myths, legends, and spiritual beliefs across the globe. Among the most well-known of these are the ancient Egyptians, who revered Sirius as a key to their agricultural calendar and associated it with the goddess Isis.

The connection between Sirius and the ancient Egyptians is often cited as evidence of the Sirians' influence on early human civilizations. According to some theories, the Sirians were deeply involved in the development of ancient Egypt, providing technological and spiritual knowledge that helped to shape one of the most advanced societies of the ancient world. The construction of the pyramids, the alignment of temples with celestial bodies, and the sophisticated understanding of astronomy and mathematics are often attributed to the Sirians' guidance. In addition to their association with Egypt, the Sirians are also linked to other ancient cultures, such as the Dogon people of West Africa. The Dogon have long been noted for their detailed knowledge of the Sirius star system, particularly the existence of Sirius B, a white dwarf companion star that is invisible to the naked eye. This knowledge, which was documented by French anthropologists in the 1930s, has led some to speculate that the Dogon's information was provided by extraterrestrial visitors, possibly the Sirians.

The Sirians are typically described as humanoid in appearance, with physical characteristics that resemble humans, but with certain features that suggest a more evolved or refined nature. Some accounts describe them as having blue or golden skin, elongated skulls, and eyes that are larger and more almond-shaped than those of humans. However, as with many extraterrestrial beings, the Sirians' appearance is often secondary to their perceived abilities and influence. One of the defining traits of the Sirians is their mastery of technology. They are often depicted as possessing advanced spacecraft, energy systems, and other technologies that far surpass anything currently known on Earth. These technologies are not only highly sophisticated but are also said to be integrated with spiritual principles, reflecting the Sirians' understanding of the interconnectedness of all things. This blend of technology and spirituality is a hallmark of Sirian culture, where science and mysticism are seen as complementary rather than opposing forces.

The Sirians' technological prowess is often linked to their role as protectors and guides for humanity. Some theories suggest that the Sirians have been working behind the scenes for millennia, subtly influencing human development and intervening in times of crisis to ensure the survival and progress of the species. This involvement is said to include the seeding of human DNA with Sirian genetic material, making humans a hybrid race with both terrestrial and extraterrestrial origins. This theory is particularly popular in certain New Age circles, where it is believed that the Sirians are helping to awaken humanity to its true potential. In addition to their technological expertise, the Sirians are also revered for their spiritual wisdom. They are often depicted as enlightened beings who have achieved a high level of consciousness and who embody qualities such as compassion, love, and understanding. The Sirians are said to be deeply committed to the spiritual evolution of humanity, offering guidance and teachings that help individuals and societies to raise their vibrational frequency and align with higher states of being.

One of the ways the Sirians are believed to impart their wisdom is through telepathic communication. Many individuals who claim to have had contact with Sirians describe receiving messages in the form of thoughts, images, or feelings, which convey complex spiritual concepts or practical advice for navigating life's challenges. These communications are often described as being filled with love and light, leaving the recipient with a sense of peace and clarity. The Sirians' teachings often emphasize the importance of balance, both within oneself and in the external world. They encourage individuals to cultivate harmony between mind, body, and spirit, and to seek balance in their relationships with others and with the Earth. This holistic approach to life is reflected in the Sirians' own culture, where technological advancement is always aligned with ethical and spiritual principles.

The Sirians are also associated with the concept of ascension, the process of raising one's consciousness to a higher level of existence. They are believed to be guiding humanity through a period of great transformation, helping individuals and the collective to move beyond the limitations of the physical world and to embrace a more expansive, multidimensional reality. This process is often described as a shift from a third-dimensional (3D) reality, characterized by duality and separation, to a fifth-dimensional (5D) reality, where unity and interconnectedness are the norm.

In the context of global events, some believe that the Sirians have played a role in preventing large-scale disasters or in mitigating the effects of conflicts and environmental crises. Their advanced technology and understanding of the cosmos are said to give them the ability to influence events on a planetary scale, ensuring that humanity's evolution continues according to a divine plan. This protective role is often likened to that of a guardian or overseer, with the Sirians acting as benevolent caretakers of Earth and its inhabitants.

Sceptics, of course, view the Sirian phenomenon with a critical eye, arguing that the stories of their involvement in human affairs are more likely a result of cultural mythology, wishful thinking, or the human tendency to attribute unexplained phenomena to higher powers. The lack of empirical evidence to support the existence of the Sirians, coupled with the highly subjective nature of most contact experiences, makes it difficult to definitively prove their reality.

However, for those who feel a connection to the Sirians, their presence is very real and deeply meaningful. The teachings and guidance attributed to the Sirians have inspired many to pursue a path of spiritual growth, technological innovation, and environmental stewardship, reflecting the values that are often associated with this advanced race. The Sirians represent a fascinating synthesis of technology and wisdom in the broader narrative of extraterrestrial contact. Whether they are seen as literal beings from another star system or as symbolic representations of humanity's potential, the Sirians offer a vision of a future where science and spirituality are united in the service of higher consciousness and collective well-being. Their influence on both ancient civilizations and modern spiritual movements suggests that the Sirians, whether real or imagined, continue to play a significant role in shaping humanity's understanding of itself and its place in the universe. As we explore the mysteries of the cosmos and seek to evolve as a species, the Sirians remind us that true mastery lies not only in technological advancement but also in the cultivation of wisdom, compassion, and balance.

The Draconians: The Reptilian Empire

The Draconians, often referred to as the Reptilian Empire, occupy one of the most feared and controversial places in the extensive lore of extraterrestrial beings. Unlike the more benevolent alien races, the Draconians are frequently depicted as malevolent and power-hungry, with a primary goal of dominating and enslaving humanity. The Draconians are said to be a highly advanced and ancient race, with a deep connection to the mythological and historical archetypes of dragons and serpents. This chapter explores the origins, characteristics, and theories surrounding the Draconians, delving into why they are perceived as one of the most dangerous extraterrestrial forces in existence.

The Draconians are typically described as large, humanoid beings with distinctly reptilian features. They are often depicted as standing between 7 to 12 feet tall, with muscular builds, scaly skin, sharp claws, and serpent-like eyes. Some accounts suggest that Draconians have wings, reminiscent of the dragons of ancient mythology, while others describe them as tail-bearing creatures with an aura of raw power and intimidation. Their appearance alone is said to inspire fear, but it is their alleged intentions and actions that have earned them their fearsome reputation.

The origins of the Draconians are often linked to the star system Alpha Draconis, also known as Thuban, located in the constellation Draco. The name "Draco" itself is Latin for "dragon," further reinforcing the connection between these beings and the dragon mythos that appears in various cultures throughout history. According to some theories, the Draconians are one of the oldest and most powerful extraterrestrial races, with an empire that spans multiple galaxies and includes numerous conquered worlds and enslaved species. One of the most persistent narratives about the Draconians is that they are the masterminds behind many of the negative events and power structures on Earth. They are often portrayed as the hidden hand behind global elites, manipulating governments, financial systems, and even religions to achieve their goals of total control over humanity. Some theories suggest that the Draconians are the true rulers of Earth, with human leaders acting as their puppets, carrying out their bidding in exchange for power and wealth.

The Draconians' methods of control are said to be varied and insidious. They are believed to possess advanced technology that allows them to manipulate human consciousness, using mind control, fear, and deception to keep humanity in a state of ignorance and subservience. This technology is often described as involving energy fields, holographic projections, and other forms of psychological manipulation that are beyond current human understanding.

In addition to their technological prowess, the Draconians are also thought to be highly skilled in genetics and bioengineering. Some theories propose that the Draconians have been involved in the manipulation of human DNA for millennia, creating hybrid beings that serve their interests or act as intermediaries between them and humanity. These hybrids, often referred to as "Reptilian hybrids" or "Draco-human hybrids," are believed to hold positions of power in various institutions, furthering the Draconians' agenda from within. The Draconians' influence is also said to extend to the spiritual realm. In some accounts, the Draconians are depicted as interdimensional beings who can operate in both the physical and non-physical planes. This ability allows them to influence not only the material world but also the spiritual and energetic realms, further enhancing their control over humanity. Some researchers and experiencers claim that the Draconians feed off negative emotions such as fear, anger, and hatred, which they intentionally provoke in order to sustain themselves.

The idea that the Draconians are involved in a cosmic battle with other extraterrestrial races is another common theme in the narrative. They are often depicted as being in conflict with more benevolent alien groups, such as the Pleiadians, Arcturians, and Sirians, who are said to be working to protect humanity from the Draconians' influence. This cosmic struggle is sometimes framed as a battle between good and evil, with humanity caught in the middle as both sides vie for control over the planet and its inhabitants.

One of the most notable proponents of the Draconian theory is David Icke, a British author and conspiracy theorist who has written extensively about the Reptilian influence on Earth. Icke's work suggests that many of the world's leaders and influential figures are, in fact, Reptilian shapeshifters who are part of a global conspiracy to enslave humanity. According to Icke, the Draconians are behind everything from wars and economic crises to environmental destruction, all of which are part of their plan to maintain dominance over the human race.

Critics of the Draconian narrative argue that these ideas are based on fear-driven speculation rather than solid evidence. They suggest that the Draconians, like many other alien races in UFO lore, may be a manifestation of deep-seated psychological fears and cultural archetypes rather than real beings. The reptilian form, in particular, taps into primal fears of predation and danger, which could explain why the Draconians are often portrayed as the ultimate villains in the extraterrestrial hierarchy.

Despite the skepticism, the Draconian narrative has gained significant traction among certain groups, particularly those involved in conspiracy theories and alternative spiritual beliefs. For these individuals, the idea of a hidden Reptilian elite controlling the world resonates with their views on power, corruption, and the unseen forces that shape human history. The Draconians, in this context, serve as a convenient explanation for the world's problems, offering a clear enemy to rally against.

In addition to their role as oppressors, some accounts also suggest that the Draconians are capable of more complex relationships with humans. There are reports of individuals who claim to have had direct contact with Draconians and describe them as intelligent, strategic, and even honorable in their own way. These accounts often emphasize the Draconians' sense of duty and loyalty to their own species and empire, suggesting that their actions, while ruthless, are motivated by a deeply ingrained sense of purpose and survival.

The psychological impact of the Draconian narrative is profound. The idea that humanity is being controlled and manipulated by a powerful, hidden force taps into feelings of powerlessness and fear, but it also offers a framework for understanding the complexities of global events. For some, the Draconians represent the ultimate adversary, a challenge that humanity must overcome in order to achieve true freedom and enlightenment.

In conclusion, the Draconians, or the Reptilian Empire, represent one of the most fearsome and controversial elements of the extraterrestrial phenomenon. Whether viewed as literal beings, symbolic representations of evil, or psychological projections, the Draconians challenge our understanding of power, control, and the forces that shape our world. Their story invites us to explore the darker aspects of the human psyche, as well as the possibility that we may not be alone in the struggle for our own destiny. As we continue to investigate the mysteries of the universe and our place within it, the Draconians will undoubtedly remain a central figure in the narrative of extraterrestrial contact, reminding us that the cosmos may be filled with both light and shadow, and that our choices may determine which prevails.

The Blue Avians: Messengers of Peace?

The Blue Avians are one of the more recent additions to the extensive catalogue of alleged extraterrestrial beings, yet they have quickly garnered attention due to their striking appearance and the profound messages they are said to convey. These beings, described as humanoid with bird-like features and brilliant blue feathers, are often portrayed as peaceful, spiritually advanced entities with a deep concern for the well-being of humanity. This chapter explores the origins, characteristics, and teachings associated with the Blue Avians, delving into their role as potential messengers of peace and spiritual enlightenment. The Blue Avians first gained widespread attention through the testimony of Corey Goode, a self-proclaimed whistle-blower who claims to have been involved in secret space programs and to have had direct contact with these beings. According to Goode, the Blue Avians are part of a group of benevolent extraterrestrial species known as the Sphere Being Alliance, which includes other beings such as the Golden Triangle-Headed beings. This alliance, Goode asserts, has been working to guide and protect humanity during a time of great transition and upheaval on Earth.

Physically, the Blue Avians are described as tall, between 8 to 10 feet, with slender, human-like bodies covered in vibrant blue feathers. Their heads are said to resemble those of birds, with large, expressive eyes that convey a deep sense of wisdom and compassion. Despite their avian features, they are bipedal and possess hands with fingers, allowing them to interact with their environment in a manner similar to humans. Their presence is often described as calming and serene, radiating an energy that is both gentle and powerful.

The messages attributed to the Blue Avians are centered around themes of peace, love, and spiritual evolution. They are said to emphasize the importance of raising one's vibrational frequency by cultivating positive emotions such as compassion, forgiveness, and gratitude. The Blue Avians encourage humanity to move away from fear, anger, and division, and to embrace a more unified and harmonious way of living. This shift in consciousness is seen as essential for navigating the challenges of the current era and for preparing humanity for the next phase of its evolution.

One of the core teachings of the Blue Avians is the principle of "Service to Others," which they contrast with the concept of "Service to Self." According to this teaching, individuals and societies that focus on helping others, promoting peace, and working for the greater good are aligned with the natural order of the universe and are more likely to experience spiritual growth and fulfillment. In contrast, those who are primarily concerned with their own power, wealth, and control are said to be on a path of spiritual stagnation or decline.

The Blue Avians are also associated with the idea of a "Great Awakening," a period of collective spiritual enlightenment that is said to be occurring on Earth. This awakening involves the breaking down of old systems and beliefs that are based on fear and control, and the emergence of new ways of thinking and being that are aligned with love, unity, and higher consciousness. The Blue Avians are believed to be playing a key role in facilitating this awakening, offering guidance and support to those who are open to receiving it. Telepathic communication is often cited as the primary method by which the Blue Avians interact with humans. Those who claim to have communicated with these beings describe the experience as clear, direct, and often accompanied by a profound sense of peace and understanding. The messages received are typically focused on personal and collective spiritual growth, encouraging individuals to examine their beliefs, behaviors, and motivations, and to make choices that are in alignment with their highest values and the well-being of others.

The Blue Avians' role as messengers of peace is further emphasized by their purported involvement in mitigating conflicts and preventing large-scale disasters. Some accounts suggest that the Blue Avians, along with other members of the Sphere Being Alliance, have intervened in human affairs at critical moments to prevent wars, environmental catastrophes, and other destructive events. This intervention is said to be carried out subtly and without direct interference, respecting humanity's free will while offering opportunities for positive change.

Despite their positive message, the Blue Avians are not without controversy. Skeptics argue that the stories of the Blue Avians, like many other accounts of extraterrestrial contact, may be the result of psychological projection, wishful thinking, or even deliberate fabrication. The vivid descriptions of these beings, coupled with the spiritual nature of their messages, have led some to suggest that the Blue Avians are more likely a product of the human imagination than actual extraterrestrial entities.

Moreover, the association of the Blue Avians with secret space programs and other conspiracy theories has further fueled skepticism. The lack of verifiable evidence to support the existence of these beings, coupled with the extraordinary nature of the claims, has led many in the scientific and mainstream communities to dismiss the Blue Avians as a modern myth or a fringe belief system.

However, for those who believe in the Blue Avians and their message, these beings represent a source of hope and inspiration during a time of global uncertainty. The teachings of the Blue Avians resonate with many who are seeking a deeper understanding of themselves and their place in the world, offering a framework for personal and collective transformation that is based on universal principles of love, compassion, and service.

In addition to their spiritual teachings, the Blue Avians are sometimes linked to ancient myths and religious symbols. Some researchers draw parallels between the Blue Avians and bird-headed deities found in various ancient cultures, such as Thoth in Egyptian mythology or Quetzalcoatl in Mesoamerican traditions. These connections suggest that the Blue Avians, if they exist, may have been interacting with humanity for much longer than is commonly recognized, potentially influencing the development of spiritual and religious thought throughout history.

The psychological impact of the Blue Avians' message is also significant. For many, the idea of a benevolent extraterrestrial race that is deeply invested in the well-being of humanity provides a sense of comfort and reassurance. The emphasis on positive emotions and spiritual growth offers a counterbalance to the fear and uncertainty that often characterize discussions of extraterrestrial contact, particularly those involving more malevolent beings like the Draconians or Reptilians.

In conclusion, the Blue Avians are a fascinating and complex aspect of the broader extraterrestrial phenomenon. Whether viewed as literal beings from another star system or as symbolic representations of humanity's highest aspirations, the Blue Avians embody a message of peace, love, and spiritual evolution that resonates with many people around the world. Their teachings challenge us to look beyond the material world and to embrace a more expansive, compassionate view of ourselves and others. As we continue to explore the mysteries of the universe and our place within it, the Blue Avians remind us that the journey toward peace and enlightenment is both a personal and collective endeavor, one that requires us to rise above our differences and to work together for the greater good.

Orions: The Dual Nature of Orion Beings

The Orion beings, often associated with the star system of Orion, are among the more complex and enigmatic figures in the extraterrestrial narrative. The stories and theories surrounding them depict a dual nature—some Orion beings are described as benevolent guides committed to humanity's spiritual evolution, while others are portrayed as malevolent entities with darker agendas. This duality makes the Orion beings particularly intriguing and difficult to categorize, as they embody both the light and shadow aspects of the extraterrestrial phenomenon. This chapter explores the origins, characteristics, and divergent roles attributed to the Orion beings, examining how they represent both the potential for enlightenment and the dangers of manipulation.

The Orion constellation, one of the most recognizable and significant star formations in the night sky, has been revered by various cultures throughout history. Its prominent stars, including Betelgeuse, Rigel, and the three stars of Orion's Belt, have inspired myths, legends, and spiritual teachings across the globe. Many ancient civilizations, such as the Egyptians and the Mayans, aligned their monuments with the stars of Orion, suggesting a deep connection between the Orion star system and human history.

In the context of extraterrestrial theories, beings from Orion are often described as highly advanced, both technologically and spiritually. However, unlike other extraterrestrial races that are typically depicted as either benevolent or malevolent, the Orion beings are often characterized by a dual nature. This duality is reflected in the diverse range of accounts and experiences reported by those who claim to have had contact with beings from Orion.

On the benevolent side, some Orion beings are described as wise and compassionate, with a deep commitment to helping humanity evolve spiritually. These beings are often associated with the principles of balance, harmony, and enlightenment. They are said to possess a profound understanding of the interconnectedness of all life and work to promote peace and unity both on Earth and throughout the cosmos. In this sense, the benevolent Orion beings are often viewed as guides or teachers, offering humanity the knowledge and tools needed to transcend its limitations and achieve a higher state of consciousness. The benevolent Orion beings are often depicted as humanoid in appearance, with some reports describing them as tall, slender, and possessing a radiant or luminous quality. Their physical features may vary, with some appearing more human-like and others having slightly elongated or ethereal forms. Regardless of their appearance, these beings are frequently described as exuding an aura of calm, wisdom, and serenity.

These benevolent entities are believed to be involved in guiding humanity through critical junctures in its development, offering subtle influence or direct communication to help individuals and societies make decisions that align with the greater good. Some accounts suggest that these Orion beings are part of a broader coalition of benevolent extraterrestrial races, such as the Pleiadians and Arcturians, working together to assist humanity during a time of great transition and potential awakening. However, not all beings from Orion are described in such positive terms. There is a darker side to the narrative, where other Orion beings are depicted as manipulative, power-hungry, and even malevolent. These beings are often associated with the lower vibrational aspects of the Orion star system and are said to be engaged in activities that seek to control or exploit humanity rather than uplift it. This duality within the Orion collective reflects a broader cosmic struggle between forces of light and darkness, with Earth and humanity often caught in the middle.

The malevolent Orion beings are sometimes described as having a more reptilian or serpentine appearance, though this varies across different accounts. These beings are frequently linked to the concept of "Service to Self," a philosophy that prioritizes personal power, control, and dominance over the well-being of others. In this context, the malevolent

Orion beings are often portrayed as being aligned with the Reptilians or other negative extraterrestrial factions that seek to manipulate humanity for their own ends.

One of the key tactics attributed to these malevolent Orion beings is deception. They are said to use advanced technology and psychological manipulation to create illusions, spread disinformation, and instill fear or division among humans. This manipulation is believed to be part of a broader agenda to maintain control over humanity, keeping it in a state of spiritual stagnation or regression. The idea that these beings may present themselves as benevolent while secretly pursuing darker goals adds a layer of complexity to the narrative, making it difficult for individuals to discern their true intentions.

The duality of the Orion beings is also reflected in various mythologies and spiritual teachings. In some traditions, the Orion star system is seen as a place of great spiritual significance, associated with wisdom, enlightenment, and the ascension of the soul. In others, Orion is linked to themes of conflict, struggle, and the battle between light and darkness. This dual symbolism suggests that the Orion beings, whether real or symbolic, represent the full spectrum of potential within the cosmos—the potential for both creation and destruction, for enlightenment and for domination.

The psychological impact of the Orion narrative is significant, particularly for those who believe they have had contact with these beings. The idea that a single star system could harbor both benevolent guides and malevolent manipulators challenges our understanding of morality and the nature of the universe. It raises questions about the inherent duality of existence and the role that different beings play in the evolution of consciousness. For some, the Orion beings represent a reflection of humanity's own dual nature—the capacity for both great good and great evil. The stories of benevolent Orion beings inspire hope and a sense of connection to higher spiritual realms, while the accounts of malevolent Orion beings serve as a cautionary tale, reminding us of the dangers of unchecked power and the potential for deception. This duality may also serve as a mirror for our own inner struggles, highlighting the importance of discernment, balance, and the pursuit of truth.

Sceptics, of course, view the Orion narrative with a critical eye, often attributing these stories to psychological projection, cultural archetypes, or the influence of popular media. The association of Orion with both light and darkness, they argue, may simply reflect the human tendency to see duality in all things—a projection of our own internal conflicts onto the cosmos.

Regardless of one's perspective, the Orion beings represent a fascinating and multifaceted aspect of the extraterrestrial phenomenon. Their dual nature challenges us to think more deeply about the complexities of the universe and the diverse forces that may be at play in our world. Whether seen as real beings from a distant star system or as symbolic representations of universal principles, the Orion beings offer a rich tapestry of ideas and possibilities to explore. The Orion beings embody the dual nature of the cosmos, representing both the potential for enlightenment and the risks of manipulation. Their presence in the narrative of extraterrestrial contact serves as a reminder that the universe is a place of both light and shadow, and that the journey toward truth and spiritual evolution requires discernment, balance, and an openness to the complexities of existence. As we continue to explore the mysteries of the stars and our place within the universe, the Orion beings challenge us to confront our own duality and to strive for a higher understanding of ourselves and the cosmos.

Zeta Reticulans: Origins and Motivations

The Zeta Reticulans, commonly referred to as "the Greys," are perhaps the most well-known and frequently reported extraterrestrial beings in modern UFO lore. Their distinctive appearance—small stature, large heads, and almond-shaped black eyes—has become almost synonymous with the concept of alien life. While much has been speculated about their actions, particularly their involvement in alleged abductions, less is definitively known about their origins and motivations. This chapter delves into the theories surrounding the Zeta Reticulans, exploring where they might come from and what drives their interactions with humanity.

The Zeta Reticulans are often associated with the star system Zeta Reticuli, a binary star system located approximately 39 light-years from Earth in the constellation Reticulum. This connection was popularized by the famous abduction case of Betty and Barney Hill in 1961. During a hypnosis session, Betty Hill described being shown a "star map" by one of the beings, which she later drew from memory. An amateur astronomer, Marjorie Fish, matched Betty's map to the Zeta Reticuli system, leading to the widespread belief that this is the home of the Greys.

The Zeta Reticulans are typically described as short, ranging from 3.5 to 5 feet tall, with spindly bodies, large, bulbous heads, and smooth, grayish skin. Their most striking feature is their large, black, almond-shaped eyes, which dominate their faces. They are usually depicted as lacking visible emotions, communicating telepathically rather than verbally, and often described as being highly intelligent but emotionally detached. These physical characteristics, combined with their reported behaviors, have led to a perception of the Greys as cold, clinical, and even sinister.

One of the most persistent narratives about the Zeta Reticulans is their involvement in abductions. Thousands of people around the world have reported being abducted by beings resembling the Greys, often describing similar experiences: being taken aboard a spacecraft, subjected to medical examinations, and sometimes being shown hybrid beings that appear to be part human and part Grey. These abductions are often characterized by a sense of powerlessness, as the abductees are unable to resist or escape, and the Greys are depicted as unemotional, efficient, and indifferent to the distress they cause.

The motivations behind these abductions are the subject of much speculation. One of the most common theories is that the Zeta Reticulans are conducting a long-term genetic experiment, possibly to create a hybrid species. Some researchers suggest that the Greys are a dying race, suffering from genetic degradation due to excessive cloning or environmental catastrophe on their home planet. To remedy this, they may be attempting to infuse their DNA with human genetic material, creating hybrids that can sustain their species. This theory is supported by the frequent reports of abductees being shown hybrid children or foetuses during their experiences.

Another theory posits that the Zeta Reticulans are involved in a broader study of human biology, psychology, and behavior. This could be part of a larger scientific mission to understand and perhaps even guide the evolution of humanity. The Greys' clinical detachment and focus on gathering genetic material, reproductive samples, and other biological data suggest that they might be scientists or researchers, conducting experiments on a planetary scale. In this view, the Greys might be acting under a directive from a higher authority or collective, possibly within a larger interstellar alliance.

Some researchers believe that the Zeta Reticulans may not be entirely autonomous in their actions. There are theories that the Greys are actually serving as intermediaries or subordinates to other, more powerful extraterrestrial races, such as the Reptilians or the Draconians. In this scenario, the Greys might be carrying out the orders of these higher beings, perhaps in exchange for protection, resources, or technological assistance. This would explain their lack of emotional engagement with their human subjects, as they are simply following orders rather than acting out of personal interest or malice. The idea that the Zeta Reticulans are part of a larger cosmic agenda is also supported by the accounts of abductees who describe interactions with other types of beings during their abductions. Some report seeing taller, more human-like figures, often described as Nordics or Pleiadians, who appear to be overseeing the actions of the Greys. Others mention encounters with Reptilian or Insectoid beings, suggesting that the Greys might be just one part of a complex hierarchy of extraterrestrial species involved in Earth's affairs.

Despite the largely negative connotations associated with the Zeta Reticulans, not all accounts depict them as malevolent. Some experiencers report more neutral or even positive interactions with these beings, describing them as teachers or guides who impart knowledge or offer assistance in times of crisis. These reports are less common but suggest that the Greys' motivations might be more nuanced than simply exploitation or control. It's possible that the Zeta Reticulans, like humans, have a range of motivations and behaviors, and that their actions are not universally hostile or benevolent. The psychological impact of encounters with the Zeta Reticulans is profound. The Greys' appearance and behavior tap into deep-seated fears of powerlessness, violation, and the unknown. For many abductees, the experience is traumatic, leading to long-lasting effects such as anxiety, depression, and post-traumatic stress disorder (PTSD). The clinical nature of the Greys' actions, combined with the sense of helplessness experienced by the abductees, contributes to the perception of the Greys as uncaring or even cruel. However, it's also possible that the Greys' actions are misunderstood due to the vast differences between human and Zeta Reticulan psychology and culture. What we interpret as coldness or indifference might simply be a lack of familiarity with human emotions or social norms. The Greys' focus on science and data collection could reflect a cultural value placed on knowledge and efficiency, rather than a lack of empathy. If the Zeta Reticulans are indeed engaged in a long-term mission involving humanity, it's likely that their motivations are complex and multifaceted, shaped by factors that we can only begin to understand.

Sceptics argue that the widespread reports of encounters with Zeta Reticulans, especially abduction scenarios, could be the result of psychological phenomena such as sleep paralysis, mass hysteria, or the influence of media and popular culture. The archetype of the Grey alien has become so ingrained in the public consciousness that it's possible people are unconsciously drawing on these images when describing unexplained experiences. While this is a plausible explanation for some cases, it doesn't account for the consistency of the descriptions and the detailed nature of many abduction reports. The Zeta Reticulans, or the Greys, represent one of the most enigmatic and controversial aspects of the extraterrestrial phenomenon. Their origins, motivations, and true nature remain shrouded in mystery, leaving us with more questions than answers. Are they scientists conducting experiments, emissaries of a higher power, or a dying race seeking to preserve their existence? Or are they simply a product of human imagination, shaped by our fears and fascination with the unknown? As we continue to explore the possibility of extraterrestrial life, the Zeta Reticulans will undoubtedly remain a central figure in the ongoing debate about humanity's place in the cosmos. Whether they are real beings or symbolic representations, the Greys challenge us to confront our deepest fears and to seek understanding in the face of the unknown.

The Andromedans: Allies from a Distant Galaxy

The Andromedans are among the more benevolent and spiritually advanced extraterrestrial races frequently mentioned in ufology and New Age circles. Originating from the Andromeda Galaxy, one of the closest galaxies to our own Milky Way, these beings are often depicted as allies of humanity, deeply invested in our spiritual growth and the protection of our planet. Their association with advanced technology, profound wisdom, and a commitment to peace and harmony has led many to view the Andromedans as some of humanity's most powerful and benevolent extraterrestrial allies. This chapter explores the origins, characteristics, and the role the Andromedans are believed to play in guiding and protecting humanity. The Andromeda Galaxy, located approximately 2.5 million light-years from Earth, has long been a subject of fascination for astronomers and spiritual seekers alike. Known for its size and beauty, Andromeda is the closest spiral galaxy to the Milky Way and is often considered a cosmic sibling to our own galaxy. The beings from this distant galaxy, known as the Andromedans, are said to have reached a level of spiritual and technological development far beyond that of humanity, allowing them to traverse vast distances across the universe and engage with civilizations like ours. The Andromedans are typically described as humanoid in appearance, though they are often depicted as taller and more physically refined than humans. Their skin is usually described as being light or glowing, and their eyes are said to be larger, often radiating a sense of deep wisdom and compassion. Some accounts suggest that Andromedans can appear in various forms, possibly due to their advanced abilities in manipulating energy and consciousness. This ability to present themselves in a way that is comforting and familiar to those they contact is seen as a reflection of their empathetic nature and their desire to foster positive interactions with humanity.

One of the most prominent figures associated with the Andromedans is Alex Collier, a self-proclaimed contactee who claims to have been in communication with Andromedan beings for several decades. According to Collier, the Andromedans are part of a larger group of extraterrestrial civilizations known as the Galactic Federation, which is committed to preserving peace and stability in the universe. The Andromedans, Collier asserts, are particularly concerned with the welfare of Earth and have been working behind the scenes to assist humanity in its spiritual evolution and to protect the planet from malevolent forces. The teachings attributed to the Andromedans often emphasize the importance of spiritual growth, the development of consciousness, and the need for humanity to evolve beyond its current state of conflict and materialism. The Andromedans are said to encourage humans to cultivate inner peace, compassion, and a sense of unity with all life. They promote the idea that humanity is at a critical juncture in its development and that the choices we make now will determine the future course of our civilization. One of the core messages of the Andromedans is the concept of ascension, the process of raising one's vibrational frequency to align with higher states of consciousness. The Andromedans are believed to be actively involved in guiding humanity through this ascension process, helping individuals and the collective to awaken to their true spiritual nature and to transcend the limitations of the physical world. This process is seen as essential for humanity to move beyond the cycles of war, greed, and environmental destruction that have plagued the planet for centuries.

The Andromedans are also associated with advanced technology, particularly in the realms of energy manipulation, space travel, and healing. They are said to possess technology that allows them to travel across galaxies, to communicate instantly over vast distances, and to heal physical and emotional ailments at an energetic level. Some contactees report that the Andromedans have shared this technology with certain individuals or groups on Earth, often with the caveat that it be used for the greater good and not for personal gain or the perpetuation of conflict.

One of the more intriguing aspects of the Andromedans is their purported involvement in the protection of Earth from external threats. Some accounts suggest that the Andromedans have played a key role in preventing large-scale disasters, such as nuclear wars or environmental catastrophes, by intervening at critical moments to ensure that humanity does not destroy itself. This protective role is often described as being carried out subtly, with the Andromedans working behind the scenes to influence events in a way that aligns with the principles of free will and non-interference. The Andromedans are also believed to be involved in monitoring and counteracting the activities of more malevolent extraterrestrial races, such as the Reptilians or certain factions of the Greys. According to some theories, the Andromedans have been engaged in a long-standing cosmic struggle with these darker forces, working to ensure that humanity remains free to pursue its spiritual evolution without being subjugated or manipulated by outside influences. This cosmic conflict is often framed as a battle between light and darkness, with the Andromedans representing the forces of light, working to protect and uplift humanity.

Despite their advanced technology and spiritual wisdom, the Andromedans are often depicted as humble and respectful of human free will. They are said to refrain from direct interference in human affairs, preferring instead to offer guidance and support to those who seek it. This approach reflects the Andromedans' belief in the importance of individual and collective sovereignty, and their desire to help humanity develop its own solutions to the challenges it faces, rather than imposing their will from above. The psychological impact of the Andromedans' message is significant, particularly for those who feel a connection to these beings. The idea of a benevolent extraterrestrial race that is deeply invested in humanity's spiritual growth offers a sense of hope and reassurance, particularly in a world that often seems dominated by conflict and division. The teachings of the Andromedans resonate with many who are seeking a deeper understanding of themselves and their place in the universe, offering a framework for personal and collective transformation that is based on universal principles of love, compassion, and unity.

Skeptics, of course, view the Andromedan narrative with a critical eye, often attributing these stories to psychological projection, cultural archetypes, or the influence of New Age spirituality. The lack of empirical evidence to support the existence of the Andromedans, coupled with the extraordinary nature of the claims, makes it difficult to definitively prove or disprove their reality. However, for those who have had personal experiences or who resonate with the teachings attributed to the Andromedans, their presence feels profoundly real and deeply meaningful. In addition to their role as spiritual guides and protectors, the Andromedans are sometimes linked to ancient myths and legends. Some researchers suggest that the Andromedans may have visited Earth in the distant past and that their influence can be seen in the religious and spiritual teachings of various ancient cultures. The connection between the Andromedans and ancient wisdom traditions adds another layer of depth to their narrative, suggesting that their relationship with humanity may be much older and more complex than is commonly recognized.

In conclusion, the Andromedans represent a powerful and positive force in the broader narrative of extraterrestrial contact. Whether viewed as literal beings from a distant galaxy or as symbolic representations of humanity's highest aspirations, the Andromedans embody a message of hope, spiritual growth, and the importance of unity and compassion. Their teachings challenge us to look beyond the material world and to embrace a more expansive, interconnected view of ourselves and the cosmos. As we continue to explore the mysteries of the universe and our place within it, the Andromedans remind us that we are not alone on our journey and that there are allies in the cosmos who are deeply invested in our success.

The Venusians: George Adamski's Encounters

The Venusians, often associated with the planet Venus, are one of the earliest extraterrestrial races introduced to the public through the accounts of George Adamski, a self-proclaimed contactee who became one of the most famous figures in the early UFO movement. Adamski's encounters with these beings, whom he described as peaceful, highly advanced, and human-like in appearance, captured the imagination of many and helped to shape the narrative of benevolent extraterrestrials during the 1950s and beyond. This chapter explores the origins, characteristics, and significance of the Venusians, focusing on Adamski's encounters and the impact they had on the broader UFO phenomenon.

George Adamski was a Polish-American who gained notoriety in the 1950s after claiming to have had multiple encounters with extraterrestrial beings from Venus. Adamski's first encounter, as detailed in his book *Flying Saucers Have Landed* (1953), allegedly took place on November 20, 1952, in the California desert. According to Adamski, he met a being named Orthon, who he described as a tall, Nordic-looking man with long, flowing hair, wearing a one-piece suit. Orthon communicated with Adamski telepathically and warned him about the dangers of nuclear weapons and the destructive path humanity was on.

Adamski's description of the Venusians stood in stark contrast to the more fearsome and alien beings that would later dominate UFO lore. He portrayed the Venusians as beautiful, peaceful, and spiritually enlightened beings who were deeply concerned about the well-being of humanity and the Earth. Adamski claimed that the Venusians, along with other extraterrestrial races from planets such as Mars and Saturn, were part of a cosmic brotherhood working to guide humanity away from war and toward a future of peace and harmony.

The Venusians, as described by Adamski, were physically similar to humans, particularly those of the Nordic race. They were often depicted as tall, with fair skin, blonde hair, and strikingly blue eyes. Their appearance was so similar to humans that Adamski claimed they could walk among us unnoticed. This idea of extraterrestrials living covertly on Earth, blending in with human society, added an intriguing element to Adamski's narrative.

In addition to their physical beauty, the Venusians were described as being technologically and spiritually advanced. Adamski claimed that they traveled in flying saucers, which were often seen by witnesses during his supposed encounters. These craft, according to Adamski, were capable of incredible speeds and maneuvers far beyond the capabilities of any earthly technology at the time. The Venusians' technology was said to be powered by a form of cosmic energy that was clean, limitless, and harmonious with the natural environment—a stark contrast to the destructive technologies that were emerging during the Cold War era.

The messages Adamski claimed to receive from the Venusians were centered on themes of peace, love, and the dangers of nuclear proliferation. Orthon and other Venusians warned that humanity's warlike tendencies and the development of nuclear weapons were putting the entire planet at risk. They urged humanity to abandon its aggressive ways and to embrace a more peaceful and cooperative existence, both with each other and with the planet.

Adamski's encounters with the Venusians were not limited to the desert meeting with Orthon. He claimed to have had several other contacts with these beings, including trips aboard their spacecraft, where he was shown various technological wonders and received further teachings. These experiences were detailed in subsequent books, including *Inside the Space Ships* (1955), where Adamski provided more insights into the Venusians' way of life, their social structure, and their philosophical and spiritual beliefs.

Adamski's accounts were met with a mixture of fascination and skepticism. On one hand, his charismatic personality and detailed descriptions of his encounters captivated many, leading to a large following and significant media attention. On the other hand, many scientists, skeptics, and even some within the UFO community dismissed his claims as fabrications or delusions. The idea that intelligent beings could live on Venus, a planet known for its extreme temperatures and inhospitable conditions, was particularly difficult for many to accept.

Despite the skepticism, Adamski's influence on the early UFO movement was profound. He was one of the first to publicly claim direct contact with extraterrestrials, and his books became bestsellers, spreading his message to a wide audience. Adamski's portrayal of the Venusians as peaceful and spiritually advanced beings helped to establish a narrative of benevolent extraterrestrials that would be echoed by other contactees in the following decades.

One of the most significant aspects of Adamski's encounters with the Venusians was the spiritual message they conveyed. Adamski's experiences resonated with the emerging New Age movement, which was beginning to take shape in the 1950s. The Venusians' emphasis on peace, love, and spiritual evolution aligned with the ideals of this movement, and many of Adamski's followers were drawn to his message not just because of the extraterrestrial element, but because of the deeper spiritual teachings he claimed to impart. In the years following Adamski's death in 1965, his legacy has been the subject of continued debate. While many dismiss his accounts as hoaxes or fantasies, others view him as a pioneer of the UFO contactee phenomenon and a key figure in the spread of the idea that extraterrestrial beings are concerned with the spiritual evolution of humanity. The concept of benevolent aliens, particularly those from Venus, became a recurring theme in the contactee movement, influencing other prominent figures such as George Van Tassel and Howard Menger.

Over time, the idea of Venusians as extraterrestrial visitors has largely fallen out of favor, particularly as scientific knowledge about Venus has advanced. The harsh conditions on Venus, with surface temperatures hot enough to melt lead and an atmosphere composed mostly of carbon dioxide, make it highly unlikely that life as we know it could exist there, let alone an advanced civilization. However, some proponents of Adamski's narrative suggest that the Venusians may not have been from the physical Venus, but rather from a parallel dimension, a higher vibrational state, or another location altogether that was simply referred to as Venus. The Venusians, as described by George Adamski, represent one of the earliest and most influential examples of benevolent extraterrestrial contact in modern UFO lore. Whether one views Adamski's accounts as genuine, symbolic, or fabricated, there is no denying the impact his stories had on the development of the contactee movement and the broader narrative of extraterrestrial life. The Venusians, with their messages of peace, love, and spiritual growth, continue to be a symbol of hope and possibility for those who believe in the existence of benevolent extraterrestrial beings. Their story serves as a reminder of the profound effect that the idea of contact with intelligent life beyond Earth can have on our understanding of ourselves, our planet, and our place in the universe.

The Lyrans: Ancestral Race of Humanoids

The Lyrans are often described as one of the most ancient and influential extraterrestrial races in the broader narrative of cosmic history. Believed to originate from the Lyra constellation, these beings are frequently depicted as the ancestral race from which many other humanoid extraterrestrial species, including humans, are descended. The Lyrans are associated with themes of origin, legacy, and the cosmic journey of consciousness, making them a central figure in the lore of extraterrestrial contact and human evolution. This chapter explores the origins, characteristics, and influence of the Lyrans, delving into their role as the progenitors of humanoid life in the galaxy. The Lyra constellation, located in the northern sky, is home to one of the brightest stars visible from Earth, Vega. In various esoteric and ufological traditions, Lyra is considered the cradle of humanoid civilization in the galaxy. According to these beliefs, the Lyrans were among the first beings to evolve into a highly advanced, space-faring civilization, possessing both technological prowess and spiritual wisdom. The Lyrans are often depicted as the ancestors of several other extraterrestrial races, including the Pleiadians, Sirians, and Arcturians, all of whom are believed to share a common genetic heritage with humanity. Physically, the Lyrans are often described as tall, humanoid beings with fair or light skin, similar to the Nordic or Pleiadian archetype. Some accounts describe them as having feline or cat-like features, reflecting their association with strength, agility, and independence. This feline connection has led some to refer to certain groups of Lyrans as the "Feline Race" or "Lion People," although these descriptions can vary widely depending on the source. In general, Lyrans are portrayed as physically imposing, with a regal or noble demeanor that reflects their ancient lineage and advanced state of being. The narrative surrounding the Lyrans is deeply intertwined with the idea of a galactic diaspora. According to many sources, the Lyrans were forced to leave their home star system in Lyra due to a cataclysmic war or conflict, which resulted in the destruction of their original planets. This event is often described as one of the earliest and most significant wars in the galaxy, involving highly advanced civilizations with powerful technologies. The reasons for this war vary among different accounts, but it is generally seen as a struggle between opposing forces of light and darkness, with the Lyrans representing a faction that sought to preserve peace, freedom, and the evolution of consciousness.

Following the destruction of their home worlds, the Lyrans embarked on a journey of exploration and colonization, spreading throughout the galaxy and seeding new civilizations. It is believed that during this diaspora, the Lyrans established colonies in various star systems, including the Pleiades, Sirius, and even Earth. These colonies eventually evolved into distinct but related species, each developing its own unique characteristics while retaining the core genetic and spiritual traits of their Lyran ancestors. The Lyrans' influence on Earth is a central theme in many of these narratives. Some theories suggest that the Lyrans were directly involved in the genetic engineering or upliftment of early human ancestors, imbuing them with qualities such as intelligence, creativity, and spiritual potential. This idea is often linked to the ancient astronaut theory, which posits that extraterrestrial beings played a crucial role in the development of human civilization by providing knowledge, technology, and spiritual guidance. The Lyrans, in this context, are seen as the original progenitors of the human race, with a deep and abiding connection to our evolutionary path. In addition to their role as creators, the Lyrans are often depicted as spiritual guides and teachers. They are said to possess a profound understanding of the nature of consciousness, the interconnectedness of all life, and the importance of maintaining harmony between technological advancement and spiritual growth. This wisdom, passed down through the ages, is believed to have influenced various ancient cultures on Earth, particularly those that emphasized the balance between science and spirituality, such as the ancient Egyptians and the civilizations of Mesoamerica.

The Lyrans' teachings are often centered around the idea of self-empowerment, the realization of one's true potential, and the importance of living in alignment with universal laws. They encourage individuals to cultivate inner strength, wisdom, and compassion, and to seek out knowledge that leads to the betterment of oneself and the collective. This emphasis on self-realization and collective responsibility reflects the Lyrans' belief in the importance of conscious evolution as the key to navigating the challenges of existence in a complex and interconnected universe.

One of the more intriguing aspects of the Lyran narrative is their association with the concept of cosmic cycles. Some sources suggest that the Lyrans, due to their ancient origins and advanced understanding of the cosmos, have a deep awareness of the cyclical nature of time, energy, and consciousness. They are believed to have knowledge of the various epochs or ages that civilizations go through, from rise to fall, and the lessons that must be learned during each cycle. This understanding is said to inform their interactions with other species, including humans, as they guide them through periods of transition and transformation.

The Lyrans are also associated with the idea of a return or reunification. According to some beliefs, the various offshoots of the Lyran race, including humans, are destined to reunite in the future, bringing together their diverse experiences and knowledge to create a new, enlightened civilization. This reunification is often seen as part of a larger cosmic plan, in which the Lyrans and their descendants play a key role in the evolution of consciousness across the galaxy. Despite the largely positive portrayal of the Lyrans, there are also narratives that suggest a more complex and nuanced view of their history. Some accounts hint at internal conflicts within the Lyran civilization, with different factions holding opposing views on how to interact with other species and whether to interfere in their development. These internal struggles are sometimes cited as a contributing factor to the wars that led to the Lyrans' diaspora, reflecting the challenges that even advanced civilizations face when dealing with power, responsibility, and the ethical implications of their actions.

Skeptics of the Lyran narrative often point to the lack of empirical evidence for the existence of these beings or their role in human history. They argue that the stories of the Lyrans, like many other elements of UFO and New Age lore, may be influenced by cultural archetypes, psychological projections, or the desire to find meaning and connection in an increasingly complex world. The similarities between the Lyran narrative and various mythological and religious stories, such as those of gods or demigods creating humanity or teaching ancient wisdom, further complicate the question of whether these beings are real or symbolic. However, for those who resonate with the Lyran narrative, the idea of an ancient, wise, and benevolent race that has played a key role in the evolution of humanity and other civilizations offers a powerful and inspiring vision of our place in the universe. The teachings attributed to the Lyrans, with their emphasis on self-empowerment, spiritual growth, and the pursuit of knowledge, continue to influence those who seek to understand the deeper mysteries of existence and the potential for humanity to evolve into a more enlightened species. The Lyrans represent a foundational element in the broader narrative of extraterrestrial contact and human evolution. Whether viewed as real beings, symbolic archetypes, or a blend of both, the Lyrans offer a rich and complex tapestry of ideas that challenge us to consider the origins of life, the interconnectedness of all beings, and the potential for conscious evolution. Their story invites us to explore our own origins, our potential for growth, and the possibility that we are part of a much larger and more ancient cosmic journey than we can currently comprehend. As we continue to seek answers to the mysteries of the universe, the Lyrans remind us that the quest for knowledge, wisdom, and self-realization is a journey that spans not just lifetimes, but eons, and that we are all connected in this grand adventure.

The MIB (Men in Black): Alien Enforcers?

The Men in Black, commonly abbreviated as MIB, are one of the most mysterious and intriguing elements within the realm of UFO and extraterrestrial lore. Often depicted as shadowy figures dressed in black suits, the MIB are said to appear after UFO sightings or encounters with extraterrestrial beings, warning witnesses to remain silent about what they have seen. The origins and motivations of the MIB are shrouded in secrecy, leading to widespread speculation about their true nature. Are they government agents, extraterrestrial beings, or something else entirely? This chapter explores the enigmatic phenomenon of the MIB, examining the theories that suggest they might be alien enforcers tasked with maintaining secrecy about extraterrestrial activity on Earth.

The Men in Black first entered popular consciousness in the 1950s, coinciding with the rise of UFO sightings and the growing interest in extraterrestrial encounters. The earliest known account of the MIB comes from Harold Dahl, who claimed to have had a run-in with them in 1947 after witnessing a UFO in the Puget Sound area of Washington state. According to Dahl, shortly after his sighting, he was approached by a man in a black suit who warned him to keep quiet about what he had seen. This encounter set the tone for many subsequent reports of MIB encounters, where witnesses to UFOs or other unexplained phenomena were intimidated into silence.

The MIB are typically described as tall, pale, and expressionless, with an almost robotic demeanor. They are often depicted wearing black suits, black hats, and sunglasses, giving them a distinct and somewhat sinister appearance. Some accounts describe the MIB as having an uncanny or otherworldly presence, with odd mannerisms, speech patterns, and behavior that suggest they are not entirely human. Witnesses have reported that the MIB seem to have an intimate knowledge of their lives, often referring to personal details that they should not have been able to know.

One of the most persistent theories about the MIB is that they are government agents, part of a secret organization tasked with maintaining the secrecy of UFO and extraterrestrial encounters.

According to this theory, the MIB operate outside the bounds of normal law enforcement or intelligence agencies, using intimidation, threats, and psychological manipulation to ensure that witnesses do not disclose what they have seen. The idea that the government would go to such lengths to suppress information about extraterrestrials suggests that the knowledge of their existence is considered highly sensitive, potentially destabilizing, or dangerous to the status quo.

However, the government agent theory does not fully explain the strange and often bizarre behavior exhibited by the MIB. Their peculiar mannerisms, lack of familiarity with common social norms, and sometimes unsettling appearance have led some to speculate that the MIB are not human at all, but rather extraterrestrial beings themselves. In this view, the MIB are seen as enforcers or agents of alien civilizations, sent to Earth to monitor and control the spread of information about extraterrestrial activity. Their mission might be to ensure that humanity remains unaware of the full extent of extraterrestrial involvement on Earth, preventing widespread panic or interference with their own agendas.

Supporters of the alien enforcer theory point to the frequent reports of MIB displaying behavior that is inconsistent with human norms. For example, some witnesses describe the MIB as having difficulty understanding or using everyday objects, such as pens, telephones, or doorknobs. Others report that the MIB seem to have an artificial or synthetic quality, with skin that appears waxy or plastic-like, and eyes that do not blink. These descriptions have led some to speculate that the MIB might be biological androids or artificially created beings designed to carry out specific tasks on behalf of their extraterrestrial creators.

Another theory suggests that the MIB might be interdimensional beings, capable of moving between different planes of existence. This idea is supported by reports of the MIB appearing and disappearing seemingly out of nowhere, as well as their ability to exert an unnerving psychological influence on those they encounter. Witnesses often describe feeling an overwhelming sense of dread or unease in the presence of the MIB, as if their very presence disrupts the natural order of reality. This interdimensional hypothesis suggests that the MIB are not bound by the same physical laws as humans, allowing them to operate in ways that seem impossible or supernatural.

The psychological impact of MIB encounters is significant. Many witnesses report feeling deeply unsettled or frightened by their experiences, often to the point of being unwilling to discuss them further. This fear and intimidation are central to the MIB phenomenon, reinforcing the idea that these beings, whatever their true nature, are determined to keep certain knowledge hidden from the public. The MIB's ability to instill fear and silence witnesses has contributed to the aura of mystery and danger that surrounds them.

Skeptics of the MIB phenomenon argue that these encounters can be explained by a combination of psychological factors, including suggestibility, stress, and the influence of popular culture. The image of the MIB, with their black suits and shadowy demeanor, has become a staple of UFO lore, and it is possible that some reports are the result of individuals projecting their fears and anxieties onto a culturally constructed archetype. Additionally, the menacing nature of the MIB could be a manifestation of the witness's own subconscious fears, particularly in the wake of a traumatic or confusing experience like a UFO sighting. However, the consistency of MIB reports across different regions and time periods suggests that there may be more to the phenomenon than simple psychological projection. The fact that witnesses often describe similar details, such as the MIB's unusual behavior, their knowledge of personal information, and their attempts to suppress UFO-related evidence, points to a pattern that is difficult to dismiss entirely as mere imagination. Even if the MIB are not literal alien enforcers, their role as a symbol of secrecy, control, and the suppression of truth resonates deeply within the broader context of UFO phenomena and conspiracy theories.

In addition to their interactions with UFO witnesses, the MIB have also been linked to other paranormal events, such as encounters with cryptids like Mothman or strange occurrences involving time anomalies or mysterious disappearances. This broader association suggests that the MIB might be connected to a wider range of unexplained phenomena, further blurring the lines between different aspects of the paranormal. This has led some researchers to speculate that the MIB are not just concerned with UFOs, but are part of a larger effort to control or manage the dissemination of information about a variety of anomalous events. The Men in Black represent one of the most enigmatic and unsettling elements of the UFO and extraterrestrial phenomenon. Whether viewed as government agents, extraterrestrial enforcers, interdimensional beings, or psychological constructs, the MIB challenge our understanding of reality, secrecy, and the lengths to which certain forces might go to keep the truth hidden. Their presence in the narratives of UFO witnesses serves as a reminder of the pervasive fear and uncertainty that often accompanies encounters with the unknown. As we continue to explore the mysteries of the universe and our place within it, the Men in Black remain a shadowy and cautionary figure, embodying the tension between revelation and concealment, knowledge and ignorance.

The Flatwoods Monster: A Unique Encounter

The Flatwoods Monster, also known as the Braxton County Monster, is one of the most bizarre and unique entities in the annals of UFO lore. This strange creature was reportedly encountered in the small town of Flatwoods, West Virginia, in September 1952, during a time when the United States was experiencing a surge of UFO sightings. The encounter with the Flatwoods Monster has since become one of the most iconic and enduring stories in the history of unexplained phenomena. This chapter explores the details of the Flatwoods Monster encounter, the theories surrounding its origin, and its lasting impact on the community and popular culture.

The story of the Flatwoods Monster begins on the evening of September 12, 1952, when two brothers, Edward and Fred May, along with their friend Tommy Hyer, witnessed a bright object streak across the sky and land on a nearby farm owned by local farmer G. Bailey Fisher. Excited and curious about what they had seen, the boys ran home to tell their mother, Kathleen May, who quickly gathered a group of people to investigate the strange sight. The group included National Guardsman Eugene Lemon, who brought a flashlight to help navigate the darkening terrain.

As the group approached the area where the object had reportedly landed, they noticed a pulsating red light on a hilltop. They also detected a foul, acrid odor in the air that made some of them feel nauseous. Undeterred, they continued up the hill, where they soon encountered something that none of them could have anticipated.

According to the witnesses, they saw a strange creature, roughly 10 to 12 feet tall, with a spade-shaped head and glowing eyes. The creature appeared to be floating or hovering above the ground and was surrounded by a misty, metallic substance. Its body was described as being dark or black, with a draped or skirt-like lower half, and it had long, claw-like hands or appendages. The creature's eyes emitted a bright orange-red glow, which added to the eerie and unsettling atmosphere of the encounter.

Eugene Lemon, who was at the front of the group, shined his flashlight on the creature, which reportedly reacted by emitting a hissing noise and gliding toward the group. Frightened, Lemon dropped his flashlight, and the group quickly fled back down the hill to safety. Once they reached town, they reported the incident to local authorities, who conducted a search of the area but found no trace of the creature or the mysterious light.

The story of the Flatwoods Monster spread quickly, capturing the attention of the national media. Newspapers across the country reported on the strange encounter, and the small town of Flatwoods was soon flooded with curiosity seekers, reporters, and UFO enthusiasts eager to learn more about the mysterious creature. The encounter was also investigated by the U.S. Air Force as part of Project Blue Book, the government's official study of UFO sightings.

Various theories have been proposed to explain the Flatwoods Monster encounter. One of the most popular explanations is that the creature was actually a misidentified owl or other large bird, seen under unusual circumstances. The bright eyes, spade-shaped head, and hovering motion could have been the result of the witnesses seeing an owl perched on a branch or another elevated surface, its eyes reflecting the light from the flashlight. The mist or metallic substance might have been vapor from the ground, and the foul odor could have been caused by natural gases or vegetation in the area.

Skeptics also suggest that the excitement and fear of the situation may have led to an exaggeration of what the witnesses saw, turning a mundane event into a more dramatic and frightening experience. The power of suggestion, combined with the influence of media coverage and the era's fascination with UFOs, may have contributed to the lasting impression of the Flatwoods Monster as a supernatural or extraterrestrial entity.

Despite these more mundane explanations, some researchers and UFO enthusiasts believe that the Flatwoods Monster was indeed an extraterrestrial being or a visitor from another dimension. They argue that the creature's strange appearance, the accompanying UFO sighting, and the physical effects experienced by the witnesses—such as nausea and irritation of the eyes and throat—are consistent with other reports of encounters with extraterrestrial beings and their craft.

Another theory suggests that the Flatwoods Monster could have been a type of robot or mechanical being, possibly sent to explore or interact with Earth. The creature's metallic appearance and the absence of typical biological features, such as a mouth or nose, lend some support to this idea. If the creature was a robot or drone, it might explain its odd behavior and the lack of any physical evidence after the encounter.

Regardless of its true nature, the Flatwoods Monster has left a lasting impact on the community of Flatwoods and on popular culture. The town has embraced its place in UFO history, with local businesses and tourism efforts capitalizing on the legend. Flatwoods is now home to several "monster" statues, gift shops, and annual events that celebrate the encounter, drawing visitors from around the world who are fascinated by the mystery.

The Flatwoods Monster has also become a part of American folklore, inspiring books, documentaries, and even appearances in video games and television shows. The creature's unique appearance and the chilling details of the encounter have cemented its place in the pantheon of unexplained phenomena, alongside other famous cases such as the Mothman of West Virginia and the Roswell UFO incident.

In conclusion, the Flatwoods Monster remains one of the most unique and intriguing encounters in the history of UFO phenomena. Whether it was a misidentified bird, a visitor from another world, or something else entirely, the Flatwoods Monster has captured the imagination of generations and continues to be a subject of fascination and debate. The encounter serves as a reminder of the enduring mystery and wonder that surrounds the unknown, and the ways in which extraordinary events can become woven into the fabric of local and national culture. As we continue to explore the possibilities of extraterrestrial life and the nature of our reality, the Flatwoods Monster stands as a testament to the power of a single, unforgettable experience to shape our collective understanding of the world around us.

The Roswell Aliens: Craft and Bodies Recovered

The Roswell incident is arguably the most famous and controversial UFO event in modern history. It centers on the alleged crash of an unidentified flying object near Roswell, New Mexico, in July 1947, and the subsequent recovery of alien bodies by the U.S. military. Over the decades, the Roswell incident has become synonymous with UFO cover-ups, sparking numerous books, documentaries, and conspiracy theories. This chapter explores the details of the Roswell incident, the accounts of the recovered craft and alien bodies, and the ongoing debate over what really happened in the New Mexico desert more than seven decades ago.

The story of the Roswell incident begins in early July 1947, when a rancher named William "Mac" Brazel discovered unusual debris scattered across his ranch, located about 75 miles north of Roswell. The debris reportedly included metallic-looking material, some of which was lightweight yet incredibly strong, as well as pieces that appeared to be part of a structure or framework. Unsure of what he had found, Brazel contacted the local sheriff, who in turn notified the nearby Roswell Army Air Field (RAAF).

On July 8, 1947, the RAAF issued a press release stating that they had recovered a "flying disc" from the crash site. This announcement made headlines across the country, fueling speculation that the military had captured a spacecraft from another world. However, just hours later, the military retracted the statement, claiming that the debris was actually from a weather balloon, not a flying saucer. The new explanation was supported by photos of military personnel posing with what appeared to be pieces of a tattered weather balloon.

For many years, the official explanation of a weather balloon was widely accepted, and the Roswell incident faded from public attention. However, in the late 1970s, new interest in the case was sparked by interviews with witnesses and former military personnel who claimed that the true story had been covered up. According to these accounts, the material recovered at the crash site was not from a weather balloon but from an extraterrestrial spacecraft, and several alien bodies were also found among the wreckage.

One of the key figures in bringing the Roswell incident back into the spotlight was Jesse Marcel, who was the intelligence officer at the RAAF in 1947 and was involved in the initial recovery of the debris. In interviews given in the late 1970s, Marcel claimed that the debris he handled was unlike anything he had ever seen before. He described it as being made of a material that was extremely light but incredibly strong, and which had properties that defied explanation, such as returning to its original shape after being crumpled. Marcel's account contradicted the official weather balloon story, leading many to believe that a cover-up had taken place.

Further claims emerged from other witnesses, including Glenn Dennis, a Roswell mortician who alleged that he was called to the Roswell Army Air Field to provide child-sized coffins and was later told by a nurse friend that she had seen alien bodies being examined at the base. According to Dennis, the bodies were small, with large heads, and were unlike anything on Earth. These claims added fuel to the growing belief that the U.S. government had recovered extraterrestrial beings at Roswell and was keeping the truth hidden from the public.

In 1980, the book *The Roswell Incident* by Charles Berlitz and William Moore brought the case back into the national spotlight, presenting interviews and evidence that supported the idea of a UFO crash and a government cover-up. The book became a bestseller and played a significant role in cementing the Roswell incident as a cornerstone of UFO conspiracy theories.

Over the years, various researchers and investigators have put forth different theories about what really happened at Roswell. Some believe that the military recovered not just one, but two crash sites, with the second site containing the bulk of the debris and the alien bodies. Others suggest that the Roswell crash involved advanced, top-secret military technology, possibly related to post-World War II experiments or the Cold War arms race, and that the UFO story was a convenient cover for these activities.

In response to the growing public interest and speculation, the U.S. Air Force released two reports in the 1990s aimed at debunking the UFO and alien body claims. The first report, published in 1994, concluded that the debris recovered at Roswell was part of Project Mogul, a top-secret program involving high-altitude balloons designed to detect Soviet nuclear tests. The second report, released in 1997, addressed the claims of alien bodies, suggesting that witnesses had likely misidentified crash test dummies used in military experiments as extraterrestrial beings.

Despite these official explanations, many people remain unconvinced, arguing that the government's changing stories and the secrecy surrounding the case point to a deliberate cover-up. The Roswell incident has become a focal point for those who believe that the U.S. government is withholding information about extraterrestrial life and UFOs. It has also fueled a broader cultural fascination with aliens, inspiring countless movies, TV shows, books, and other media.

The Roswell incident has also had a lasting impact on the town of Roswell itself, which has embraced its association with UFOs and extraterrestrial life. Roswell is now home to the International UFO Museum and Research Center, and the town hosts an annual UFO Festival that attracts visitors from around the world. The legacy of the Roswell incident has transformed the town into a symbol of the ongoing search for truth in the face of official secrecy.

In conclusion, the Roswell incident remains one of the most enduring and debated events in the history of UFO phenomena. The conflicting accounts, the government's handling of the case, and the subsequent emergence of new witnesses and evidence have all contributed to the belief that something extraordinary may have happened in the New Mexico desert in 1947.

Whether the Roswell incident involved an extraterrestrial spacecraft, a military experiment gone wrong, or something else entirely, it has become a symbol of the broader questions surrounding UFOs and the possibility of alien life. As new information continues to emerge and the debate over Roswell persists, the incident serves as a reminder of the enduring human fascination with the unknown and the lengths to which people will go to uncover the truth.

The Phoenix Lights: Mass Sighting or Alien Craft?

The Phoenix Lights is one of the most well-documented and widely witnessed UFO events in modern history. On the evening of March 13, 1997, thousands of people across the state of Arizona, as well as parts of Nevada and Sonora, Mexico, reported seeing a massive, V-shaped formation of lights moving silently across the night sky. The event, which has come to be known as "The Phoenix Lights," has sparked decades of debate, with theories ranging from a military exercise to an extraterrestrial spacecraft. This chapter explores the details of the Phoenix Lights incident, the various explanations that have been proposed, and its lasting impact on the UFO community and popular culture.

The Phoenix Lights event began around 7:30 p.m. local time when people in the small town of Henderson, Nevada, reported seeing a large, V-shaped object with six lights moving across the sky. Over the next few hours, similar sightings were reported in Prescott, Arizona, and eventually in the Phoenix metropolitan area, where the phenomenon was seen by thousands of people, including police officers, pilots, and residents from all walks of life. The object was described as being enormous—some witnesses estimated it to be over a mile wide—and it moved silently and slowly across the sky.

The lights on the object were described as being white or amber and evenly spaced along the edges of the V-shape. Some witnesses reported seeing a solid structure connecting the lights, while others believed the lights were separate objects flying in formation. As the object moved over Phoenix, it passed directly overhead in some areas, blocking out the stars and creating a sense of awe and fear among those who witnessed it.

In addition to the V-shaped formation of lights, there were also reports of other strange lights in the sky that night. Around 10 p.m., a series of bright orbs appeared over the Estrella Mountains, southwest of Phoenix. These lights hovered in place for several minutes before gradually disappearing. This secondary event was captured on video by multiple witnesses and became a central focus of the investigation and media coverage that followed.

The Phoenix Lights generated widespread media attention and quickly became a topic of intense public interest. Local news stations aired interviews with witnesses, and video footage of the lights was shown repeatedly. The event also attracted the attention of national and international media, leading to widespread speculation about the nature of the phenomenon.

In the days following the event, the U.S. military offered an explanation for the lights, claiming that they were the result of a training exercise involving A-10 Warthog aircraft from the Maryland Air National Guard, which were dropping flares over the Barry M. Goldwater Range, southwest of Phoenix. According to the military, the flares were responsible for the lights seen in the sky around 10 p.m. However, this explanation did not account for the earlier sightings of the V-shaped formation, which had occurred several hours earlier and over a much larger area.

Many witnesses and UFO researchers were skeptical of the military's explanation, arguing that the characteristics of the lights—such as their slow, silent movement and the apparent size of the object—did not match those of military flares or aircraft. The sheer number of witnesses, the consistency of their descriptions, and the duration of the sightings led many to believe that the Phoenix Lights were something far more extraordinary than a military exercise.

One of the most notable aspects of the Phoenix Lights incident is the credibility of the witnesses who came forward. Among them was Fife Symington, the governor of Arizona at the time, who initially made light of the event by holding a press conference where he had an aide dress up as an alien. However, in later years, Symington admitted that he had also seen the lights that night and described the object as being "otherworldly." His admission added significant weight to the argument that the Phoenix Lights were not a simple case of misidentified military activity.

The Phoenix Lights also became a flashpoint for discussions about government secrecy and the possibility of an extraterrestrial presence on Earth. Many people were frustrated by what they perceived as a lack of transparency and a dismissive attitude from the government and military officials. This sentiment was compounded by the fact that no definitive explanation for the earlier V-shaped formation of lights was ever provided.

Over the years, various theories have been proposed to explain the Phoenix Lights. Some skeptics argue that the V-shaped formation could have been a series of aircraft flying in close formation, with their lights creating the illusion of a single, massive object. However, this explanation has been challenged by witnesses who insist that the object they saw was solid, blocking out the stars as it passed overhead.

Another theory suggests that the lights could have been part of a secret military project, possibly involving experimental aircraft or advanced stealth technology. However, the scale of the sightings, the number of witnesses, and the lack of any clear military presence in the area at the time make this explanation difficult to substantiate.

For many people, the most compelling explanation is that the Phoenix Lights were the result of an extraterrestrial craft visiting Earth. The sheer size of the object, its silent movement, and the coordinated nature of the lights all suggest something beyond current human capabilities. The idea that an alien spacecraft could have flown over one of the largest cities in the United States without being intercepted or explained by the authorities is both thrilling and unsettling, fueling speculation and debate for decades.

The Phoenix Lights incident has had a lasting impact on the UFO community and popular culture. It has been the subject of numerous documentaries, books, and television programs, and continues to be a key reference point in discussions about UFOs and extraterrestrial life. The event also inspired the 2007 film "The Phoenix Lights," which dramatized the events of that night and explored the various theories surrounding the phenomenon.

In conclusion, the Phoenix Lights remain one of the most compelling and mysterious UFO events in modern history. Whether the lights were the result of a military exercise, an extraterrestrial craft, or something else entirely, the incident has left an indelible mark on the public consciousness. The sheer number of witnesses, the credibility of many of those who came forward, and the enduring mystery of what exactly was seen in the skies over Arizona continue to make the Phoenix Lights a subject of fascination and debate. As we continue to explore the possibilities of life beyond Earth and the potential for contact with extraterrestrial civilizations, the Phoenix Lights stand as a powerful reminder of the mysteries that still exist in our world and the universe beyond.

Whitley Strieber's Visitors: An Ongoing Contact

Whitley Strieber's experiences with what he calls "the Visitors" are among the most detailed, intense, and controversial accounts of alien contact ever recorded. Strieber, a best-selling author, first publicly shared his encounters with these beings in his 1987 book *Communion*, which became a cultural phenomenon and significantly influenced the public's perception of alien abduction.

Strieber's ongoing contact with the Visitors has been both a source of profound insight and deep personal struggle, raising questions about the nature of these entities, their intentions, and the broader implications for humanity. This chapter delves into Strieber's experiences, the characteristics of the Visitors, and the lasting impact of his story on the UFO and alien contact narrative.

Whitley Strieber was already an established author of horror and science fiction before his life took a dramatic turn in December 1985. While staying at his cabin in upstate New York, Strieber had a terrifying experience that would change his life forever. He described waking up in the middle of the night to find himself paralysed, surrounded by strange beings who took him from his bed and subjected him to a series of unsettling procedures. These beings, which he later referred to as the Visitors, were not easily categorized as simply extraterrestrial or human. They appeared in various forms, some resembling the typical "Greys" with large, almond-shaped eyes, while others had more insectoid or humanoid features.

In *Communion*, Strieber detailed these encounters and the profound impact they had on him. He described a range of emotions, from fear and confusion to awe and curiosity, as he tried to make sense of what was happening to him. The book struck a chord with many readers who had experienced similar phenomena, and it quickly became a bestseller. *Communion* brought the concept of alien abduction into the mainstream, and Strieber became a central figure in the discussion about contact with non-human entities.

One of the most striking aspects of Strieber's encounters with the Visitors is the ambiguity surrounding their nature and intentions. Unlike the more straightforward narratives of benevolent or malevolent extraterrestrials, Strieber's Visitors defy easy classification. They are elusive, appearing to him in different forms and communicating in ways that are often symbolic or indirect. Strieber has described them as being both physically present and somehow existing outside the conventional understanding of space and time.

The Visitors are often depicted as deeply enigmatic, with their true purpose remaining unclear even to Strieber after decades of contact. Some experiences seemed to involve painful or invasive procedures, leading Strieber to initially fear the Visitors and question their intentions. However, over time, he also reported experiences that suggested a more complex relationship, one that involved not just fear but also a sense of connection, learning, and even spiritual awakening.

Strieber's relationship with the Visitors evolved as he continued to document his experiences in subsequent books, including *Transformation* (1988), *Breakthrough* (1995), and *The Secret School* (1997). In these works, he explored the possibility that the Visitors were not simply aliens from another planet but beings from another dimension, time travelers, or even manifestations of some deeper aspect of human consciousness. This broader interpretation of the Visitors added a new layer of complexity to Strieber's narrative and challenged conventional ideas about the nature of reality.

One of the central themes in Strieber's work is the idea that the Visitors are somehow connected to humanity's evolution, both on a physical and spiritual level. He has speculated that their interest in humans might involve genetic or consciousness-related experiments, aimed at guiding or accelerating our development. This theory aligns with broader themes in UFO and alien contact literature, where extraterrestrials are often seen as either guardians or manipulators of human destiny.

Strieber's experiences with the Visitors have had a profound impact on his personal life, leading him to explore various spiritual practices and philosophies in an attempt to understand the nature of his encounters. He has studied and written about topics such as out-of-body experiences, meditation, and the nature of the soul, all of which he believes are related to the Visitors' interest in humanity. This exploration has led Strieber to view his experiences not just as alien encounters but as part of a larger spiritual journey.

Despite the deeply personal and often unsettling nature of his experiences, Strieber has been remarkably open about his ongoing contact with the Visitors. He has shared his story not only through his books but also through lectures, interviews, and his popular website, Unknown Country, where he continues to explore these topics and engage with others who have had similar experiences. Strieber's openness has made him a polarizing figure, with some viewing him as a brave pioneer in the exploration of human consciousness, while others dismiss his accounts as delusions or fabrications.

One of the most controversial aspects of Strieber's narrative is the question of whether the Visitors are physically real or a psychological phenomenon. Strieber himself has acknowledged the possibility that his experiences could be the result of some form of psychological or neurological anomaly. However, he has also argued that the intensity and consistency of the experiences, combined with their impact on his life and the lives of many others who have had similar encounters, suggest that there is something more at play.

Strieber's work has had a lasting impact on the UFO community and on the broader discussion of human consciousness and the nature of reality. *Communion* and its sequels have inspired countless others to come forward with their own experiences, contributing to the growing body of literature on alien contact and abduction phenomena. The idea that these encounters might be part of a broader spiritual or consciousness-related experience has also influenced the way many people approach the subject of UFOs and extraterrestrial life, moving beyond the simple question of "Are we alone?" to explore deeper philosophical and existential questions.

In conclusion, Whitley Strieber's encounters with the Visitors represent one of the most complex and compelling narratives in the field of UFO and alien contact literature. His ongoing relationship with these enigmatic beings challenges our understanding of reality, consciousness, and the nature of extraterrestrial life. Whether the Visitors are aliens, interdimensional beings, or something else entirely, Strieber's experiences offer a unique and thought-provoking perspective on the mysteries of human existence. As we continue to explore the possibilities of life beyond Earth and the potential for contact with other intelligences, Strieber's story serves as a reminder of the profound and often unsettling ways in which these encounters can shape our understanding of ourselves and the universe.

Bob Lazar's Revelations: Working at S-4

Bob Lazar is one of the most controversial and intriguing figures in the world of UFO and extraterrestrial studies. His claims of working at a secretive site known as S-4, located near the infamous Area 51, and his detailed descriptions of reverse engineering alien technology have had a profound impact on the UFO community and have fueled countless conspiracy theories. Lazar's revelations have sparked debates about government secrecy, the existence of extraterrestrial life, and the potential for advanced, hidden technologies. This chapter delves into Bob Lazar's story, the specifics of his claims, and the broader implications of his alleged experiences.

Bob Lazar first came into the public eye in 1989 when he was interviewed by investigative reporter George Knapp for a Las Vegas television station. In the interview, Lazar, using the pseudonym "Dennis" at the time to protect his identity, claimed that he had been employed by the U.S. government to work on extraterrestrial technology at a site known as S-4, located near the highly classified Area 51 military base in Nevada. According to Lazar, S-4 was a highly secretive facility where several recovered alien spacecraft were being reverse-engineered in an effort to understand and replicate their advanced technology.

Lazar's most explosive claim was that he had personally worked on one of these extraterrestrial craft. He described the craft as being saucer-shaped, with a propulsion system that utilized an element called "Element 115" to generate gravity waves. According to Lazar, the alien spacecraft's propulsion system was capable of bending space and time, allowing it to travel vast distances almost instantaneously—a concept that aligns with theoretical ideas about warp drives and gravity manipulation in modern physics.

Element 115, which was unknown to science at the time of Lazar's claims, was said to be the key to the craft's advanced propulsion system. Lazar described how the element was used in a reactor that produced a powerful gravity wave, which could be manipulated to propel the craft. He claimed that the element was incredibly rare and had been synthesized in small quantities for use in the alien technology. Interestingly, years after Lazar's revelations, Element 115 (Moscovium) was officially added to the periodic table in 2003, though its synthesized form is highly unstable and decays rapidly, raising questions about the feasibility of its use in the manner Lazar described.

Lazar's story also included detailed descriptions of the interior of the craft and the various technologies he encountered. He spoke of seats that were too small for human beings, leading him to conclude that the craft was designed for extraterrestrial beings. He also described the controls of the craft as being operated by the mind, suggesting a level of technological sophistication far beyond anything available on Earth at the time.

Lazar's claims have been met with both intrigue and skepticism. On one hand, his detailed descriptions of the technology and his apparent knowledge of certain scientific principles have led many in the UFO community to believe that he is telling the truth. On the other hand, critics have pointed out several inconsistencies in his story and have questioned his credentials. For example, Lazar claimed to have degrees from the Massachusetts Institute of Technology (MIT) and the California Institute of Technology (Caltech), but there are no records of him attending these institutions. Lazar has countered this by suggesting that the government erased his academic and employment records as part of a cover-up to discredit him.

In addition to the controversy surrounding his credentials, some skeptics argue that Lazar's descriptions of the alien technology are too speculative and lack concrete evidence. While his explanations of gravity wave propulsion and Element 115 are intriguing, they are also highly theoretical and have not been demonstrated or proven in any practical sense. Critics also point out that the idea of reverse engineering alien technology, while fascinating, is difficult to verify without physical evidence or corroborating testimony from others who worked at S-4.

Despite the skepticism, Lazar's story has had a lasting impact on the UFO community and popular culture. His revelations have become a cornerstone of the modern UFO narrative, particularly in discussions about government secrecy and the possibility that advanced alien technology is being hidden from the public. Lazar's claims have also contributed to the mystique surrounding Area 51, which has long been rumored to be a site of secretive military projects and extraterrestrial research.

In the years following his initial revelations, Lazar has remained a somewhat elusive figure, giving occasional interviews and participating in documentaries, but generally avoiding the public spotlight. His reluctance to engage with the media and his insistence on the truth of his story have only added to the mystique surrounding him. The 2018 documentary *Bob Lazar: Area 51 & Flying Saucers*, directed by Jeremy Corbell, brought Lazar's story back into the public eye, introducing a new generation to his claims and reigniting the debate over their veracity.

One of the most significant aspects of Lazar's story is its broader implications for our understanding of technology, science, and government secrecy. If Lazar's claims are true, it would suggest that the U.S. government has access to technologies far beyond what is publicly known and that this technology is of extraterrestrial origin. This raises profound questions about the nature of human progress, the role of secrecy in scientific advancement, and the potential consequences of withholding such knowledge from the public.

Lazar's revelations also touch on deeper philosophical questions about humanity's place in the universe. The idea that we are not alone and that extraterrestrial civilizations have visited Earth has captivated the imagination of millions of people. Lazar's story, whether true or not, taps into this collective fascination and serves as a reminder of the enduring mystery and wonder that surrounds the possibility of contact with other intelligent beings.

In conclusion, Bob Lazar's revelations about his work at S-4 and his claims of reverse engineering alien technology remain some of the most controversial and intriguing elements of modern UFO lore. While his story has been met with both belief and skepticism, its impact on the UFO community and popular culture is undeniable. Lazar's account challenges our understanding of science, technology, and government secrecy, and raises profound questions about the nature of reality and our place in the cosmos. As the debate over his claims continues, Lazar's story serves as a powerful reminder of the mysteries that still exist in our world and the potential for extraordinary discoveries just beyond the limits of our current understanding.

Area 51: Epicenter of Alien Technology

Area 51, a highly classified U.S. Air Force facility located in the Nevada desert, has long been the subject of intense speculation, mystery, and conspiracy theories. For decades, it has been widely rumored to be the epicenter of secret research and development projects involving advanced alien technology, particularly related to the reverse engineering of extraterrestrial spacecraft. The association of Area 51 with UFOs and aliens has made it one of the most iconic and enigmatic locations in popular culture. This chapter explores the history of Area 51, the claims of alien technology being studied there, and the broader implications of its reputation as a hub of extraterrestrial research.

Area 51 is officially known as the Nevada Test and Training Range, a part of the larger Nellis Air Force Base complex. It is located in the remote Groom Lake area, about 83 miles north-northwest of Las Vegas. The facility was established in the 1950s as a testing ground for the U-2 spy plane, a top-secret reconnaissance aircraft developed during the Cold War. The site's isolation and vast airspace made it an ideal location for testing advanced aircraft and conducting highly classified military projects.

For many years, the very existence of Area 51 was denied by the U.S. government. It was not until the 1990s that the government officially acknowledged the facility's presence, following a series of legal challenges and Freedom of Information Act requests. Despite this acknowledgment, much of what occurs at Area 51 remains shrouded in secrecy, fueling ongoing speculation and conspiracy theories about its true purpose.

The association of Area 51 with extraterrestrial technology can be traced back to the late 1970s and early 1980s, when reports began to surface about unusual activities and sightings in the area. However, it was Bob Lazar's explosive claims in 1989 that truly catapulted Area 51 into the spotlight as a focal point of alien conspiracy theories. Lazar, as discussed in the previous chapter, claimed to have worked at a nearby facility called S-4, where he allegedly participated in the reverse engineering of alien spacecraft recovered by the U.S. government.

According to Lazar, S-4 was located just a short distance from Area 51 and was accessible only by a heavily guarded road. He described a series of hangars built into the side of a mountain, where several flying saucers were stored and studied. Lazar's account included detailed descriptions of the alien technology, including the use of Element 115 to generate gravity waves for propulsion, and the efforts to understand and replicate the capabilities of the extraterrestrial craft.

Lazar's revelations brought Area 51 into the public consciousness as a place where alien technology was allegedly being studied and developed. His claims have been met with both fascination and skepticism, but they have undeniably contributed to the enduring mystique of Area 51 as a hub of extraterrestrial research.

The secrecy surrounding Area 51, combined with the government's reluctance to disclose information about the activities conducted there, has only added to the speculation that the facility is involved in more than just the development of advanced military aircraft. Over the years, numerous former employees, contractors, and alleged insiders have come forward with stories of encountering strange phenomena at the base, including sightings of unidentified flying objects, alien beings, and highly advanced technologies that defy conventional understanding.

One of the most persistent rumours about Area 51 is that it houses the remnants of extraterrestrial spacecraft recovered from crash sites, most notably from the infamous Roswell incident of 1947. According to various accounts, the wreckage of the Roswell UFO, along with the bodies of its alien occupants, was transported to Area 51 for study. While there is no definitive evidence to support this claim, it remains a central element of the Area 51 mythology.

In addition to the alleged reverse engineering of alien technology, Area 51 is also rumored to be the site of ongoing experiments involving human-alien hybridization, time travel, and other highly speculative projects. Some conspiracy theories suggest that the U.S. government is working in collaboration with extraterrestrial beings, who provide advanced technology in exchange for access to human subjects or resources. These theories are often dismissed by sceptics as unfounded and sensational, but they continue to capture the imagination of the public.

The cultural impact of Area 51 cannot be overstated. The facility has been featured in countless books, movies, television shows, and video games, often depicted as the ultimate repository of government secrets and alien technology. Films like "Independence Day" and "Paul," as well as television series like "The X-Files," have reinforced the idea that Area 51 is the epicenter of extraterrestrial activity on Earth.

The speculation surrounding Area 51 reached a peak in 2019 with the "Storm Area 51" event, a social media phenomenon that began as a joke but quickly went viral. The event, which called for people to "storm" the base to "see them aliens," attracted widespread media attention and highlighted the enduring fascination with the site. While the actual turnout was much smaller than anticipated, the event underscored the deep cultural resonance of Area 51 as a symbol of hidden knowledge and government secrecy.

Despite the intrigue, much of what is known about Area 51 suggests that its primary focus has always been on the development and testing of advanced military aircraft. Over the years, several ground-breaking aircraft have been developed and tested at the facility, including the U-2 spy plane, the SR-71 Blackbird, and the F-117 Nighthawk stealth fighter. The secrecy surrounding these projects, along with the unusual shapes and capabilities of the aircraft, may have contributed to the sightings of unidentified flying objects in the area.

However, the possibility that Area 51 also serves as a site for the study of extraterrestrial technology cannot be entirely ruled out. The facility's remoteness, strict security measures, and the government's history of withholding information about its activities have all contributed to the belief that something extraordinary may be happening there. Whether or not Area 51 is truly the epicenter of alien technology, it remains a potent symbol of the unknown and the potential for hidden truths that lie just beyond our reach.

In conclusion, Area 51 stands as one of the most enigmatic and culturally significant locations in the world. While its primary function as a testing ground for advanced military aircraft is well-documented, the facility's association with extraterrestrial technology and UFOs has made it a focal point of conspiracy theories and public fascination. The enduring mystery of Area 51 speaks to our collective curiosity about the unknown and our desire to uncover the secrets that may be hidden within its guarded boundaries. As the debate over the true nature of Area 51 continues, the site will likely remain a symbol of the tantalizing possibilities that exist at the intersection of science, secrecy, and the unexplained.

The Betty and Barney Hill Case: First Abduction

The Betty and Barney Hill case is widely regarded as the first widely publicized claim of alien abduction in the United States and has since become a cornerstone of UFO lore. The couple's encounter in 1961 introduced the concept of alien abduction to the public and set the stage for countless other accounts of similar experiences. This chapter delves into the details of the Hill case, exploring the events of that night, the subsequent investigation, and the lasting impact of their story on the UFO community and popular culture.

The Encounter

On the night of September 19, 1961, Betty and Barney Hill, a married couple from Portsmouth, New Hampshire, were returning home from a vacation in Canada. As they drove through the White Mountains of New Hampshire, Betty noticed a bright light in the sky that appeared to be following them. Initially thinking it was a star or a plane, the couple continued on their way, but the light grew larger and closer as they drove. Betty, curious and somewhat concerned, urged Barney to stop the car so they could get a better look.

Barney eventually pulled over, and the couple used binoculars to observe the object more closely. What they saw was unlike anything they had ever seen before. The object was disc-shaped, with rows of windows along its edge, and it appeared to be rotating. Barney, a World War II veteran, initially thought it might be a military aircraft, but as the object descended toward them, he became increasingly alarmed. Through the binoculars, he claimed to see humanoid figures inside the craft, staring back at him.

Terrified, Barney hurried back to the car, telling Betty that they needed to leave immediately. As they sped down the road, the object reportedly moved directly over their vehicle, emitting a series of beeping and buzzing sounds. The next thing the Hills remembered was finding themselves 35 miles further down the road with little recollection of how they got there. Both Betty and Barney felt an overwhelming sense of confusion and anxiety as they continued their drive home.

The Aftermath

Once home, the Hills began to notice strange things. Their watches had stopped working, Barney's shoes were scuffed, and Betty's dress was torn and covered in an unknown pink substance. They also experienced intense anxiety and nightmares about the encounter. Disturbed by the events of that night, Betty contacted the local Air Force base to report the incident. She was interviewed by Major Paul W. Henderson, who filed a report with Project Blue Book, the Air Force's official UFO investigation program. Although Henderson dismissed the sighting as an unidentified aircraft, the Hills were not satisfied with this explanation. In the weeks following the encounter, Betty began experiencing vivid nightmares in which she and Barney were taken aboard the UFO by strange beings who conducted medical examinations on them. These dreams left her deeply shaken, and she shared them with Barney, who was initially reluctant to believe that they were anything more than nightmares. However, both Betty and Barney felt that something had happened to them that night that they could not fully remember. In 1963, the Hills sought the help of Dr. Benjamin Simon, a well-respected Boston psychiatrist and neurologist, in an attempt to recover their lost memories through hypnosis. Over several sessions, Dr. Simon hypnotized both Betty and Barney separately and had them recount the events of that night. Under hypnosis, both of the Hills provided detailed and consistent accounts of being abducted by extraterrestrial beings and taken aboard a spacecraft.

The Abduction Experience

According to the Hills' hypnotic recollections, after the beeping sounds, they were stopped by a group of humanoid beings who escorted them onto the UFO. The beings were described as being short, with large, hairless heads, slanted eyes, and grayish skin—an early description of what would later become known as the "Greys." Once aboard the craft, the Hills reported being separated and subjected to a series of medical examinations. Betty described having a long needle inserted into her navel, which she was told was a pregnancy test, while Barney recalled having a device placed over his genitals and samples of his sperm taken. Both Betty and Barney reported that the beings communicated with them telepathically and seemed to be particularly interested in human reproduction. Betty also recalled being shown a "star map" by one of the beings, which she later drew under hypnosis. This map purportedly showed the location of the beings' home star system in relation to Earth's solar system. Although the map has been the subject of much speculation and analysis over the years, its exact meaning remains unclear.

The Investigation and Public Response

The Hills' account of their abduction quickly gained attention, both from the UFO community and the general public. In 1965, their story was published in the book *The Interrupted Journey* by John G. Fuller, which brought the case to a much wider audience. The book's publication, along with subsequent media coverage, helped to popularize the concept of alien abduction and made the Hills' case one of the most famous UFO encounters in history. The Hills' experience also sparked considerable debate and skepticism. Dr. Benjamin Simon, while believing that the Hills were sincere in their beliefs, suggested that their recollections might be a product of a shared delusion or the result of Betty's dreams, which Barney had internalized. Critics also pointed to inconsistencies in their story and questioned the reliability of hypnosis as a method for recovering memories. Despite the skepticism, the Hills' story resonated with many people, particularly those who had experienced similar encounters. Their case became a template for future abduction reports, with many of the details—such as the Greys, medical examinations, and telepathic communication—appearing in subsequent accounts. The Hills' experience also helped to shape the broader narrative of alien abduction, influencing everything from science fiction to psychological studies.

The Legacy of the Hill Case

The Betty and Barney Hill case is significant not only because it was the first widely publicized alien abduction account but also because it set the stage for how such encounters would be perceived and reported in the years to come. The details of their story have become deeply embedded in the cultural consciousness, influencing countless other reports of alien abductions and contributing to the development of the modern UFO phenomenon. The case has also been the subject of numerous books, documentaries, and films, further cementing its place in the annals of UFO history. Despite the ongoing debate over the veracity of the Hills' account, their story remains one of the most compelling and influential in the history of alien encounters. The Betty and Barney Hill case stands as a landmark event in the study of UFOs and alien abductions. Whether viewed as a genuine encounter with extraterrestrial beings or as a psychological phenomenon, the Hills' story has had a profound impact on the way we think about the possibility of contact with otherworldly intelligences. Their experience continues to be a source of fascination, debate, and inspiration, serving as a reminder of the enduring mystery and wonder that surrounds the question of whether we are alone in the universe.

The Travis Walton Experience: Fire in the Sky

The Travis Walton experience, often referred to as the "Fire in the Sky" incident, is one of the most well-known and controversial cases of alleged alien abduction. Walton's encounter in 1975 not only gained widespread attention but also sparked debates that continue to this day about the nature of his experience. This chapter explores the details of Walton's account, the investigation that followed, and the lasting impact of his story on the UFO community and popular culture.

The Incident

On November 5, 1975, Travis Walton was working as part of a logging crew in the Apache-Sitgreaves National Forest near Snowflake, Arizona. Walton, then 22 years old, and his six coworkers were driving home after a long day of work when they encountered a mysterious object in the sky. As the crew's truck made its way through the dense forest, they saw a bright light ahead and soon realized it was coming from a hovering, disc-shaped object. The object was described as being metallic and emitting a strong, bright light that illuminated the surrounding area. Curious and perhaps driven by a sense of adventure, Walton got out of the truck and approached the object despite the protests of his co-workers. As he neared the craft, Walton was suddenly struck by a beam of light or energy that sent him flying through the air, knocking him unconscious. Panicked by what they had witnessed, Walton's coworkers fled the scene, driving quickly back to the town of Snowflake to report the incident to the authorities. They claimed that Walton had been taken by the UFO, a claim that was met with skepticism by local law enforcement. A search party was organized, but Walton was nowhere to be found.

The Aftermath

Walton's disappearance sparked a massive search effort that involved law enforcement, volunteers, and even helicopters, but there was no sign of him. For five days, Walton was missing, and rumors began to circulate that his coworkers had either harmed him or that the entire story was a hoax. The crew members were subjected to polygraph tests to determine if they were telling the truth about the incident. Remarkably, all but one of the crew members passed the tests, which seemed to lend credibility to their story.

Then, on November 10, 1975, Walton suddenly reappeared, disoriented and confused, near Heber, Arizona, about 15 miles from where he had disappeared. He claimed to have no memory of the five days he had been missing, except for fragmented and terrifying images of being aboard a spacecraft with strange beings.

Walton's Account

After his return, Walton gradually recovered memories of what had happened to him during those five days. He claimed that after being struck by the beam of light, he regained consciousness inside a strange room, lying on a table. The room was filled with medical-like instruments, and Walton quickly realized he was not alone. Standing over him were several small beings with large heads and eyes, similar to the "Greys" commonly described in other abduction cases. According to Walton, the beings appeared to be conducting some sort of examination on him. Frightened and in pain, he attempted to fight them off but was unable to overpower them. He described the beings as having smooth, pale skin, and wearing tight-fitting suits. Walton eventually managed to escape from the room and ran through a series of corridors, finding himself in another part of the craft.

In this new area, Walton encountered what he described as more human-like beings, who were taller and had more normal-looking facial features. They wore helmets and blue uniforms and did not speak to him, but they guided him back to the room where he had initially awakened. Walton claimed that these beings placed a mask over his face, causing him to lose consciousness again. The next thing he remembered was waking up on the side of a road, with the craft hovering above him before it quickly sped away into the sky.

The Investigation and Public Response

Walton's story quickly became a media sensation, drawing attention from UFO researchers, skeptics, and the general public. The incident was investigated by several groups, including the Aerial Phenomena Research Organization (APRO) and the National Enquirer, which offered a cash reward for the best UFO story of the year. Walton's case was also examined by the famous UFO researcher Dr. J. Allen Hynek, who was intrigued by the details of the encounter.

Walton underwent multiple polygraph tests, some of which he passed and others that produced inconclusive or contradictory results. These mixed results fueled ongoing debate over the credibility of his account. Skeptics argued that the incident was a hoax, possibly orchestrated by Walton and his co-workers to gain fame or financial reward. They pointed to inconsistencies in Walton's story and the possibility of suggestibility under hypnosis as reasons to doubt his claims. However, Walton and his supporters have consistently maintained that his experience was genuine. Walton has stood by his story for decades, repeatedly stating that he has no doubt about the reality of what happened to him. He even underwent medical examinations, which revealed some anomalies, though nothing definitively proving or disproving his account. In 1978, Walton published a book titled *The Walton Experience*, in which he detailed his encounter and the aftermath. His story was further popularized by the 1993 movie *Fire in the Sky*, which dramatized the events leading up to and following the abduction. While the film took some creative liberties with the story, it brought Walton's experience to a broader audience and cemented his place in UFO lore.

The Legacy of the Travis Walton Experience

The Travis Walton experience remains one of the most compelling and controversial cases in the history of UFO phenomena. Unlike many other abduction stories, Walton's account is supported by the testimony of multiple witnesses who saw the UFO and the subsequent disappearance. The physical evidence, while circumstantial, combined with Walton's consistency in retelling his story over the years, has kept the case alive in the public consciousness. The incident has inspired numerous books, documentaries, and articles, and continues to be a subject of debate among UFO researchers and sceptics alike. For those who believe Walton's account, it stands as one of the most credible examples of alien abduction, providing insights into the possible nature and intentions of extraterrestrial beings. For sceptics, it serves as a cautionary tale about the power of suggestion, the fallibility of memory, and the potential for deception. The Travis Walton experience is a defining case in the study of alien abduction phenomena. Whether one views it as a genuine encounter with extraterrestrial beings or as an elaborate hoax, there is no denying the impact it has had on the UFO community and popular culture. Walton's story challenges our understanding of reality, raising questions about the nature of consciousness, the limits of human knowledge, and the possibility that we are not alone in the universe. As with many UFO cases, the truth may never be fully known, but the mystery of what happened to Travis Walton on that fateful night in 1975 continues to captivate and intrigue people around the world.

The Rendlesham Forest Incident: UK's Roswell

The Rendlesham Forest Incident, often referred to as "Britain's Roswell," is one of the most well-documented and debated UFO events in history. Occurring over several nights in December 1980, near the RAF Bentwaters and RAF Woodbridge military bases in Suffolk, England, the incident involved multiple military personnel witnessing unexplained lights and strange phenomena in the forest. The Rendlesham Forest Incident has since become one of the most significant and controversial UFO cases, drawing comparisons to the Roswell incident due to its impact and the ongoing debates it has sparked. This chapter explores the details of the Rendlesham Forest Incident, the official investigation, and its enduring legacy.

The Incident

The Rendlesham Forest Incident began in the early hours of December 26, 1980, when security personnel at RAF Woodbridge, a base used by the United States Air Force (USAF), noticed strange lights descending into the nearby Rendlesham Forest. At first, they believed it might be a downed aircraft, and a small team was dispatched to investigate. Among the first to arrive at the scene were Staff Sergeant Jim Penniston, Airman First Class John Burroughs, and others from the base's security team.

As they entered the forest, the men encountered a series of bright, pulsating lights that seemed to move through the trees. Penniston described seeing a metallic, triangular craft approximately three meters wide and two meters high, hovering or resting on the forest floor. He claimed to have approached the object, noting strange hieroglyphic-like symbols on its surface. Penniston later stated that he touched the craft, which felt warm to the touch, and after a few moments, the craft suddenly lifted off the ground and disappeared into the night sky at incredible speed.

Burroughs and other witnesses corroborated Penniston's account of the lights and the presence of a mysterious object, although their descriptions varied slightly. Some reported seeing a glowing object with no clear structure, while others saw lights moving erratically through the trees. Despite these differences, all agreed that something highly unusual had occurred.

The following morning, Penniston, Burroughs, and others returned to the site in daylight. They found triangular impressions on the ground where the craft had allegedly landed, as well as broken branches and scorch marks on the trees. Radiation levels at the site were reportedly higher than normal, further adding to the mystery.

The Subsequent Nights

The strange phenomena did not end with the first night. Over the next two nights, more unusual lights were seen in the forest and in the sky above the military bases. On December 28, Lieutenant Colonel Charles Halt, the deputy base commander, led a team into the forest to investigate. Halt carried a portable tape recorder and documented his observations as they occurred, creating an audio record that has since become one of the most important pieces of evidence in the case.

During his investigation, Halt and his team observed a series of flashing lights in the sky, as well as a glowing object that moved through the trees. At one point, the object was reported to emit a beam of light that shone down near their location, which Halt later described as being "like a laser beam." The object then split into multiple smaller lights that moved rapidly through the sky. Halt's audio recording captures his and his team's reactions as they witnessed these events, providing a real-time account of their experiences.

The Official Investigation

The Rendlesham Forest Incident quickly attracted the attention of both the British Ministry of Defence (MoD) and the USAF. However, despite the compelling eyewitness accounts and physical evidence, the MoD officially concluded that the incident posed no threat to national security and did not warrant further investigation. This decision was met with frustration by those involved, particularly Halt, who believed that the events they witnessed were not adequately explained or taken seriously by higher authorities. The lack of a thorough investigation fueled suspicions of a cover-up, similar to the controversies surrounding the Roswell incident in the United States. Many UFO researchers and enthusiasts have argued that the MoD and the USAF downplayed or dismissed the incident to avoid public panic or to conceal knowledge of advanced technology—whether extraterrestrial or secretive military projects.

Theories and Explanations

Over the years, various theories have been proposed to explain the Rendlesham Forest Incident. Skeptics have suggested that the lights seen by the military personnel could have been misidentified natural or man-made phenomena. Some explanations include the nearby Orfordness Lighthouse, which emits a powerful light that could be seen through the trees, and the possibility of a meteor or other celestial event that coincided with the sightings. Others have speculated that the incident was a result of secret military exercises or tests involving advanced technology, possibly conducted without the knowledge of the base personnel. This theory posits that the lights and strange objects witnessed by the soldiers were part of an experimental aircraft or drone, and that the unusual effects, such as the radiation levels and beam of light, were related to this technology. However, these explanations have not satisfied all of those involved in the incident, particularly Penniston and Halt, who continue to assert that what they witnessed was not of human origin. Penniston has gone so far as to claim that he received telepathic messages from the craft when he touched it, revealing a binary code that he later documented. The code, according to Penniston, contained coordinates and messages that have been interpreted by some as evidence of extraterrestrial contact.

The Legacy of the Rendlesham Forest Incident

The Rendlesham Forest Incident has become one of the most famous and enduring UFO cases in the world, often referred to as the "British Roswell" due to its similarities with the American incident in terms of its impact and the controversy it has generated. The case has been the subject of numerous books, documentaries, and television programs, and it continues to be a focus of research and debate among UFO enthusiasts and sceptics alike. The incident has also had a lasting impact on the lives of those who were involved. Many of the witnesses have reported experiencing ongoing psychological and physical effects, and several have expressed frustration and disappointment with the official response to the incident. Despite the lack of definitive answers, the case remains a powerful reminder of the potential for unexplained phenomena to challenge our understanding of the world. In recent years, the Rendlesham Forest Incident has continued to attract attention, with new evidence and interpretations periodically emerging. In 2010, Halt signed an affidavit reaffirming his belief that the objects he and his team witnessed were "extraterrestrial in origin" and criticizing the MoD's handling of the case. This statement has further fueled the debate and has kept the case in the public eye. The Rendlesham Forest Incident stands as one of the most significant and perplexing UFO cases in history. The combination of multiple credible eyewitnesses, physical evidence, and the involvement of military personnel has made it a landmark event in the study of unexplained phenomena. Whether the incident was the result of extraterrestrial contact, secret military technology, or a series of misidentified natural events, its legacy as the "British Roswell" continues to captivate and intrigue those who seek to uncover the truth behind the mysterious lights in Rendlesham Forest.

The Pascagoula Abduction: Unforgettable Night

The Pascagoula Abduction is one of the most famous and well-documented alien abduction cases in UFO history. The incident, which took place on the night of October 11, 1973, in Pascagoula, Mississippi, involved two men, Charles Hickson and Calvin Parker, who claimed to have been abducted by strange, robotic beings while fishing on the banks of the Pascagoula River. The harrowing details of their experience, combined with the subsequent investigation and public attention, have made the Pascagoula Abduction an unforgettable event in the annals of UFO lore. This chapter explores the events of that night, the aftermath, and the enduring impact of the Pascagoula Abduction on the UFO community.

The Abduction

On the evening of October 11, 1973, 42-year-old Charles Hickson and 19-year-old Calvin Parker were fishing off a pier on the west bank of the Pascagoula River. As the sun set and darkness fell, the two men suddenly noticed a strange, bluish light reflecting off the water. When they looked up, they were astonished to see a large, oval-shaped craft hovering just above the ground about 30 feet away from them. The craft emitted a bright, blue light and made a faint, whirring sound as it descended.

Before the men could react, an opening appeared on the side of the craft, and three strange beings emerged and floated toward them. The beings were unlike anything Hickson and Parker had ever seen. They were about five feet tall, with wrinkled, grayish skin and no visible eyes. Their heads were conical, and they had pointed, carrot-like protrusions where their ears and noses should have been. The beings had stiff, robotic movements, and their hands ended in pincer-like claws. The beings grabbed Hickson and Parker and, according to their accounts, floated them into the craft. Inside, Hickson and Parker found themselves in a brightly lit, featureless room. Hickson later described how one of the beings examined him with a large, eye-like device that hovered in front of his face, emitting a series of clicking noises. He felt paralysed and unable to move, but he did not feel pain. Parker, meanwhile, claimed that he was so terrified that he blacked out and had only vague recollections of what happened to him during the encounter. After what felt like an eternity but was likely only a matter of minutes, Hickson and Parker were taken back outside the craft and left on the pier where they had been fishing. The strange beings re-entered the craft, which then lifted off the ground, hovered briefly, and shot off into the sky, disappearing from sight. Dazed and terrified, Hickson and Parker sat in stunned silence for a few moments before Hickson suggested they report the incident to the authorities.

The Aftermath

Hickson and Parker drove to the nearby town of Gautier, where they found a payphone and called Keesler Air Force Base to report the incident. They were told that the Air Force no longer handled UFO reports and were directed to contact local law enforcement. Reluctantly, the men drove to the Jackson County Sheriff's Office, where they recounted their story to Sheriff Fred Diamond and Captain Glenn Ryder.

The officers were skeptical of the men's claims but noted that both Hickson and Parker appeared genuinely frightened and shaken by the experience. To determine if they were telling the truth, the officers left the two men alone in a room that was secretly being recorded. The idea was that if Hickson and Parker were fabricating the story, they would likely discuss it when they thought they were alone. However, the recording revealed that both men continued to express fear and confusion about what had happened, suggesting that they were genuinely traumatized by the experience.

The story quickly made headlines, and the Pascagoula Abduction became a national sensation. UFO investigators, including the renowned Dr. J. Allen Hynek, who was involved in Project Blue Book, took an interest in the case. Both Hickson and Parker underwent polygraph tests, which indicated that they were not lying about the events of that night. However, as with most polygraph results, these findings were not definitive proof of their claims. Hickson, who was more open about discussing the incident, gave several interviews and even appeared on talk shows to recount his experience. He was adamant that what he and Parker had witnessed was real and not a hallucination or a hoax. Parker, on the other hand, was deeply traumatized by the incident and largely avoided the spotlight, seeking to put the experience behind him.

Public Reaction and Skepticism

As with most UFO cases, the Pascagoula Abduction was met with a mix of belief, skepticism, and outright disbelief. Some people were convinced that Hickson and Parker had indeed experienced something extraordinary, citing their consistent stories, the physical evidence of their distress, and the fact that they had little to gain from fabricating such a tale. Others, however, dismissed the incident as a hoax or a case of mistaken perception, possibly triggered by stress, fatigue, or alcohol consumption. Skeptics pointed to the bizarre appearance of the beings and the lack of physical evidence as reasons to doubt the story. Some suggested that the men had concocted the story for attention or financial gain, though Hickson and Parker never made much money from their experience. Others speculated that the encounter could have been a case of sleep paralysis or a shared hallucination, though the details of the story seemed too complex and consistent for such explanations.

The Legacy of the Pascagoula Abduction

Despite the skepticism, the Pascagoula Abduction has endured as one of the most compelling UFO cases on record. The incident has been the subject of numerous books, documentaries, and articles, and it continues to be a topic of interest for UFO researchers and enthusiasts. The story was given new life in 1983 when Charles Hickson published a book titled *UFO Contact at Pascagoula*, in which he detailed the events of that night and their aftermath. In 2018, Calvin Parker, who had largely remained silent about the incident for decades, published his own book, *Pascagoula – The Closest Encounter: My Story*, in which he shared his perspective on the abduction and the impact it had on his life. Parker's decision to come forward after so many years added new depth to the story and reignited public interest in the case.

In addition to the personal accounts of Hickson and Parker, the Pascagoula Abduction has also been the subject of ongoing research and investigation. In recent years, previously unreleased audio recordings from the original police interviews have surfaced, providing further insight into the men's state of mind immediately following the encounter. The Pascagoula Abduction is often cited as one of the best-documented abduction cases, due to the credibility of the witnesses, the involvement of law enforcement, and the detailed accounts provided by Hickson and Parker. Whether one believes their story or not, the case remains a significant and influential part of UFO history. The Pascagoula Abduction is an unforgettable chapter in the annals of UFO lore. The strange and terrifying experience recounted by Charles Hickson and Calvin Parker has captivated and mystified people for decades, raising questions about the nature of alien encounters and the possibility of life beyond Earth. While the truth of what happened that night in Pascagoula may never be fully known, the case continues to stand as a powerful reminder of the enduring mystery of the UFO phenomenon and the profound impact that such experiences can have on those who live through them. As with many of the most compelling UFO cases, the Pascagoula Abduction challenges our understanding of reality and the boundaries of human experience, leaving us to wonder what might lie beyond the world we know.

The Varginha Incident: Brazil's Alien Encounter

The Varginha Incident, often referred to as "Brazil's Roswell," is one of the most famous and controversial UFO events in South America. The incident, which took place in January 1996 in the city of Varginha, Brazil, involved multiple sightings of strange creatures and a possible UFO crash. The case quickly became a national sensation and drew international attention, with comparisons being made to the Roswell incident due to its significance and the level of government secrecy that allegedly surrounded it. This chapter explores the details of the Varginha Incident, the key witnesses and their accounts, the investigation that followed, and the lasting impact of the case on Brazil's UFO community.

The Sightings

The Varginha Incident began on January 20, 1996, when three young women—Liliane and Valquíria Fátima Silva, and their friend Kátia Andrade Xavier—claimed to have encountered a strange, humanoid creature while walking through a vacant lot in the Jardim Andere neighborhood of Varginha. The girls described the creature as being about five feet tall, with brown, oily skin, a large head, and large, red eyes. The being appeared to be crouching or hunched over and seemed to be in distress. The girls also noticed that it had three rounded protrusions on its head, which they described as resembling horns.

Terrified by what they had seen, the girls ran home and told their mother, who later reported the incident to the authorities. News of the sighting spread quickly, and within hours, other reports began to surface of strange creatures and unusual activity in the area. According to some accounts, military and emergency personnel were seen conducting operations in the vicinity, leading to speculation that they were involved in the capture of the creature.

In the days following the initial sighting, more witnesses came forward with their own accounts of strange phenomena. Some reported seeing a UFO crash or strange lights in the sky, while others claimed to have seen military trucks transporting a strange, large container through the streets of Varginha. These reports fueled rumors that the Brazilian military had recovered an extraterrestrial being—or beings—and were involved in a cover-up.

The Military's Role

One of the most significant aspects of the Varginha Incident is the alleged involvement of the Brazilian military and their response to the situation. According to several witnesses, the military was quick to arrive at the scene after the creature was sighted and was seen conducting operations in the area. Some locals reported that they saw soldiers capturing the creature, placing it in a box or a net, and taking it away in a military vehicle.

In the days that followed, there were additional reports of military personnel blocking off roads and cordoning off areas where UFOs were reportedly seen. Witnesses also claimed that the military confiscated camera equipment and film from those who attempted to photograph the events. This heightened the sense of secrecy surrounding the incident and led to widespread speculation that the Brazilian government was hiding something extraordinary.

Adding to the mystery, several witnesses who claimed to have seen the creature or witnessed military activity reported being intimidated or threatened by authorities. This has led many to believe that a significant cover-up was in place, similar to the alleged suppression of information following the Roswell incident in the United States.

The Death of a Soldier

One of the most tragic and mysterious elements of the Varginha Incident is the death of a soldier who was allegedly involved in the recovery of the creature. A young soldier, Marco Eli Chereze, who was reportedly part of the military team that captured the creature, died under suspicious circumstances just a few weeks after the incident. Chereze's family claimed that he fell ill shortly after the operation, suffering from severe symptoms that doctors could not explain. His condition rapidly deteriorated, and he died in the hospital. Some have speculated that Chereze's death was caused by exposure to a toxic substance or pathogen carried by the creature, while others believe that his death was the result of foul play to keep him silent. The military has denied any connection between Chereze's death and the Varginha Incident, attributing his death to natural causes, but this has done little to quell the rumours.

The Investigation

The Varginha Incident attracted the attention of Brazilian UFO researchers and investigators, who launched their own inquiries into the events. One of the most prominent investigators was Ufologist and researcher Ademar José Gevaerd, who conducted numerous interviews with witnesses and military personnel. Gevaerd's investigation suggested that at least two extraterrestrial beings were involved, one of which was captured and taken to a local hospital before being transferred to a military facility.

Gevaerd and other researchers also uncovered reports that doctors at the hospital where the creature was allegedly taken were instructed to remain silent about what they had seen. There were also claims that the creature had been examined by a team of doctors, who later found themselves under pressure from the authorities to keep quiet. Despite the best efforts of researchers, the Brazilian government and military have consistently denied any involvement in or knowledge of the incident. Official explanations have dismissed the sightings as a case of mistaken identity, attributing the creature seen by the girls to a deformed human or animal, possibly a homeless person or a sickly animal that had wandered into the area.

The Legacy of the Varginha Incident

The Varginha Incident remains one of the most significant and mysterious UFO cases in Brazil, often referred to as the "Brazilian Roswell." Despite the official denials and lack of concrete evidence, the incident has had a lasting impact on the UFO community in Brazil and around the world.

The case has been the subject of numerous books, documentaries, and television programs, both in Brazil and internationally. It has also inspired debates and discussions among UFO researchers and enthusiasts, with many believing that the incident represents one of the best-documented cases of extraterrestrial contact. The incident has also had a profound effect on the city of Varginha itself. The city has embraced its connection to the UFO phenomenon, with a UFO-shaped water tower, themed monuments, and an annual UFO festival that draws visitors from across the globe. Varginha has become a focal point for UFO tourism in Brazil, and the legacy of the incident continues to shape the city's identity. The Varginha Incident remains an enigmatic and controversial event in the history of UFO phenomena. Whether it was a case of extraterrestrial contact, a misidentified terrestrial phenomenon, or an elaborate hoax, the incident has captured the imagination of people around the world and continues to be a subject of fascination and debate. The alleged involvement of the military, the death of a soldier, and the numerous eyewitness accounts have only added to the mystery, making the Varginha Incident one of the most compelling UFO cases of all time. As with many UFO incidents, the truth of what happened in Varginha in January 1996 may never be fully known. However, the impact of the event on the city, the country, and the global UFO community is undeniable. The Varginha Incident stands as a powerful reminder of the enduring mystery of UFOs and the possibility that we are not alone in the universe.

J. Allen Hynek's Legacy: Scientific Ufology

J. Allen Hynek is often regarded as the father of "scientific ufology," a term that reflects his rigorous and systematic approach to the study of unidentified flying objects (UFOs). Over the course of his career, Hynek transitioned from being a skeptic and debunker of UFO phenomena to becoming one of its most respected advocates, advocating for serious scientific investigation into the mystery of UFOs. His work laid the foundation for modern UFO research and has had a lasting impact on the field. This chapter explores J. Allen Hynek's legacy, his contributions to ufology, and the ways in which his scientific approach continues to influence the study of UFOs.

Early Career and Skepticism

J. Allen Hynek began his career as an astronomer, earning his Ph.D. in astrophysics from the University of Chicago in 1935. He was a respected academic and worked as a professor of astronomy at Ohio State University, as well as an astrophysicist at the Smithsonian Astrophysical Observatory. Hynek's expertise in astronomy led him to be recruited by the U.S. Air Force in 1948 as a scientific consultant for Project Sign, the first official U.S. government study of UFOs. Initially, Hynek was a skeptic. He believed that UFO sightings could be easily explained as misidentifications of natural phenomena, man-made objects, or psychological effects. As part of Project Sign (and later Project Grudge and Project Blue Book), Hynek's role was to investigate and debunk UFO reports. In many cases, he did just that, attributing sightings to mundane causes such as weather balloons, astronomical objects, or aircraft. However, as Hynek continued his work, he began to encounter cases that defied easy explanation. He became increasingly frustrated with the Air Force's tendency to dismiss or downplay credible reports and began to question whether the UFO phenomenon might deserve more serious scientific attention.

The Turning Point

The turning point in Hynek's views on UFOs came during the 1950s and 1960s, when he was involved in investigating several high-profile UFO cases that could not be easily explained. One such case was the 1953 sighting over Ellsworth Air Force Base in South Dakota, where multiple witnesses, including military personnel, reported seeing a large, unidentified object that was tracked on radar. Despite a thorough investigation, no satisfactory explanation could be found. Another pivotal moment came with the 1964 Lonnie Zamora incident in Socorro, New Mexico. In this case, a police officer named Lonnie Zamora reported seeing a landed UFO and two small humanoid figures near it. Zamora's credibility as a witness, combined with physical evidence at the scene, convinced Hynek that this was not a case that could be easily dismissed. Hynek's growing doubts about the official explanations for UFO sightings culminated in his decision to publicly advocate for the scientific study of the phenomenon. In 1966, during a wave of UFO sightings in Michigan, Hynek faced intense scrutiny from both the public and the media after he suggested that some of the sightings might have been caused by "swamp gas," a natural phenomenon. The backlash he received from this statement made him realize that the public was deeply concerned about the issue, and that dismissive explanations would not suffice. This experience solidified his resolve to approach UFOs with greater scientific rigor.

The Classification System and the Close Encounter Scale

One of Hynek's most enduring contributions to ufology is the development of a classification system for UFO sightings. This system, which he first introduced in his 1972 book *The UFO Experience: A Scientific Inquiry*, categorizes UFO sightings into different types based on the nature of the encounter:

1. **Nocturnal Lights**: Unexplained lights seen in the night sky.
2. **Daylight Discs**: Unidentified objects seen during daylight hours.
3. **Radar-Visual Cases**: UFOs that are simultaneously observed visually and tracked on radar.

Hynek's most famous contribution to UFO terminology is the "Close Encounter" classification, which describes sightings where the observer is in close proximity to a UFO. He divided close encounters into three categories:

Close Encounters of the First Kind: Sightings of a UFO within 500 feet, where the object is clearly seen.

Close Encounters of the Second Kind: Close sightings that involve physical effects, such as interference with vehicles, animals, or the environment.

Close Encounters of the Third Kind: Close sightings where occupants or beings are seen in or near the UFO.

This classification system helped to standardize the reporting and investigation of UFO sightings and remains a cornerstone of ufology. The term "Close Encounters of the Third Kind" became widely known after the release of Steven Spielberg's 1977 film of the same name, for which Hynek served as a technical advisor.

The Center for UFO Studies (CUFOS)

In 1973, Hynek founded the Center for UFO Studies (CUFOS), an organization dedicated to the scientific investigation of UFO phenomena. CUFOS aimed to collect, analyze, and archive UFO reports, and to promote a serious, evidence-based approach to the study of UFOs. Under Hynek's leadership, CUFOS became a hub for UFO research, attracting both professional scientists and amateur researchers who shared a commitment to understanding the phenomenon. CUFOS conducted its own investigations into UFO sightings, worked to develop better methods for gathering and analyzing data, and published a journal to disseminate its findings to the public and the scientific community. Hynek's work with CUFOS was instrumental in legitimizing the study of UFOs and in advocating for greater openness and transparency in government UFO investigations.

Hynek's Legacy and Impact

J. Allen Hynek's legacy in the field of ufology is profound. His insistence on a scientific approach to the study of UFOs helped to elevate the subject from the realm of fringe speculation to a legitimate area of inquiry. Hynek's work demonstrated that UFO sightings could be investigated systematically and that some cases warranted serious consideration rather than dismissal. Hynek's influence extends beyond the field of ufology. His work has inspired generations of researchers, scientists, and enthusiasts to approach the UFO phenomenon with an open mind and a commitment to empirical evidence. His emphasis on critical thinking, skepticism, and the importance of scientific inquiry continues to resonate with those who seek to understand the mysteries of UFOs and their potential implications for humanity. Hynek's legacy is also reflected in the ongoing debates about the nature of UFOs and the need for government transparency. In recent years, the U.S. government has taken steps toward greater openness regarding UFOs, acknowledging the existence of the phenomenon and releasing previously classified information. Hynek's early advocacy for serious investigation into UFOs laid the groundwork for these developments and has helped to shape the modern discourse on the subject. J. Allen Hynek's contributions to ufology are immeasurable. His scientific approach, innovative classification system, and tireless advocacy for serious study have left an indelible mark on the field. Hynek's legacy as the father of scientific ufology endures, and his work continues to inspire those who seek to explore the mysteries of the unknown with curiosity, rigor, and an unwavering commitment to the pursuit of truth.

Stanton Friedman: Pursuing the Truth

Stanton Friedman was one of the most prominent and influential figures in the field of ufology. A nuclear physicist by training, Friedman devoted much of his life to the study and investigation of UFOs, earning a reputation as a tireless advocate for the serious, scientific examination of the phenomenon. Known for his rigorous approach, compelling public speaking, and dedication to uncovering the truth, Friedman became a key figure in bringing the UFO phenomenon into the mainstream. This chapter explores Stanton Friedman's career, his contributions to ufology, and the legacy he left in his relentless pursuit of the truth.

Early Career and Transition to Ufology

Stanton T. Friedman was born on July 29, 1934, in Elizabeth, New Jersey. He studied at the University of Chicago, where he earned a bachelor's degree in 1955 and a master's degree in 1956, both in physics. Friedman began his career as a nuclear physicist, working on advanced nuclear propulsion systems for companies like General Electric, Westinghouse, and McDonnell Douglas. His work involved top-secret projects related to nuclear aircraft, rockets, and power plants, giving him a solid background in science and engineering. Friedman's interest in UFOs was sparked in the late 1950s when he came across a report on UFOs that intrigued him. This curiosity led him to begin researching the phenomenon in depth. By 1970, Friedman had decided to leave his work in nuclear physics to focus full-time on ufology. He became a lecturer and researcher, traveling across the United States and Canada to speak about UFOs and investigate cases.

Advocacy for the Extraterrestrial Hypothesis

One of Friedman's most significant contributions to ufology was his staunch advocacy for the Extraterrestrial Hypothesis (ETH)—the idea that some UFOs are spacecraft from other planets, piloted by intelligent beings. Friedman argued that the evidence for UFOs was compelling and that many credible sightings could not be easily dismissed as misidentifications, hoaxes, or natural phenomena. He believed that the only logical explanation for certain well-documented cases was that they involved extraterrestrial visitors. Friedman's scientific background lent credibility to his arguments, and he became known for his ability to present complex ideas in a clear, persuasive manner. He often challenged skeptics, emphasizing that the dismissal of UFOs by the scientific community was more about a lack of investigation than a lack of evidence. Friedman frequently pointed out that many scientists were quick to dismiss UFOs without seriously studying the available data, which he believed was a grave mistake.

Investigating the Roswell Incident

Stanton Friedman is perhaps best known for his work on the Roswell incident, which he helped to bring back into the public eye. In 1978, Friedman interviewed Jesse Marcel, a retired U.S. Air Force intelligence officer who had been involved in the recovery of debris from a crash site near Roswell, New Mexico, in 1947. Marcel told Friedman that the debris was not from a weather balloon, as the official story claimed, but from an extraterrestrial spacecraft. Friedman's interview with Marcel marked the beginning of a renewed interest in the Roswell incident, which had largely been forgotten by the public. Friedman conducted extensive research into the case, interviewing other witnesses and gathering documentation that suggested a cover-up by the U.S. government. His work was instrumental in establishing Roswell as a key event in UFO history and led to numerous books, documentaries, and films about the incident.

In 1980, Friedman co-authored the book *The Roswell Incident* with William Moore, which presented the evidence they had gathered and argued that the U.S. government had recovered an alien spacecraft and its occupants. The book became a bestseller and solidified Friedman's reputation as a leading UFO researcher.

Public Speaking and Debates

Stanton Friedman was a prolific public speaker, giving hundreds of lectures on UFOs at universities, conferences, and other venues around the world. He was known for his engaging and authoritative speaking style, which combined scientific rigor with a passion for the subject. Friedman's lectures often focused on the evidence for UFOs, the inadequacies of the skeptical arguments, and the need for a serious, scientific investigation of the phenomenon.

Friedman was also a frequent participant in debates with sceptics and debunkers. He enjoyed challenging those who dismissed UFOs out of hand and was known for his ability to dismantle their arguments with facts and logic. One of his most famous debates was with the astrophysicist Carl Sagan, with whom he sparred over the reality of UFOs and the likelihood of extraterrestrial visitation. Friedman argued that Sagan and other sceptics were ignoring or misrepresenting the evidence and that their position was based more on ideology than science.

The UFO Cover-Up and Government Secrecy

Throughout his career, Stanton Friedman was a vocal critic of government secrecy regarding UFOs. He believed that there was a concerted effort by governments, particularly the U.S. government, to suppress information about UFOs and extraterrestrial life. Friedman argued that this cover-up was motivated by a desire to maintain control over advanced technology, avoid public panic, and protect national security.

Friedman's views on government secrecy were rooted in his experience working on classified projects as a nuclear physicist. He understood the lengths to which governments would go to keep sensitive information hidden and believed that the truth about UFOs was being deliberately concealed from the public. He often cited the fact that many UFO sightings involved military personnel and that the U.S. government had a long history of denying or downplaying such incidents.

In his book *Top Secret/Majic* (1996), Friedman detailed his investigation into the Majestic 12 (MJ-12) documents, which allegedly revealed a secret government group tasked with handling UFO-related matters. While the authenticity of the MJ-12 documents has been widely debated, Friedman believed that they were at least partially genuine and that they provided evidence of a government cover-up.

Legacy and Influence

Stanton Friedman's legacy in ufology is immense. He is widely regarded as one of the most important and influential figures in the field, and his work has inspired countless others to take the study of UFOs seriously. Friedman's dedication to uncovering the truth about UFOs, his rigorous investigative methods, and his ability to communicate complex ideas to the public have left a lasting impact on the field.

Friedman's work on the Roswell incident helped to elevate it to the status of the most famous UFO case in history, and his advocacy for the Extraterrestrial Hypothesis continues to influence discussions about the nature of UFOs. He played a key role in legitimizing the study of UFOs as a scientific endeavor and challenged both the scientific community and the public to confront the possibility that we are not alone in the universe.

In addition to his work as a researcher and speaker, Friedman was a prolific author, writing numerous books and articles on UFOs. His books, including *Crash at Corona* (with Don Berliner) and *Science Was Wrong* (with Kathleen Marden), remain influential and continue to be widely read by those interested in the UFO phenomenon.

Stanton Friedman passed away on May 13, 2019, but his contributions to ufology continue to resonate. He is remembered not only for his ground-breaking research but also for his unwavering commitment to the pursuit of truth, regardless of where it might lead. Friedman's work serves as a powerful reminder that the search for answers about UFOs and extraterrestrial life is a serious and worthy endeavor, one that requires both scientific rigor and an open mind.

In conclusion, Stanton Friedman's career in ufology was marked by his relentless pursuit of the truth about UFOs and his dedication to bringing the subject into the mainstream. His work on the Roswell incident, his advocacy for the Extraterrestrial Hypothesis, and his challenges to government secrecy have left an indelible mark on the field. Friedman's legacy as a pioneering UFO researcher and a passionate advocate for the scientific study of UFOs continues to inspire and influence those who seek to understand the mysteries of the universe.

Dr. Steven Greer: Disclosing the Hidden

Dr. Steven Greer is a prominent figure in the field of ufology, known for his efforts to disclose information about UFOs and extraterrestrial encounters that he believes has been hidden by governments and military organizations around the world. As a physician turned UFO researcher and advocate, Greer has dedicated his life to exposing what he claims is a widespread cover-up of the truth about extraterrestrial life and advanced technologies. His work has sparked both admiration and controversy, as he continues to push for greater transparency and public awareness regarding the UFO phenomenon. This chapter explores Dr. Steven Greer's career, his contributions to the disclosure movement, and the impact of his work on the global UFO community.

Early Life and Career

Steven M. Greer was born on June 28, 1955, in Charlotte, North Carolina. He pursued a career in medicine, earning his medical degree from the James H. Quillen College of Medicine at East Tennessee State University in 1987. Greer specialized in emergency medicine and worked as a physician in various hospitals. However, despite his successful medical career, Greer's interest in UFOs and extraterrestrial life began at a young age and eventually led him to a very different path.

Greer's interest in UFOs was reignited in the 1990s, when he began to investigate the phenomenon more seriously. He claims to have had his own experiences with UFOs and extraterrestrial beings, which deepened his conviction that the truth about these encounters was being deliberately hidden from the public. In 1993, Greer founded the Center for the Study of Extraterrestrial Intelligence (CSETI), an organization dedicated to the peaceful contact with extraterrestrial civilizations and the promotion of public awareness about UFOs.

The Disclosure Project

One of Dr. Steven Greer's most significant contributions to ufology is the Disclosure Project, an initiative he launched in 1993 with the goal of convincing government insiders, military personnel, and other witnesses to come forward and share what they know about UFOs and extraterrestrial encounters. Greer believes that there are thousands of individuals who have been involved in top-secret projects related to UFOs and who possess valuable information that could help the public understand the true nature of the phenomenon.

The Disclosure Project reached a major milestone on May 9, 2001, when Greer organized a press conference at the National Press Club in Washington, D.C. During the event, more than 20 military, intelligence, and government witnesses testified about their experiences with UFOs and extraterrestrial technologies. These witnesses, who included retired military officers, FAA officials, and defense contractors, provided detailed accounts of their encounters and called for congressional hearings on the subject.

The press conference received significant media attention and was broadcast on major news networks. However, the events of September 11, 2001, overshadowed the disclosure efforts, and the momentum generated by the press conference was largely lost. Despite this setback, Greer continued to advocate for disclosure, and the Disclosure Project remains one of the most well-known efforts to bring hidden UFO information to light.

The Orion Project and Free Energy

In addition to his work on UFO disclosure, Dr. Greer has also been involved in efforts to develop and promote advanced energy technologies that he believes could revolutionize the world. In 2007, Greer launched the Orion Project, an initiative aimed at identifying, funding, and developing new energy technologies that are based on principles of "zero-point energy" or other unconventional sources. Greer argues that these technologies have the potential to provide clean, limitless energy, but that they have been suppressed by powerful interests who are invested in maintaining the status quo.

Greer's work in this area is rooted in his belief that the same forces that are covering up the truth about UFOs are also preventing the public from accessing advanced technologies that could eliminate the need for fossil fuels and reduce global dependence on centralized energy systems. He has claimed that some of these technologies have been derived from recovered extraterrestrial craft and that their development could have a transformative impact on society.

Despite the ambitious goals of the Orion Project, it has faced significant challenges, including skepticism from the scientific community and difficulties in securing funding. Critics argue that the claims made by Greer and others about zero-point energy are not supported by credible scientific evidence and that the technology is, at best, speculative.

The CE-5 Initiative

Another key aspect of Dr. Steven Greer's work is the CE-5 Initiative, which stands for "Close Encounters of the Fifth Kind." This initiative promotes the idea that humans can establish direct, peaceful communication with extraterrestrial beings through meditation, group consciousness, and other practices. According to Greer, the CE-5 protocol allows individuals to initiate contact with extraterrestrial civilizations, bypassing the need for government or military intervention.

The CE-5 Initiative is based on the belief that extraterrestrial beings are not hostile, but rather are concerned with the spiritual and environmental welfare of humanity. Greer argues that these beings are waiting for humans to demonstrate a willingness to engage in peaceful, cooperative interactions before making more overt contact. The CE-5 protocol involves group meditations, the use of lights and sounds to signal extraterrestrial craft, and the setting of positive intentions to invite contact.

The CE-5 Initiative has gained a following among those who are interested in spiritual and consciousness-based approaches to UFO contact. However, it has also faced criticism from sceptics who argue that the experiences reported by participants are more likely to be the result of psychological or hallucinatory effects than actual contact with extraterrestrial beings.

Films and Media Presence

Dr. Steven Greer has been a prolific author and filmmaker, using these mediums to spread his message about UFOs, disclosure, and advanced energy technologies. His books, such as *Hidden Truth, Forbidden Knowledge* and *Unacknowledged: An Exposé of the World's Greatest Secret*, provide detailed accounts of his investigations and the testimonies of witnesses involved in the Disclosure Project.

In recent years, Greer has produced several documentaries that have reached a wide audience. One of his most well-known films, *Sirius* (2013), explores the UFO phenomenon, the suppression of advanced energy technologies, and the discovery of a small humanoid figure known as the "Atacama Humanoid," which some claimed was of extraterrestrial origin. The film received significant attention, though the Atacama Humanoid was later determined by scientists to be the remains of a human child with genetic abnormalities.

Another of Greer's films, *Unacknowledged* (2017), focuses on the secrecy surrounding UFOs and the efforts to bring this information to the public. The documentary includes interviews with former government and military officials who support Greer's claims of a cover-up and explores the potential implications of disclosure for society.

Legacy and Controversy

Dr. Steven Greer's work has made him one of the most influential and polarizing figures in the UFO community. His dedication to disclosure and his efforts to bring hidden information to light have earned him a loyal following, as well as significant criticism. Supporters praise Greer for his courage in challenging powerful institutions and for his commitment to exploring the spiritual dimensions of the UFO phenomenon.

However, Greer has also faced criticism from skeptics and some within the UFO community. Critics argue that Greer's claims are often sensational and lack verifiable evidence. Some have questioned the credibility of the witnesses he has presented, while others have expressed concern that his emphasis on consciousness-based contact methods may detract from more scientific approaches to UFO research.

Despite the controversy, Dr. Steven Greer's impact on the field of ufology is undeniable. His work has brought the issue of UFO disclosure into the public eye and has inspired many to question the official narratives surrounding extraterrestrial encounters and advanced technologies. Whether one agrees with his methods and conclusions or not, Greer's influence on the discourse around UFOs and the push for greater transparency is significant.

Dr. Steven Greer's legacy in the field of ufology is marked by his relentless pursuit of disclosure and his efforts to expose what he believes are hidden truths about UFOs and advanced technologies. Through the Disclosure Project, the Orion Project, the CE-5 Initiative, and his films and writings, Greer has worked to raise public awareness and challenge the secrecy that he argues surrounds the UFO phenomenon. His work has sparked debate, inspired many, and contributed to the ongoing discussion about the nature of extraterrestrial life and the implications of contact for humanity.

As the global conversation about UFOs continues to evolve, Dr. Steven Greer's contributions to the movement for disclosure remain a vital part of the narrative. His efforts to bridge the gap between scientific inquiry, spiritual exploration, and public advocacy have left a lasting impact on the way we think about UFOs and the potential for human contact with extraterrestrial civilizations.

The Aldebarans: Nazis and Extraterrestrial Links

The connection between the Aldebarans and the Nazis is one of the more controversial and speculative topics in the realm of ufology and conspiracy theories. The Aldebarans, supposedly extraterrestrial beings from a star system 65 light-years away in the Taurus constellation, are said to have played a role in influencing Nazi ideology and technological advancements. These claims, while lacking substantial evidence, have been the subject of intense debate and fascination, particularly within the context of Nazi occultism and the mythos surrounding UFOs and advanced technologies. This chapter explores the origins of the Aldebaran-Nazi connection, the theories surrounding it, and the impact of these ideas on both ufology and historical interpretations of the Nazi regime.

Origins of the Aldebaran-Nazi Connection

The connection between the Aldebarans and the Nazis primarily stems from post-war speculation and the writings of several authors who have explored the occult and esoteric aspects of the Third Reich. One of the central figures in this narrative is the Vril Society, a secretive and allegedly mystical group that, according to some sources, existed in Germany before and during the Nazi era. The Vril Society is said to have believed in the existence of a powerful, ancient energy source called "Vril," which could be harnessed to achieve incredible feats, including the development of advanced technology.

According to these theories, the Vril Society, along with the Thule Society—another occult group with connections to early Nazi ideology—believed that the Aryan race had descended from a master race of extraterrestrials who originated from the Aldebaran star system. These beings were supposedly highly advanced, both technologically and spiritually, and had visited Earth in ancient times. The Vril Society members, it is claimed, sought to reestablish contact with these extraterrestrials to gain access to their knowledge and power.

The idea of a connection between the Nazis and extraterrestrial beings from Aldebaran gained traction in part due to the work of authors like Louis Pauwels and Jacques Bergier, whose 1960 book *The Morning of the Magicians* explored the idea of Nazi occultism and its potential links to advanced, otherworldly technology. This book, along with other speculative works, contributed to the development of a narrative that intertwined Nazi ideology, occult practices, and extraterrestrial influences.

The Vril Society and UFO Technology

One of the most persistent aspects of the Aldebaran-Nazi connection is the claim that the Nazis, under the guidance of the Vril Society and with the assistance of Aldebaran extraterrestrials, developed advanced flying saucer technology. These claims often focus on the idea that the Nazis were able to build anti-gravity craft, sometimes referred to as "Vril saucers" or "Haunebu," which were powered by Vril energy or other exotic propulsion methods.

According to these theories, the Nazis' supposed development of flying saucer technology was part of a larger plan to create a technologically superior Aryan empire, with the goal of establishing a New World Order. Some proponents of these ideas argue that the Nazis were able to escape defeat at the end of World War II by fleeing to secret bases in Antarctica or even off-planet, taking their advanced technology with them. However, these claims are widely regarded as speculative and lacking in credible evidence. Mainstream historians and UFO researchers generally dismiss the notion that the Nazis developed functioning flying saucers or had contact with extraterrestrials. The idea of Nazi UFOs is often seen as a combination of post-war myth-making, Cold War-era conspiracy theories, and the blending of historical fact with science fiction.

Aldebarans and Nazi Ideology

Another aspect of the Aldebaran-Nazi connection is the idea that the supposed extraterrestrial influence extended beyond technology to the ideological underpinnings of the Nazi regime. Some theorists suggest that the Nazi belief in a pure Aryan race and their obsession with eugenics and racial purity were influenced by the idea of an extraterrestrial master race from Aldebaran.

This theory posits that Nazi leaders, particularly those involved in occult practices, believed that they were carrying out the will of their extraterrestrial ancestors by attempting to create a pure, dominant race on Earth. The Nazis' interest in ancient civilizations, such as the search for the lost city of Atlantis and expeditions to Tibet, is sometimes cited as evidence of their belief in these extraterrestrial connections.

However, it is important to note that these ideas are highly speculative and not supported by historical evidence. While the Nazis did indeed engage in occult practices and were interested in mysticism and pseudo-scientific racial theories, the connection to extraterrestrials from Aldebaran is largely the product of post-war conspiracy theories and esoteric writings rather than documented historical fact.

Impact on Ufology and Conspiracy Theories

The Aldebaran-Nazi connection has had a significant impact on certain segments of ufology and conspiracy theory culture. It has contributed to the broader narrative of secret Nazi technology, including the idea that the Nazis developed UFOs and may have had contact with extraterrestrial beings. These ideas are often tied to other conspiracy theories, such as the notion that world governments are hiding the truth about UFOs and advanced technology from the public.

The idea of Nazi UFOs and extraterrestrial connections has also found its way into popular culture, appearing in films, television shows, and books. These stories often blend elements of science fiction, historical fiction, and conspiracy theory, creating a complex and sometimes confusing narrative that blurs the line between fact and fiction.

Critics of the Aldebaran-Nazi connection argue that these theories can be problematic, as they sometimes serve to sensationalize or distort the historical reality of the Nazi regime. By focusing on fantastical ideas like extraterrestrial influence and secret technology, these theories may distract from the true horrors of the Holocaust and the atrocities committed by the Nazis during World War II.

The connection between the Aldebarans and the Nazis is a highly speculative and controversial topic that has captured the imagination of certain segments of the ufology and conspiracy theory communities. While these ideas are rooted in post-war myth-making and esoteric writings, they have nonetheless become a part of the broader narrative surrounding UFOs, advanced technology, and the occult. It is important to approach the Aldebaran-Nazi connection with a critical eye, recognizing the lack of credible evidence and the potential for these theories to distort historical understanding. While the idea of extraterrestrial influence on the Nazi regime is intriguing, it remains firmly in the realm of speculation and should be considered as such. Ultimately, the Aldebaran-Nazi connection serves as a reminder of how easily history can be intertwined with myth and how conspiracy theories can take on a life of their own, blending fact and fiction in ways that can be both fascinating and problematic. As with all aspects of ufology and conspiracy theory, it is essential to separate well-supported facts from speculative or fantastical claims and to approach these topics with a balanced and informed perspective.

The Ebens: Extraterrestrial Biological Entities

The term "Ebens," short for Extraterrestrial Biological Entities, refers to an alleged species of extraterrestrial beings that are said to have been involved in direct contact and exchanges with humans, particularly through secretive U.S. government programs. The story of the Ebens has gained prominence within certain circles of ufology and conspiracy theory, largely due to claims surrounding a clandestine operation known as "Project Serpo." According to these accounts, the Ebens are a highly advanced and peaceful extraterrestrial species from the Zeta Reticuli star system, who have had significant interactions with Earth. This chapter explores the origins of the Eben narrative, the details of the alleged contact and exchange program, and the impact of these claims on the UFO community.

Origins of the Eben Narrative

The story of the Ebens is closely tied to the alleged Project Serpo, a supposed exchange program between the U.S. government and an extraterrestrial civilization. The existence of Project Serpo first came to light in 2005 when an anonymous source, claiming to be a retired government official, began releasing information online through UFO researcher Victor Martinez. This source, often referred to as "Anonymous," claimed that in the 1960s, the U.S. government had entered into an agreement with a race of extraterrestrials known as the Ebens. According to the narrative, the Ebens were the occupants of a spacecraft that crashed near Roswell, New Mexico, in 1947. This crash led to the recovery of both the craft and its occupants—one of whom allegedly survived and was taken into custody by the U.S. military. The surviving Eben was said to have communicated with the U.S. government and facilitated the establishment of a formal exchange program, which would later become known as Project Serpo.

Project Serpo: The Alleged Exchange Program

The central claim of the Project Serpo narrative is that in 1965, a group of 12 U.S. military personnel—10 men and 2 women—were sent on an expedition to the Ebens' home planet, which is said to orbit one of the stars in the Zeta Reticuli system. This exchange program allegedly lasted for 13 years, during which time the human team lived among the Ebens, studying their culture, technology, and way of life. According to the story, the Ebens were a peaceful and advanced species with a society based on cooperation and mutual respect. They were said to possess technology far beyond anything known on Earth, including advanced spacecraft, energy systems, and medical capabilities. The Eben home planet, sometimes referred to as "Serpo," was described as being similar to Earth in some respects, with a breathable atmosphere and a habitable environment, though it also had significant differences, such as a longer day and harsher climate conditions. The alleged members of the Serpo expedition reportedly faced various challenges during their time on the Eben planet, including adjusting to the different gravity, environmental conditions, and Eben social norms. Some members of the team are said to have died during the mission, while others chose to remain on Serpo permanently. Those who returned to Earth after the mission allegedly brought back valuable knowledge and information about the Ebens and their technology.

The Ebens: Characteristics and Culture

The Ebens are described as being small, humanoid beings with an average height of about four feet. They are said to have a similar appearance to the "Greys" often reported in UFO encounters, with large heads, slanted eyes, and small bodies. However, unlike the cold, emotionless depictions of the Greys in some accounts, the Ebens are portrayed as warm, caring, and deeply spiritual beings.

According to the narrative, the Eben society is highly organized and operates on principles of cooperation, community, and respect for all life forms.

The Ebens are said to have no concept of war or violence, and their technology is used to improve their quality of life and maintain harmony within their society. Their medical knowledge is reported to be far advanced, allowing them to cure diseases and extend life spans far beyond human capabilities. The Ebens are also described as being deeply connected to their environment and the cosmos, with a profound understanding of energy and the interconnectedness of all things. They are said to possess a collective consciousness, allowing them to communicate telepathically and share knowledge and experiences in a way that is incomprehensible to humans.

The Controversy and Skepticism

The story of the Ebens and Project Serpo has been met with significant skepticism and controversy within the UFO community and beyond. Critics argue that the entire narrative is based on unverified claims and that there is no credible evidence to support the existence of Project Serpo or the Ebens. The information provided by the anonymous source has been scrutinized, with many pointing out inconsistencies, logical flaws, and a lack of corroborating evidence. Skeptics also note that the narrative shares similarities with various science fiction themes, leading some to believe that the story may be a hoax or a fabrication designed to mislead or entertain. The fact that the information was released anonymously and through informal channels has further fueled doubts about its authenticity. However, despite the skepticism, the story of the Ebens has gained a following among those who believe in the possibility of government cover-ups and extraterrestrial contact. Some proponents of the narrative argue that the lack of concrete evidence is due to the highly secretive nature of the program and the government's efforts to suppress the truth. They point to the consistency of certain details across various UFO accounts and the plausibility of an exchange program as reasons to consider the story seriously.

Impact on Ufology and Popular Culture

The narrative of the Ebens and Project Serpo has had a notable impact on certain segments of the UFO community. It has contributed to the broader discourse on extraterrestrial contact, government secrecy, and the potential for interplanetary exchange programs. The idea of an alien species with advanced technology and a peaceful society has also captured the imagination of many, leading to discussions about the possibilities of human-alien cooperation and the lessons humanity could learn from such a civilization. The story of the Ebens has also influenced popular culture, inspiring books, documentaries, and online discussions. The idea of extraterrestrial biological entities, advanced alien civilizations, and secret government programs has become a recurring theme in science fiction and conspiracy theory genres, further blurring the lines between fact and fiction. The story of the Ebens, as presented through the narrative of Project Serpo, is one of the more elaborate and controversial tales in the world of ufology. While the lack of verifiable evidence and the anonymous nature of the claims have led many to dismiss the story as a hoax or a work of fiction, it has nonetheless captured the interest of those who are open to the possibility of extraterrestrial contact and government cover-ups. The Ebens, as they are described in the narrative, represent an idealized vision of an advanced, peaceful, and spiritually enlightened extraterrestrial civilization. Whether or not such beings exist, the story of the Ebens serves as a reminder of humanity's enduring fascination with the unknown and the potential for life beyond our planet. As with many aspects of ufology, the truth of the Eben narrative remains elusive, but it continues to inspire curiosity, debate, and speculation about the nature of extraterrestrial life and the possibility of contact with civilizations far more advanced than our own. Whether viewed as a serious possibility or a compelling work of science fiction, the story of the Ebens and Project Serpo remains a fascinating chapter in the ongoing exploration of the UFO phenomenon.

The Khazarians: Mysteries of the Cosmic Jews

The concept of the "Khazarians" and their connection to ancient or cosmic mysteries is a topic that merges history, conspiracy theories, and speculative fiction. The Khazarian narrative has been invoked in various contexts, often linked with controversial and sometimes misleading ideas about hidden histories, ancient civilizations, and even extraterrestrial connections. This chapter will explore the historical background of the Khazars, the evolution of the "Khazarian" narrative in modern conspiracy theories, and the implications of these ideas within the broader context of ufology and mysticism.

The Historical Khazars

The Khazars were a semi-nomadic Turkic people who established a powerful empire in Eastern Europe between the 7th and 10th centuries. The Khazar Khaganate, as it was known, controlled a vast territory that included parts of modern-day Russia, Ukraine, and Kazakhstan. The Khazars were known for their military prowess, their strategic location along trade routes between the Byzantine Empire and the Islamic Caliphates, and their religious tolerance.

One of the most intriguing aspects of Khazar history is the claim that the Khazarian elite converted to Judaism in the 8th or 9th century, making the Khazar Empire one of the few known examples of a state adopting Judaism as its official religion. This conversion has been the subject of much debate among historians, with some seeing it as a strategic move to maintain political independence from both the Christian Byzantine Empire and the Muslim Caliphates.

The Khazar Empire eventually declined and fell in the 10th century, and the fate of the Khazarian people remains a topic of historical speculation. Some scholars believe that the Khazars were assimilated into surrounding populations, while others suggest that they migrated to other regions, including Eastern Europe.

The Khazarian Narrative in Conspiracy Theories

In modern times, the historical Khazars have been the subject of various conspiracy theories, particularly those that suggest a hidden or alternative history involving the Khazarians as a secretive or powerful group. One of the most persistent and controversial theories is the idea that the Khazarians are the ancestors of Ashkenazi Jews, and that this lineage has been kept hidden or deliberately obscured.

This theory, popularized by the book *The Thirteenth Tribe* (1976) by Arthur Koestler, posits that Ashkenazi Jews are primarily descended from the Khazars rather than from the ancient Israelites. While Koestler's work was intended to challenge traditional ideas about Jewish identity and to foster a sense of unity, it has been misused by some to promote anti-Semitic ideas and to question the legitimacy of Jewish heritage. Mainstream historians and genetic studies have largely discredited the theory, showing that Ashkenazi Jews have Middle Eastern origins, though the Khazar hypothesis persists in some fringe circles.

In the context of conspiracy theories, the "Khazarian" narrative has been expanded to include ideas about secret societies, global control, and even extraterrestrial origins. Some theorists claim that the Khazarians, or a group descended from them, are involved in a global conspiracy to control financial systems, governments, and media. These ideas often intersect with broader conspiracy theories about the "Illuminati," "Reptilians," or other shadowy organizations.

Cosmic Connections and Mystical Interpretations

In the realm of ufology and mysticism, the Khazarians have occasionally been linked to more fantastical ideas about cosmic origins or connections with ancient extraterrestrial civilizations. These narratives are typically speculative and draw on the broader mythology of lost civilizations, hidden knowledge, and ancient aliens.

Some esoteric interpretations suggest that the Khazarians were not merely a historical people but were connected to cosmic forces or otherworldly beings. In these narratives, the Khazarians are portrayed as guardians of ancient, arcane knowledge or as part of a cosmic struggle between different extraterrestrial or interdimensional factions. These ideas are often woven into larger stories about the origins of human civilization, the role of secret societies, and the hidden history of humanity's interactions with extraterrestrial beings.

While these cosmic interpretations of the Khazarians are largely speculative and lack historical or scientific evidence, they reflect a broader trend in ufology and esotericism to reinterpret history through the lens of ancient alien theories and mystical traditions. These narratives often blend elements of history, mythology, and science fiction to create complex and sometimes contradictory stories about the past, present, and future of humanity.

The Impact of the Khazarian Narrative

The various narratives surrounding the Khazarians, whether historical, conspiratorial, or mystical, have had a significant impact on discussions of history, identity, and power. The historical reality of the Khazar Empire is an important part of the medieval history of Eastern Europe and the Jewish diaspora. However, the distortion of this history in modern conspiracy theories has had troubling implications, particularly when used to promote divisive or harmful ideologies.

In the context of ufology and mysticism, the Khazarian narrative serves as an example of how historical figures and events can be reinterpreted and repurposed to fit alternative or speculative frameworks. While these interpretations can be fascinating and thought-provoking, they also highlight the challenges of distinguishing between historical fact and imaginative fiction, especially in a field as complex and contested as ufology.

The story of the Khazarians, both as a historical people and as a subject of modern conspiracy theories and mystical interpretations, is a multifaceted and often controversial topic. While the historical Khazars played a significant role in the medieval history of Eastern Europe, their legacy has been reshaped and reinterpreted in ways that extend far beyond their original context.

The use of the Khazarian narrative in conspiracy theories and cosmic speculation reflects broader trends in the reinterpretation of history and the blending of fact and fiction. As with many aspects of ufology and esotericism, it is important to approach these narratives with a critical eye, recognizing the potential for distortion and the influence of ideological agendas.

Ultimately, the mysteries of the Khazarians—whether historical, conspiratorial, or cosmic—serve as a reminder of the enduring human fascination with the unknown and the complex ways in which we construct meaning from the past. Whether viewed as a lost empire, a hidden lineage, or a cosmic mystery, the Khazarians continue to capture the imagination of those who seek to uncover the deeper truths of history and the universe.

The Archons: Controllers from the Shadows

The concept of the Archons originates from Gnostic texts, where they are described as powerful entities that exert control over the material world and humanity. In the context of modern esotericism, conspiracy theories, and ufology, the Archons have been reinterpreted as shadowy controllers who manipulate reality, often acting as the hidden hand behind governments, institutions, and even extraterrestrial phenomena. This chapter explores the origins of the Archons in Gnostic thought, their reinterpretation in contemporary mysticism and conspiracy theories, and their significance in discussions about control, power, and the nature of reality.

The Gnostic Origins of the Archons

The Archons are first mentioned in Gnostic texts, a collection of early Christian writings that present an alternative view of the world, creation, and the divine. Gnosticism, which emerged in the first few centuries of the Common Era, is characterized by its dualistic worldview, which posits a stark distinction between the material world and the spiritual realm. Gnostics believed that the material world was created by a lesser deity, often identified as the Demiurge, who was flawed or even malevolent.

In Gnostic cosmology, the Archons are servants of the Demiurge, acting as rulers or controllers of the material world. They are often depicted as powerful but malevolent entities who seek to keep humanity trapped in the physical realm, preventing them from attaining spiritual enlightenment and reconnecting with the true divine source. The Archons are seen as agents of deception, creating illusions and false realities to keep human beings ignorant of their true nature.

Gnostic texts, such as the Nag Hammadi Library, describe the Archons as cosmic gatekeepers who control the planets and the stars, exerting influence over the minds and souls of humanity. They are often portrayed as entities that thrive on fear, ignorance, and suffering, feeding off the negative energies that they perpetuate in the world. In this sense, the Archons represent the forces of darkness and materialism that Gnostics sought to transcend through spiritual knowledge (gnosis).

Modern Reinterpretations of the Archons

In contemporary esoteric thought and conspiracy theories, the concept of the Archons has been reinterpreted and expanded, often merging with other ideas about extraterrestrial beings, secret societies, and hidden control structures. These modern interpretations build on the Gnostic idea of the Archons as controllers but place them in a more elaborate cosmology that incorporates UFOs, advanced technology, and global conspiracies.

One of the most influential figures in popularizing the modern interpretation of the Archons is British author and conspiracy theorist David Icke. Icke has written extensively about the Archons, describing them as interdimensional beings who manipulate human reality from behind the scenes. According to Icke, the Archons operate through a network of secret societies and elites, controlling governments, corporations, and religious institutions to maintain their grip on humanity.

Icke's version of the Archons is closely tied to his broader theories about the "Reptilian" beings, whom he claims are a race of shape-shifting extraterrestrials that have infiltrated human society at the highest levels. In this narrative, the Archons are the ultimate puppet masters, using the Reptilians as their enforcers to carry out their agenda on Earth. Icke suggests that the Archons' goal is to keep humanity in a state of fear, conflict, and division, preventing people from awakening to their true spiritual potential.

Archons in Ufology and Alien Encounters

The concept of the Archons has also found a place in ufology, where it is sometimes used to explain certain aspects of alien encounters and the broader UFO phenomenon. Some researchers and experiencers have drawn parallels between the Archons of Gnostic thought and the Greys or other extraterrestrial beings reported in UFO encounters. In this context, the Archons are seen as non-physical or interdimensional entities that influence or even control the actions of these extraterrestrial beings.

For example, some narratives suggest that the Greys are not independent entities but rather biological drones or avatars controlled by the Archons. This idea aligns with the Gnostic view of the Archons as deceivers, suggesting that what people perceive as extraterrestrial encounters may actually be manifestations of the Archons' manipulation of reality. In this interpretation, the Archons use UFOs and alien abductions as tools to create confusion, fear, and misinformation, furthering their control over human consciousness.

Additionally, the Archons are sometimes linked to the phenomenon of mind control and psychological manipulation. Some theories propose that the Archons have the ability to implant thoughts, emotions, or false memories in human minds, shaping people's perceptions and beliefs to serve their agenda. This idea resonates with the Gnostic view of the Archons as entities that create false realities, keeping humanity trapped in a cycle of ignorance and suffering.

The Role of the Archons in Conspiracy Theories

The Archons have become a key component in many modern conspiracy theories, often serving as the ultimate explanation for the hidden forces that control the world. In these narratives, the Archons are depicted as the architects of a grand conspiracy that spans centuries, if not millennia, influencing every aspect of human society, from politics and economics to religion and culture.

Some conspiracy theorists argue that the Archons are responsible for the creation and perpetuation of hierarchical systems of power, such as monarchies, empires, and modern nation-states. These systems, according to the theory, are designed to concentrate power in the hands of a few, creating a controlled and compliant population that is easier to manipulate. The Archons are also often blamed for major global conflicts, economic crises, and other disasters, which are seen as deliberate strategies to create fear, division, and chaos.

In this view, the ultimate goal of the Archons is to maintain their control over humanity by preventing people from realizing their true spiritual nature. The Archons are said to use a variety of methods to achieve this, including propaganda, censorship, technological surveillance, and the manipulation of history and science. Some conspiracy theorists even suggest that the Archons are behind the suppression of knowledge about extraterrestrial life and advanced technologies, which they fear could empower humanity and disrupt their control.

Significance and Impact of the Archon Narrative

The concept of the Archons has had a significant impact on both esoteric thought and modern conspiracy culture. It provides a powerful metaphor for understanding the forces of control, deception, and manipulation that many people perceive in the world. Whether interpreted literally or symbolically, the Archons represent the idea that there are hidden forces working behind the scenes to shape reality and limit human potential.

The Archon narrative also resonates with broader themes in Gnosticism and other spiritual traditions that emphasize the struggle between light and darkness, knowledge and ignorance, freedom and control. In this sense, the Archons serve as a symbol of the obstacles that individuals and societies must overcome in their quest for truth, enlightenment, and liberation.

However, the modern reinterpretation of the Archons also raises important questions about the line between myth, metaphor, and reality. While the idea of the Archons can be a useful tool for exploring concepts of power and control, it can also be problematic when taken literally or used to justify extreme or harmful beliefs. As with all conspiracy theories, it is important to approach the Archon narrative with critical thinking and discernment, recognizing its symbolic value while remaining aware of the potential for distortion or misuse.

The Archons, as conceived in Gnostic thought and reinterpreted in modern esotericism and conspiracy theories, represent a compelling and complex narrative about control, power, and the nature of reality. Whether viewed as literal beings, metaphysical entities, or symbolic representations of the forces that shape our world, the Archons offer a powerful lens through which to examine the challenges of human existence and the quest for spiritual liberation.

As with many aspects of esoteric and conspiracy theory culture, the Archon narrative blurs the line between myth and reality, inviting us to question the nature of the world around us and the unseen forces that may influence it. Whether we see the Archons as malevolent controllers, cosmic deceivers, or simply as metaphors for the struggles we face in life, their story serves as a reminder of the importance of seeking truth, knowledge, and freedom in a world that often seems dominated by hidden forces and unseen powers.

Inner Earth Beings: Hollow Earth Theories

The concept of Inner Earth Beings and the Hollow Earth Theory is one of the most enduring and fascinating ideas in the realm of alternative history, conspiracy theories, and speculative fiction. This theory suggests that beneath the Earth's surface lies a vast, hidden world inhabited by advanced civilizations, strange creatures, and even extraterrestrial beings. The Hollow Earth Theory has captivated imaginations for centuries, blending elements of mythology, science fiction, and pseudoscience. This chapter explores the origins of the Hollow Earth Theory, the various interpretations of Inner Earth Beings, and the impact of these ideas on both popular culture and fringe scientific communities.

The Origins of the Hollow Earth Theory

The idea of a Hollow Earth can be traced back to ancient mythology and folklore, where many cultures described subterranean realms inhabited by gods, giants, or other mystical beings. For example, the ancient Greeks believed in the existence of Hades, an underworld ruled by the god of the same name, while the Norse mythology speaks of Svartálfaheim, the land of the dwarves beneath the Earth.

The concept began to take on a more scientific veneer in the 17th century when the English astronomer and mathematician Edmond Halley, known for Halley's Comet, proposed a theory that the Earth might be hollow. Halley suggested that the Earth consisted of a hollow shell with multiple concentric layers and a central core, each of which could be inhabited and potentially luminous. His theory was based on observations of the Earth's magnetic field and was an early attempt to explain its anomalies.

In the 18th and 19th centuries, the Hollow Earth Theory was further popularized by figures such as John Cleves Symmes Jr., an American army officer who proposed that the Earth was hollow and contained large openings at the poles, through which one could access the inner world. Symmes even petitioned the U.S. government to fund an expedition to the North Pole to find these entrances, although his request was never granted. His ideas, however, inspired other writers and thinkers, leading to the development of a rich body of literature on the subject.

Inner Earth Beings: Agartha, Shambhala, and More

One of the most enduring aspects of the Hollow Earth Theory is the belief in advanced civilizations that exist within the Earth. These civilizations are often described as being technologically and spiritually superior to surface-dwelling humans, and they are sometimes credited with influencing human history or even guiding the development of humanity.

One of the most famous Inner Earth civilizations is Agartha, a legendary city said to exist at the Earth's core. The concept of Agartha is rooted in Tibetan and Indian traditions, where it is often associated with the mythical land of Shambhala, a hidden kingdom believed to be a place of peace and enlightenment. In these traditions, Agartha is depicted as a utopian society ruled by wise beings, sometimes referred to as the "Masters" or "Elders," who possess advanced knowledge and technology. It is said that Agartha is accessible through secret tunnels or portals located in remote parts of the world, such as the Himalayas or the polar regions.

Another common element in Hollow Earth narratives is the presence of various beings, ranging from giant humanoids to reptilian creatures, who inhabit the inner realms. Some accounts describe these beings as ancient, possibly pre-human, civilizations that have lived underground for millennia, either to escape a cataclysm on the surface or because they have always existed in these hidden realms.

In certain interpretations, these Inner Earth Beings are linked to extraterrestrials, with the idea that the Earth's interior serves as a base or sanctuary for advanced alien races. These beings are sometimes portrayed as benevolent, working to protect the Earth and its inhabitants, while in other narratives, they are depicted as hostile or indifferent to humanity.

The Hollow Earth in Modern Ufology and Conspiracy Theories

The Hollow Earth Theory has been integrated into various aspects of modern ufology and conspiracy theories, often serving as an explanation for unexplained phenomena or as part of a broader narrative about secret knowledge and hidden truths.

One of the most common connections between Hollow Earth and UFOs is the idea that UFOs originate from within the Earth rather than from outer space. Proponents of this theory argue that the advanced technology and craft observed in UFO sightings could belong to the civilizations that dwell within the Earth. These Inner Earth beings are said to have developed their technology independently of surface-dwelling humans, allowing them to create vehicles capable of extraordinary feats.

Another related theory suggests that some of the world's most famous explorers and scientists were aware of the Hollow Earth and even visited it. For instance, the famous polar explorer Admiral Richard E. Byrd is often cited in Hollow Earth literature. Byrd's expeditions to the North and South Poles have been reinterpreted by some to suggest that he discovered entrances to the inner world and encountered its inhabitants. Although there is no concrete evidence to support these claims, Byrd's reputed statements and diaries have become a cornerstone of Hollow Earth lore.

The Hollow Earth Theory has also been linked to various other conspiracy theories, such as the idea that the Earth's true history has been hidden from the public by powerful elites who wish to keep humanity ignorant of its origins and potential. In this narrative, the Inner Earth civilizations are either allies or adversaries of these elites, working behind the scenes to shape the course of human events.

Hollow Earth in Popular Culture

The Hollow Earth Theory has had a significant impact on popular culture, inspiring countless works of fiction, from literature and film to video games and comic books. One of the earliest and most famous examples is Jules Verne's *Journey to the Center of the Earth* (1864), a novel that follows a group of adventurers as they descend into a vast underground world filled with prehistoric creatures and other wonders. Verne's work helped to popularize the idea of a Hollow Earth and set the stage for future explorations of the concept in fiction.

In the 20th century, the Hollow Earth continued to be a popular theme in science fiction and fantasy. H.P. Lovecraft, for example, incorporated the idea of ancient subterranean civilizations in his Cthulhu Mythos, where forgotten races and eldritch horrors dwell in hidden caverns beneath the Earth's surface. The concept also appeared in comic books, such as Marvel's Savage Land, a hidden prehistoric world located in Antarctica, and in films like *The Mole People* (1956) and *Godzilla vs. Kong* (2021), where the Hollow Earth is portrayed as a realm inhabited by massive creatures and ancient civilizations.

In addition to fiction, the Hollow Earth Theory has inspired various pseudo-documentaries, podcasts, and online discussions that continue to explore the possibility of an inner world. The theory has a dedicated following among those interested in alternative history, unexplained phenomena, and the mysteries of the Earth.

Criticisms and Scientific Rejection

Despite its enduring popularity in certain circles, the Hollow Earth Theory has been thoroughly discredited by mainstream science. Geologists and physicists point to a wealth of evidence, including seismic data, the study of Earth's magnetic field, and the principles of gravity, that demonstrate the Earth is not hollow but consists of a solid crust, a viscous mantle, and a dense core.

Seismic waves generated by earthquakes, for instance, travel through the Earth's interior in patterns that are consistent with a solid and layered structure, rather than a hollow one. Additionally, the gravitational behavior of the Earth, which has been measured and studied in great detail, would be vastly different if the planet were hollow. The density of the Earth, as inferred from its gravitational pull and the behavior of seismic waves, also aligns with the presence of a solid core.

The scientific community considers the Hollow Earth Theory to be a pseudoscience, lacking empirical evidence and rooted more in mythology and speculative fiction than in verifiable research. While the idea of a Hollow Earth remains a fascinating concept, it is not supported by the body of scientific knowledge accumulated over centuries of study.

The idea of Inner Earth Beings and the Hollow Earth Theory has captivated imaginations for centuries, blending ancient mythology with modern conspiracy theories and speculative fiction. Whether as a hidden utopia, a refuge for ancient civilizations, or the origin of UFOs, the Hollow Earth serves as a symbol of humanity's enduring curiosity about the unknown and the possibility that the world is far more mysterious than it appears.

While the scientific community has thoroughly debunked the Hollow Earth Theory, its appeal persists in certain corners of popular culture and alternative thought. For those who believe, or simply find the idea intriguing, the Hollow Earth represents a world of endless possibilities, a hidden realm waiting to be discovered. As with many ideas that straddle the line between myth and reality, the Hollow Earth continues to inspire wonder, debate, and exploration, reminding us of the power of the human imagination to envision worlds beyond our own.

The Ashtar Command: Galactic Federation

The Ashtar Command, often referred to as part of a broader Galactic Federation, is a concept that originated in the mid-20th century and has since become a central theme in certain New Age, ufology, and spiritual circles. The Ashtar Command is described as an extraterrestrial organization dedicated to overseeing and assisting humanity during times of great change, often portrayed as a benevolent force working to ensure the peaceful evolution of Earth and its inhabitants. This chapter explores the origins of the Ashtar Command, its role within the broader concept of the Galactic Federation, and its significance within New Age spirituality and ufology.

Origins of the Ashtar Command

The concept of the Ashtar Command first emerged in the 1950s through the channeling activities of George Van Tassel, a former aviation engineer turned UFO contactee and spiritual leader. Van Tassel claimed to have received telepathic messages from an extraterrestrial being named Ashtar, who identified himself as the commander of a vast fleet of spacecraft operating in Earth's vicinity. According to Van Tassel, Ashtar and his command were part of a larger intergalactic organization responsible for overseeing the spiritual and physical well-being of humanity.

Van Tassel was one of the earliest figures in the UFO contactee movement, which was characterized by individuals who claimed to have direct contact with benevolent extraterrestrial beings. These beings were often portrayed as advanced, enlightened, and concerned with the future of humanity. Van Tassel's claims about Ashtar and the Ashtar Command quickly gained a following, particularly among those who were interested in UFOs, spirituality, and alternative beliefs about the cosmos.

The messages attributed to Ashtar often focused on themes of peace, love, and the need for humanity to overcome its destructive tendencies. Ashtar was described as a figure of great wisdom and compassion, whose mission was to guide humanity through a period of transformation and to help avert global catastrophes. The Ashtar Command was said to be a fleet of highly advanced extraterrestrial beings who worked in harmony with other benevolent civilizations within a larger organization known as the Galactic Federation or the Galactic Confederation.

The Galactic Federation: A Cosmic Alliance

The Ashtar Command is often depicted as a key component of the Galactic Federation, a term used to describe a vast alliance of extraterrestrial civilizations that work together to maintain peace and order in the galaxy. The Galactic Federation is portrayed as a highly organized, hierarchical structure that includes representatives from numerous star systems and planets, all united by a common purpose: the promotion of spiritual evolution, peace, and cooperation among sentient beings.

In this narrative, the Galactic Federation operates under the guidance of advanced spiritual beings, often referred to as Ascended Masters, who possess deep wisdom and understanding of the cosmic laws that govern the universe. The Federation is said to monitor the activities of various planets, including Earth, and to intervene when necessary to prevent destructive events or to assist in the spiritual awakening of a civilization.

The concept of the Galactic Federation has been popularized by various channelers and spiritual teachers over the decades, each adding their own interpretations and details to the narrative. The Federation is often described as having a non-interventionist policy, meaning that it generally allows civilizations to evolve on their own unless direct intervention is necessary to prevent a catastrophe or to protect the integrity of the galaxy.

Channeling and Messages from the Ashtar Command

The Ashtar Command's messages have primarily been conveyed through channeling, a practice in which individuals claim to receive telepathic communications from extraterrestrial beings, spiritual entities, or higher-dimensional consciousnesses. Since Van Tassel's initial contact with Ashtar, numerous other channelers have claimed to receive messages from Ashtar and other members of the Ashtar Command.

These messages typically emphasize themes of love, unity, and the importance of raising one's consciousness to align with the higher frequencies of the universe. The Ashtar Command is often depicted as watching over Earth during times of crisis, offering guidance and support to those who seek to raise their spiritual awareness. Messages from the Ashtar Command have often predicted significant global events, such as natural disasters, political upheavals, and shifts in human consciousness, sometimes referred to as "The Great Awakening" or "Ascension."

One of the central tenets of the Ashtar Command's teachings is the idea that humanity is on the verge of a major transformation, often described as a shift from the third dimension (associated with the physical, material world) to the fifth dimension (associated with spiritual enlightenment and higher consciousness). This transition is believed to be accompanied by a period of cleansing or purification, during which old systems and beliefs that no longer serve humanity's highest good will be dismantled.

The Ashtar Command's messages also frequently refer to the idea of "Disclosure," the anticipated revelation of the existence of extraterrestrial life and the true nature of humanity's relationship with other civilizations in the cosmos. According to these messages, the Ashtar Command and the Galactic Federation are preparing humanity for this eventual disclosure, which will lead to a new era of cooperation and peace on Earth.

Criticism and Skepticism

The Ashtar Command and the broader concept of the Galactic Federation have been met with both enthusiasm and skepticism. While many people find comfort and inspiration in the messages of love, peace, and spiritual growth associated with the Ashtar Command, others view these ideas as speculative or even deceptive.

Critics argue that the Ashtar Command narrative lacks empirical evidence and is based largely on subjective experiences, such as channeling, which cannot be independently verified. Some skeptics suggest that the messages attributed to Ashtar and other extraterrestrial beings may be the result of psychological phenomena, such as the subconscious mind projecting its own desires and beliefs, rather than genuine communications from otherworldly sources.

Additionally, the prediction of specific global events by the Ashtar Command has often been problematic, as many of these predictions have failed to materialize as foretold. This has led some to question the validity of the messages and the authenticity of the channelers who convey them.

However, supporters of the Ashtar Command emphasize the symbolic and spiritual value of the messages, suggesting that the teachings are meant to inspire positive change and personal growth, regardless of their literal accuracy. For many, the Ashtar Command represents a hopeful vision of the future, one in which humanity transcends its current limitations and embraces a more enlightened, harmonious way of living.

Impact on New Age Spirituality and Ufology

The Ashtar Command has had a significant impact on New Age spirituality, ufology, and related movements. It has contributed to the development of a cosmology that blends elements of traditional spirituality with modern concepts of extraterrestrial life, creating a unique framework for understanding humanity's place in the universe.

In New Age circles, the Ashtar Command is often invoked as a source of spiritual guidance and support, particularly during times of personal or global crisis. The idea of a benevolent extraterrestrial force watching over humanity aligns with broader New Age beliefs in the interconnectedness of all life, the importance of spiritual evolution, and the existence of higher dimensions of consciousness.

In the field of ufology, the Ashtar Command represents one of many narratives about extraterrestrial contact and the role of UFOs in human history. While some ufologists focus on the physical evidence of UFO sightings and encounters, others are drawn to the more metaphysical aspects of the phenomenon, such as the messages conveyed by beings like Ashtar.

The Ashtar Command's teachings have also influenced the broader discourse on the potential for peaceful coexistence with extraterrestrial civilizations. The idea that humanity is being guided and protected by advanced beings from other star systems resonates with those who believe that contact with extraterrestrial life could be a positive and transformative experience.

The Ashtar Command and the concept of the Galactic Federation represent a fascinating blend of New Age spirituality, ufology, and speculative cosmology. Whether viewed as literal truth, symbolic myth, or a combination of both, the narrative of the Ashtar Command offers a hopeful vision of a future in which humanity evolves into a more enlightened and peaceful species, guided by the wisdom of benevolent extraterrestrial beings.

While the Ashtar Command has been met with skepticism and criticism, it continues to inspire and uplift those who resonate with its messages of love, unity, and spiritual growth. In a world often characterized by conflict and uncertainty, the idea of a cosmic alliance dedicated to the well-being of humanity provides a source of comfort and inspiration for many.

As with all aspects of ufology and New Age thought, the Ashtar Command invites us to explore the boundaries of our understanding, to consider the possibility that we are not alone in the universe, and to reflect on the potential for a more harmonious and enlightened future for all beings. Whether one sees the Ashtar Command as a literal presence or a powerful metaphor, its message of hope and transformation remains a compelling and enduring part of the spiritual and cosmic landscape.

The Black Eyed Children: Alien Hybrids?

The phenomenon of the Black Eyed Children, sometimes referred to as BEKs (Black Eyed Kids), is one of the most unsettling and mysterious topics in modern paranormal lore. These entities are described as children or young teens with pale skin, lifeless black eyes, and a deeply unsettling presence. Encounters with Black Eyed Children typically involve them appearing at the doors of homes, asking to be let in, or approaching individuals in isolated places. Theories about their origins vary widely, with some suggesting that they are alien-human hybrids, demonic entities, or even a new type of cryptid. This chapter explores the origins of the Black Eyed Children phenomenon, various accounts and encounters, and the theories that seek to explain what they might be.

Origins of the Black Eyed Children Phenomenon

The Black Eyed Children phenomenon gained widespread attention in the late 1990s, largely due to a story shared by a Texas-based journalist named Brian Bethel. In 1996, Bethel recounted an eerie encounter he had with two young boys who approached his car one night in a parking lot in Abilene, Texas. According to Bethel, the boys asked for a ride, but something about their demeanor and the intense blackness of their eyes filled him with an overwhelming sense of dread. Despite their insistence, Bethel did not let them into his car, and the encounter left him deeply shaken.

Bethel's account was one of the first widely publicized reports of Black Eyed Children, and it quickly spread across the internet, sparking interest and fear in equal measure. Since then, numerous other reports of encounters with Black Eyed Children have surfaced, with many people describing similar experiences of being approached by pale, black-eyed children who exude an inexplicable sense of malevolence.

While the phenomenon may have gained popularity in the 1990s, some researchers suggest that stories of black-eyed beings have existed in folklore and mythology for much longer. Tales of dark, soulless eyes are often associated with demonic possession, vampirism, and other supernatural occurrences, leading some to speculate that the Black Eyed Children are a modern iteration of these older legends.

Characteristics and Common Encounter Scenarios

Accounts of encounters with Black Eyed Children share several common characteristics:

Appearance: Black Eyed Children are typically described as being between the ages of 6 and 16, with pale or ashen skin and eyes that are completely black, lacking any white sclera or iris. They often wear outdated or ill-fitting clothing, adding to their unsettling appearance.

Behavior: These children are usually described as calm, polite, and eerily articulate, often using language that seems overly formal for their age. They typically ask for permission to enter a home, car, or other private space, often under the pretense of needing help. However, their requests are accompanied by a sense of urgency and an underlying threat.

Psychological Effects: Witnesses often report feeling an overwhelming sense of fear, dread, or unease during these encounters, even before noticing the children's black eyes. Some describe the sensation as a primal fear, as if their instincts are warning them of imminent danger. This intense emotional response is a hallmark of Black Eyed Children encounters.

Mysterious Disappearances: In many cases, witnesses report that the children vanish suddenly and inexplicably if they are denied entry or if the witness manages to escape. These disappearances often add to the eerie and supernatural nature of the encounters.

Theories about the Nature of Black Eyed Children

The enigmatic nature of Black Eyed Children has given rise to numerous theories about what they might be. While there is no consensus, several prominent ideas have emerged:

Alien Hybrids: One of the most popular theories is that Black Eyed Children are alien-human hybrids, possibly the result of extraterrestrial experimentation or breeding programs. The theory posits that these beings are attempting to integrate into human society or gather information for their alien progenitors. Their black eyes, which resemble the classic depiction of the Greys, and their strange, otherworldly demeanor, are often cited as evidence of their extraterrestrial origin.

Demons or Malevolent Spirits: Another theory is that Black Eyed Children are demonic entities or malevolent spirits that take on the guise of children to exploit human compassion and gain access to their victims. This idea is supported by the intense fear and dread that witnesses often feel, which some interpret as a natural response to the presence of evil. The children's insistence on being invited in also parallels traditional vampire lore, where the creature cannot enter a home without permission.

Cryptids or Supernatural Beings: Some researchers suggest that Black Eyed Children may be a new type of cryptid or supernatural being, unrelated to aliens or demons. These beings could represent an unknown species or a manifestation of energy that preys on fear. In this view, Black Eyed Children might be similar to other mysterious entities like the Mothman or Slender Man, existing on the fringes of reality and interacting with humans in ways that defy explanation.

Urban Legend or Mass Hysteria: Skeptics argue that the Black Eyed Children phenomenon is a modern urban legend, fueled by the power of suggestion and the internet's ability to spread stories quickly. According to this theory, the growing number of reports is a result of people being influenced by existing stories, leading them to misinterpret ordinary encounters or fabricate experiences. The psychological effects described in these encounters, such as the overwhelming sense of fear, could be attributed to the influence of suggestibility and the human tendency to experience heightened emotions in response to perceived threats.

Cultural Impact and Popularity

Since their emergence in the 1990s, Black Eyed Children have become a staple of internet folklore and paranormal discussions. The phenomenon has been featured in books, movies, and television shows, often as a symbol of hidden dangers or as a representation of primal fears. Their eerie, unsettling nature has made them a popular subject for horror fiction, where they are portrayed as enigmatic and malevolent forces that defy understanding. The popularity of Black Eyed Children has also led to numerous hoaxes and fabricated stories, further complicating the task of discerning genuine encounters from fictional accounts. Despite this, the phenomenon continues to captivate those interested in the paranormal, with new reports and theories emerging regularly.

The Black Eyed Children phenomenon remains one of the most intriguing and unsettling mysteries in the realm of the paranormal. Whether they are alien hybrids, demonic entities, cryptids, or simply the product of modern urban legend, the accounts of these eerie children tap into deep-seated fears and the unknown aspects of our reality.

The enduring popularity of Black Eyed Children in paranormal lore speaks to the human fascination with the unknown and the unexplainable. As with many such phenomena, the truth behind these encounters may never be fully understood, but the stories continue to evoke a sense of wonder, fear, and curiosity.

For those who have encountered Black Eyed Children, the experience is often life-altering, leaving them with more questions than answers and a lingering sense of unease. As long as these reports continue, the mystery of the Black Eyed Children will persist, reminding us of the strange and unexplained aspects of our world that remain beyond our comprehension.

Hybrid Programs: Creating a New Species

The concept of hybrid programs, particularly those involving the creation of a new species through the combination of human and extraterrestrial DNA, is one of the more provocative and complex ideas in ufology and conspiracy theory circles. These programs are often depicted as secret, ongoing efforts to engineer a hybrid race that possesses the best traits of both humans and extraterrestrials. Proponents of these theories suggest that such programs could be part of a larger agenda—whether benevolent or malevolent—aimed at influencing the future evolution of humanity. This chapter delves into the origins of hybrid program theories, the characteristics attributed to these hybrid beings, the motivations behind such programs, and the impact of these ideas on popular culture and the UFO community.

Origins of Hybrid Program Theories

The idea of hybrid programs has its roots in various reports of alien abductions that began to surface prominently in the mid-20th century. Many abductees claimed that during their experiences, they were subjected to medical procedures that appeared to involve reproductive experimentation. These accounts often described encounters with extraterrestrials, typically the Greys, who performed procedures that involved the extraction of eggs or sperm, as well as the implantation of embryos.

One of the most influential cases in the development of hybrid program theories is that of Betty and Barney Hill, who claimed to have been abducted by extraterrestrials in 1961. Under hypnosis, Betty Hill recounted being subjected to a procedure that involved the extraction of eggs, a detail that has been echoed in numerous other abduction reports. These stories contributed to the growing belief that extraterrestrials were interested in human reproduction and genetic material. Over time, the idea emerged that these reproductive procedures were not merely for study but were part of a deliberate effort to create a hybrid species. This theory gained further traction with the work of researchers such as Budd Hopkins, David Jacobs, and John Mack, who documented and analyzed abduction cases in which the creation of hybrid beings was a recurring theme. These researchers suggested that the hybrids were part of a covert program with profound implications for the future of humanity.

Characteristics of Hybrid Beings

Descriptions of hybrid beings vary, but they typically combine human and extraterrestrial traits. Common characteristics attributed to hybrids include:

Physical Appearance: Hybrids are often described as having a blend of human and alien features. They may have a humanoid form but with certain alien characteristics, such as large, almond-shaped eyes, elongated limbs, or unusually smooth, pale skin. Some hybrids are said to be nearly indistinguishable from humans, while others retain more pronounced extraterrestrial traits.

Enhanced Abilities: Hybrids are often believed to possess abilities beyond those of ordinary humans. These abilities might include heightened intelligence, telepathy, psychic powers, or advanced healing capabilities. Some accounts suggest that hybrids have a greater understanding of complex technologies or possess a deep spiritual awareness.

Emotional and Social Traits: In some narratives, hybrids are depicted as having a more refined emotional state, often described as being more compassionate, empathetic, or spiritually advanced than humans. However, they are also sometimes portrayed as struggling with human emotions and social norms, leading to feelings of isolation or confusion.

Purpose and Mission: Many accounts suggest that hybrids have a specific purpose or mission, often related to the evolution or enlightenment of humanity. Some are believed to be integrated into human society to help guide humanity through future challenges, while others are seen as potential leaders of a new era of human existence.

Motivations behind Hybrid Programs

Theories about the motivations behind hybrid programs are diverse and often reflect the broader worldview of those who propose them. Some of the most common explanations include:

Survival of the Extraterrestrial Species: One of the most frequently cited motivations is the idea that extraterrestrials are creating hybrids to ensure the survival of their own species. Some theories suggest that these beings, particularly the Greys, are suffering from genetic decline or infertility and require human DNA to restore their genetic health. By creating hybrids, they can preserve their species while also adapting to life on Earth.

Spiritual Evolution: Another perspective is that hybrid programs are part of a cosmic plan to elevate the spiritual consciousness of humanity. In this view, the hybrids are seen as "star children" or "indigo children" who have been sent to Earth to help guide humanity through a period of spiritual awakening. The blending of human and extraterrestrial DNA is believed to produce beings with a greater capacity for love, empathy, and understanding, which are necessary for humanity's evolution.

Preparation for Disclosure: Some theorists believe that hybrid programs are being conducted in preparation for a future disclosure of extraterrestrial contact. The hybrids, in this scenario, are being integrated into human society to facilitate this transition and to help humanity adapt to the reality of extraterrestrial life. The hybrids may serve as ambassadors or intermediaries between humans and extraterrestrials.

Control and Manipulation: On the more sinister end of the spectrum, some theories suggest that hybrid programs are part of a broader agenda of control and manipulation. In this view, the hybrids are being created to infiltrate and dominate human society, ultimately leading to the subjugation or replacement of the human race. This perspective often ties into larger conspiracy theories about a global elite working in conjunction with extraterrestrials to establish a New World Order.

Impact on Popular Culture and Ufology

The concept of hybrid programs has had a significant impact on popular culture, influencing books, films, television shows, and other media. The idea of beings that are part human and part alien taps into deep-seated fears and fascinations about identity, evolution, and the unknown. In science fiction, hybrids are often portrayed as powerful but conflicted figures, caught between two worlds and struggling to find their place in the universe.

Films like *The X-Files* series, *Species* (1995), and *The 4400* (2004-2007) explore themes related to hybridization, often depicting hybrids as both a threat and a hope for the future. In these narratives, hybrids are sometimes portrayed as a bridge between humanity and a larger cosmic community, while in others, they are depicted as potential harbingers of destruction. Within the UFO community, hybrid programs remain a topic of intense debate and speculation. For some, the idea of hybrid beings offers a compelling explanation for the strange and often frightening experiences reported by abductees. For others, it raises unsettling questions about the nature of reality, the future of humanity, and the intentions of the extraterrestrial beings involved.

Skepticism and Criticism

As with many aspects of ufology and conspiracy theories, hybrid programs have been met with skepticism and criticism. Mainstream scientists and skeptics argue that there is no credible evidence to support the existence of hybrid beings or the claims made by those who report such experiences. They suggest that the stories of hybrid programs are likely the result of psychological phenomena, cultural influences, or hoaxes rather than actual encounters with extraterrestrial entities.

Critics also point out that the narratives surrounding hybrid programs often reflect broader societal anxieties, such as fears of genetic engineering, loss of identity, or the erosion of traditional boundaries between humans and other forms of life. In this view, the hybrid program theories can be seen as a modern myth that addresses these fears in a symbolic or allegorical way. Despite the lack of empirical evidence, the idea of hybrid programs continues to capture the imagination of many and remains a potent symbol of the potential and peril of human evolution in a rapidly changing world.

Hybrid programs, as a concept, represent one of the most provocative and enigmatic aspects of modern ufology and conspiracy theory. Whether viewed as a genuine extraterrestrial agenda, a symbolic narrative, or a speculative fiction, the idea of creating a new species through the blending of human and alien DNA raises profound questions about the future of humanity and our place in the cosmos.

For those who believe in the reality of hybrid programs, these beings are a sign of humanity's potential to evolve beyond its current limitations, guided by the wisdom and technology of advanced extraterrestrial civilizations. For others, the concept serves as a metaphor for the complex and often unsettling changes that humanity faces in the modern world.

As with many elements of the UFO phenomenon, the truth behind hybrid programs may never be fully known. However, the ongoing interest in these theories reflects a deep and enduring curiosity about the mysteries of life, the possibilities of genetic manipulation, and the potential for a future in which humans are no longer the sole intelligent beings on Earth. Whether real or imagined, the idea of hybrid programs challenges us to think about what it means to be human and what the next step in our evolutionary journey might entail.

Underground Bases: Hidden Alien Facilities

The concept of underground bases, particularly those believed to be hidden alien facilities, is a pervasive and intriguing aspect of modern conspiracy theories and ufology. These secretive locations are often depicted as highly advanced installations where extraterrestrial beings and government or military personnel collaborate on a range of activities, from technological research to genetic experiments. The idea of hidden underground bases ties into broader themes of government secrecy, extraterrestrial contact, and the possibility that humanity is not alone in its technological and scientific endeavors. This chapter explores the origins of the underground base narrative, famous alleged sites, the activities purportedly conducted within these facilities, and the impact of these ideas on popular culture and the UFO community.

Origins of the Underground Base Narrative

The notion of underground bases can be traced back to various sources, including Cold War-era fears of nuclear conflict, accounts of secret government projects, and reports of UFO sightings in remote areas. The idea gained significant traction in the latter half of the 20th century, particularly as stories of secret military installations and alien encounters began to proliferate.

One of the earliest and most influential proponents of the underground base theory was a man named Phil Schneider, a former government contractor who claimed to have worked on the construction of secret underground facilities in the United States. Schneider's most famous claims involve the alleged existence of an underground base at Dulce, New Mexico, which he described as a massive complex where human and extraterrestrial scientists collaborated on a variety of sinister projects. Schneider's accounts, delivered through lectures and presentations in the 1990s, included descriptions of battles between humans and aliens within these underground bases, genetic experiments on both humans and extraterrestrials, and advanced technology far beyond what is known to the public. Schneider's death under mysterious circumstances in 1996 further fueled speculation and conspiracy theories about the existence of these hidden facilities.

Famous Alleged Underground Bases

Several locations around the world are frequently mentioned in connection with underground alien bases. These sites are often remote, heavily guarded, or associated with unusual activity, leading to speculation about what might be hidden beneath the surface.

Dulce Base, New Mexico: Perhaps the most famous of all alleged underground bases, Dulce Base is said to be located beneath the Archuleta Mesa on the Colorado-New Mexico border. According to various accounts, Dulce Base is a sprawling underground facility where joint human-alien experiments are conducted. These experiments are rumored to include genetic manipulation, mind control, and the development of advanced weapons. Reports of strange lights, UFO sightings, and cattle mutilations in the area have all contributed to the mystique surrounding Dulce.

Area 51, Nevada: While Area 51 is primarily known as a highly classified U.S. Air Force facility associated with the development and testing of experimental aircraft, some conspiracy theorists believe that it also houses underground facilities where extraterrestrial beings and technology are stored. The secrecy surrounding Area 51, combined with its association with UFO lore, has made it a focal point for speculation about hidden alien bases.

The Pine Gap Facility, Australia: Pine Gap is a joint U.S.-Australian military facility located in the remote outback of Australia. Officially, it serves as a satellite tracking station and intelligence-gathering site. However, some theories suggest that Pine Gap has extensive underground facilities where alien technology is reverse-engineered, and extraterrestrial beings collaborate with human scientists. The remote location and the high level of secrecy surrounding the facility have contributed to its reputation as a potential underground base.

Cheyenne Mountain Complex, Colorado: The Cheyenne Mountain Complex, located near Colorado Springs, is a well-known military installation that houses the operations center for NORAD (North American Aerospace Defense Command). While the facility's primary purpose is to monitor airspace and provide missile defense, some theorists believe that it also includes deep underground levels where extraterrestrial beings are involved in classified projects.

The S4 Facility, Nevada: Allegedly located near Area 51, the S4 facility is said to be a secret underground base where recovered alien spacecraft are stored and studied. The existence of S4 was popularized by Bob Lazar, a controversial figure who claimed to have worked at the facility in the late 1980s. According to Lazar, the U.S. government is actively reverse-engineering alien technology at S4, including propulsion systems that defy the known laws of physics.

Activities Allegedly Conducted in Underground Bases

The activities purportedly carried out within these underground bases vary depending on the source, but several common themes emerge:

Genetic Experiments: One of the most prevalent claims about underground bases is that they are sites of advanced genetic experimentation. These experiments allegedly involve the creation of human-alien hybrids, cloning, and the manipulation of DNA to produce new life forms. Some reports suggest that these experiments are conducted in collaboration with extraterrestrial beings, who provide the necessary technology and knowledge.

Reverse Engineering of Alien Technology: Another frequent claim is that underground bases are used to study and reverse-engineer alien technology recovered from crashed UFOs. This technology is said to include advanced propulsion systems, energy sources, and materials with properties unknown to modern science. The goal of these efforts is often described as the development of new weapons, aircraft, or other military applications.

Interrogation and Communication with Aliens: Some theories propose that underground bases are used to house extraterrestrial beings, either as guests or captives, and that human scientists and military personnel engage in communication and interrogation with these beings. These interactions are said to focus on understanding alien intentions, acquiring knowledge about their civilizations, and negotiating agreements or alliances.

Mind Control and Psychological Experimentation: There are also claims that underground bases are sites of mind control and psychological experimentation, often involving both human and extraterrestrial subjects. These experiments allegedly aim to develop techniques for controlling or influencing the human mind, potentially for use in military or covert operations.

Preparation for Disclosure or Invasion: Some theorists believe that underground bases are being used to prepare for an eventual disclosure of extraterrestrial contact or even an alien invasion. In this scenario, the bases serve as secure locations where governments can coordinate defense strategies, communicate with extraterrestrial allies or adversaries, and develop the technology needed to survive and thrive in a post-disclosure world.

Impact on Popular Culture and Ufology

The idea of underground alien bases has had a profound impact on popular culture, influencing books, films, television shows, and video games. These narratives often depict secretive government operations, hidden facilities, and the tension between human and extraterrestrial forces.

Movies like *The X-Files* series, *Independence Day* (1996), and *Stranger Things* (2016) explore themes of government secrecy, hidden bases, and the existence of otherworldly beings. In these stories, underground bases are often portrayed as places where dark and dangerous activities take place, with far-reaching consequences for humanity.

Within the UFO community, the idea of underground bases remains a popular and enduring topic of discussion. Theories about these facilities often intersect with broader conspiracy narratives, such as those involving the New World Order, government cover-ups, and the potential for extraterrestrial contact or conflict. For many, the idea of hidden alien bases serves as a powerful symbol of the unknown and the potential dangers that may lie beneath the surface of our world.

Skepticism and Criticism

As with many aspects of ufology and conspiracy theories, the idea of underground alien bases has been met with skepticism and criticism. Mainstream scientists, military experts, and government officials generally dismiss the claims about these facilities as unfounded and lacking credible evidence.

Critics argue that the stories of underground bases are likely the result of a combination of misinformation, exaggeration, and the human tendency to imagine hidden dangers. They point out that many of the supposed "whistle-blowers" who have come forward with information about these bases have been unable to provide verifiable evidence to support their claims.

Additionally, the logistics of constructing and maintaining large underground bases, especially in remote or hostile environments, are often cited as a major challenge. Skeptics suggest that the secrecy and scale required to operate such facilities without detection would be extremely difficult, if not impossible, to achieve.

Despite these criticisms, the idea of underground alien bases continues to capture the imagination of those who are open to the possibility of extraterrestrial involvement in human affairs. For believers, these hidden facilities represent a tantalizing glimpse into a world of advanced technology, secret knowledge, and the potential for profound discoveries about the nature of the universe.

The concept of underground bases as hidden alien facilities is a compelling and complex aspect of modern conspiracy theory and ufology. Whether seen as a genuine threat, a secretive operation, or a metaphor for the unknown, these bases serve as a powerful symbol of humanity's fascination with the mysteries that lie beneath the surface.

While the existence of such bases remains unproven and highly speculative, the narratives surrounding them continue to inspire debate, curiosity, and exploration. As with many elements of the UFO phenomenon, the truth behind underground alien bases may never be fully known, but their enduring appeal reflects a deep and persistent interest in the hidden aspects of our world and the possibility that we are not alone. Whether real or imagined, the idea of underground bases challenges us to consider the limits of human knowledge and the potential for discovery in places we have yet to explore. It invites us to ask questions about the nature of secrecy, power, and the unknown, and to reflect on the ways in which we seek to understand the mysteries of the universe.

Dolores Cannon's Hypnotherapy: Recollections of Past Lives with Aliens

Dolores Cannon was a pioneering hypnotherapist and past-life regressionist whose work has had a profound impact on the fields of metaphysics, spirituality, and ufology. Over the course of her career, Cannon developed a unique method of hypnotherapy that she called "Quantum Healing Hypnosis Technique" (QHHT), through which she explored her clients' past lives, memories, and experiences, including those involving extraterrestrial beings. Her work has been influential in shaping the narratives around alien encounters, soul journeys, and the interconnectedness of consciousness across different lifetimes and dimensions. This chapter delves into Dolores Cannon's approach to hypnotherapy, the key themes of her work, and the significance of her findings in the broader context of ufology and spiritual exploration.

Dolores Cannon's Background and Hypnotherapy Techniques

Dolores Cannon began her career as a traditional hypnotherapist in the 1960s. However, her work took a dramatic turn when she inadvertently regressed a client to a past life, an experience that sparked her interest in past-life regression and the exploration of consciousness. Over time, Cannon refined her techniques and developed QHHT, a method that involved guiding clients into a deep state of trance where they could access memories of past lives, other dimensions, and even interactions with non-human entities.

QHHT is distinct from other forms of hypnotherapy in that it not only explores past lives but also connects clients with what Cannon referred to as the "Subconscious," a higher aspect of the self that possesses vast knowledge and understanding. Through this connection, clients were able to access profound insights about their current life, past incarnations, and the nature of reality itself.

Cannon's sessions often revealed information that went beyond personal healing, touching on universal themes such as the evolution of the soul, the purpose of human existence, and the role of extraterrestrial beings in humanity's spiritual journey. Her clients frequently recounted experiences that seemed to defy conventional understanding, including encounters with aliens, memories of lives on other planets, and participation in intergalactic missions.

Key Themes in Dolores Cannon's Work

Dolores Cannon's body of work is vast, encompassing numerous books, lectures, and workshops. Some of the key themes that emerge from her research include:

Past Lives and Reincarnation: One of the central tenets of Cannon's work is the concept of reincarnation—the belief that the soul undergoes multiple lifetimes, each one contributing to its growth and evolution. Through QHHT, many of Cannon's clients accessed memories of past lives, sometimes on Earth, and sometimes on other planets or in other dimensions. These past-life recollections often provided insights into the challenges and lessons of their current lives, suggesting that each incarnation is part of a broader spiritual journey.

Alien Encounters and Extraterrestrial Origins: A significant portion of Cannon's work deals with clients who recalled interactions with extraterrestrial beings. These encounters were often described as having occurred in other lifetimes or even in parallel realities. Some clients remembered being part of extraterrestrial civilizations before choosing to incarnate on Earth. Others recounted abductions or visitations that were framed as positive, transformative experiences rather than the traumatic events often depicted in popular culture.

The Volunteer Souls and the New Earth: One of Cannon's most famous concepts is that of the "Three Waves of Volunteers." According to her findings, many souls currently incarnated on Earth are volunteers who have come from other planets, dimensions, or planes of existence to assist humanity during a time of great transition. These volunteers are here to help raise the vibrational frequency of the planet and to guide humanity through the shift to a "New Earth"—a higher-dimensional state of being characterized by love, peace, and spiritual enlightenment.

Healing and Spiritual Awakening: Cannon's work emphasized the healing potential of understanding past lives and the greater cosmic context of one's existence. Many clients reported profound physical, emotional, and spiritual healing after undergoing QHHT sessions, often as a result of insights gained from their past-life experiences or their connection to the Subconscious. Cannon believed that by accessing this higher knowledge, individuals could release deep-seated traumas, fears, and limiting beliefs, leading to greater well-being and spiritual awakening.

The Nature of Reality and Multidimensional Existence: Throughout her sessions, Cannon encountered numerous accounts that challenged conventional notions of reality. Clients described experiences that suggested the existence of multiple dimensions, parallel universes, and alternate timelines. These narratives often depicted a reality that is far more fluid and interconnected than commonly understood, with consciousness playing a central role in shaping one's experience of the world.

Impact on Ufology and Spirituality

Dolores Cannon's work has had a significant impact on both ufology and the broader spiritual community. Her research has provided a unique perspective on the phenomenon of alien encounters, one that frames these experiences not as isolated incidents but as part of a larger, multidimensional reality.

In the context of ufology, Cannon's findings challenge the more conventional narratives of alien abductions that emphasize fear and victimization. Instead, her work suggests that many alien encounters may be part of a prearranged soul contract or mission, with extraterrestrial beings serving as guides, teachers, or collaborators in the evolution of human consciousness. This perspective has resonated with those who seek a more positive and empowering understanding of their experiences with extraterrestrials.

In the realm of spirituality, Cannon's teachings have contributed to the growing interest in past-life regression, reincarnation, and the exploration of consciousness. Her concept of the "Volunteer Souls" has particularly influenced the New Age movement, providing a framework for understanding the sense of mission and purpose that many people feel in their lives. Her work has inspired countless individuals to explore their own spiritual paths, often leading to profound personal transformation.

Cannon's influence extends beyond her immediate field, as her ideas have permeated popular culture and alternative spirituality. Concepts like the New Earth, the Three Waves of Volunteers, and the healing potential of past-life regression have become part of the broader discourse on spiritual awakening and the evolution of consciousness.

Criticism and Controversy

While Dolores Cannon's work has garnered a large following, it has also faced criticism, particularly from sceptics and those in the scientific community. Critics argue that the information obtained through QHHT and similar methods is highly subjective and cannot be independently verified. They suggest that the experiences recounted by clients may be influenced by suggestion, imagination, or cultural narratives rather than being literal recollections of past lives or encounters with extraterrestrial beings.

Some psychologists and hypnotherapists caution that past-life regression can lead to the creation of false memories, especially in highly suggestible individuals. They argue that while such sessions can be therapeutic, the information obtained should be interpreted with caution and not taken as objective truth.

Despite these criticisms, many practitioners and clients of QHHT report profound benefits from the process, including healing, spiritual growth, and a greater understanding of their life's purpose. For those who resonate with Cannon's teachings, the insights gained through her methods are seen as valuable and transformative, regardless of their verifiability.

Legacy and Continuing Influence

Dolores Cannon passed away in 2014, but her legacy continues to thrive through her books, lectures, and the work of practitioners who have been trained in QHHT. Her teachings have inspired a global community of spiritual seekers, many of whom continue to explore the themes of past lives, extraterrestrial encounters, and the evolution of consciousness.

Cannon's books, such as *The Convoluted Universe* series, *Keepers of the Garden*, and *The Three Waves of Volunteers and the New Earth*, remain popular among those interested in metaphysics and spiritual exploration. Her work has also influenced other researchers and authors in the fields of ufology, past-life regression, and spiritual healing.

The continuing interest in Cannon's work reflects a broader cultural shift toward exploring the mysteries of consciousness and the possibility of life beyond Earth. In a world where the boundaries of reality are increasingly being questioned, Cannon's teachings offer a framework for understanding the interconnectedness of all life and the role that extraterrestrial beings may play in the ongoing evolution of humanity.

Dolores Cannon's hypnotherapy and her exploration of past lives with aliens have left an indelible mark on the fields of ufology and spirituality. Through her pioneering work, she has expanded the boundaries of what is possible in the exploration of consciousness, offering a vision of a reality that is far more complex and interconnected than commonly understood.

Whether one views her findings as literal truth, symbolic representations, or therapeutic narratives, the impact of Cannon's work on those who have experienced it is undeniable. Her teachings continue to inspire and empower individuals to explore their own spiritual paths, to seek healing and understanding, and to embrace the possibility that we are all part of a vast, multidimensional universe.

As the exploration of consciousness and the mysteries of existence continue to evolve, Dolores Cannon's work remains a guiding light for those who seek to understand the deeper truths of who we are, where we come from, and what our purpose may be in this ever-unfolding cosmic journey.

The Anshar: Inner Earth Inhabitants

The Anshar are a group of beings often described in modern esoteric and ufological narratives as advanced, highly evolved inhabitants of the Inner Earth. These beings are said to have existed on Earth for millennia, living in hidden subterranean cities and possessing advanced spiritual and technological knowledge. The Anshar, as described by certain modern sources, are part of a larger narrative about the existence of ancient, wise civilizations that have chosen to remain hidden from surface-dwelling humanity but may soon emerge to play a more active role in guiding humanity through a period of global transformation. This chapter explores the origins of the Anshar narrative, the characteristics attributed to these beings, their supposed interactions with surface humans, and the broader implications of their existence within the context of modern esotericism and ufology.

Origins of the Anshar Narrative

The Anshar are primarily known through the accounts of Corey Goode, a controversial figure in the ufology and esoteric communities who claims to have had extensive contact with various extraterrestrial and Inner Earth civilizations. Goode's claims, which have been shared through various online platforms, conferences, and documentaries, have significantly shaped the modern understanding of the Anshar.

According to Goode, the Anshar are a race of advanced beings who have lived in vast, technologically sophisticated cities beneath the Earth's surface for many thousands of years. These beings are believed to be descendants of an ancient civilization that predates much of known human history. Goode suggests that the Anshar have remained hidden from the surface world, maintaining a non-interventionist stance while observing and occasionally influencing human events from behind the scenes.

The Anshar narrative fits within a broader tradition of Inner Earth mythology, which includes various ancient cultures, secretive civilizations, and advanced beings said to inhabit the Earth's subterranean realms. These ideas have been part of human folklore for centuries, but the Anshar represent a modern iteration of these themes, blending them with contemporary ideas about extraterrestrial contact, spiritual ascension, and global transformation.

Characteristics of the Anshar

The Anshar are described as tall, slender beings with a distinctly human-like appearance, though their features are often said to be more refined or ethereal. They are typically depicted as having long, white or blonde hair, pale or glowing skin, and large, expressive eyes. Their physical form is sometimes described as slightly elongated or otherworldly, reflecting their advanced nature and the different environment in which they live.

Key characteristics attributed to the Anshar include:

Advanced Technology: The Anshar are said to possess technology far beyond what is known on the surface of the Earth. This includes advanced transportation systems, such as anti-gravity craft or portal technology, as well as sophisticated methods of communication, healing, and energy generation. Their cities are described as being powered by clean, renewable energy sources and incorporating architectural designs that harmonize with the natural environment.

Spiritual Wisdom: The Anshar are often portrayed as highly spiritual beings who have attained a level of consciousness and enlightenment far beyond that of most humans. They are said to live in harmony with the Earth and the cosmos, following principles of love, peace, and balance. The Anshar's spiritual practices are believed to include meditation, telepathy, and other forms of consciousness expansion.

Longevity and Health: Due to their advanced technology and spiritual practices, the Anshar are believed to have significantly longer lifespans than surface humans. They are said to be immune to many of the diseases and physical ailments that affect humans, and their societies are free from the conflict, poverty, and environmental degradation that plague the surface world.

Non-Interventionist Philosophy: The Anshar are often described as adhering to a philosophy of non-intervention, choosing to remain hidden from surface humanity while observing and subtly influencing events when necessary. However, some accounts suggest that the Anshar are preparing for a time when they will make their presence known more openly, possibly as part of a broader plan to assist humanity during a period of global transformation.

The Anshar and Human Interaction

According to the narratives surrounding the Anshar, these beings have occasionally interacted with surface humans throughout history, particularly with individuals who possess a certain level of spiritual awareness or who have been chosen to serve as intermediaries. These interactions are said to take place in a variety of ways, including:

Telepathic Communication: The Anshar are believed to be capable of telepathic communication, allowing them to convey messages and guidance to certain individuals on the surface. These communications are often described as subtle, appearing as intuitive insights or vivid dreams, and are intended to help guide humans along their spiritual path.

Physical Encounters: Some individuals claim to have had direct physical encounters with the Anshar, either through being taken to their subterranean cities or through meetings in secluded locations on the surface. These encounters are often described as deeply transformative, with the Anshar imparting wisdom, healing, or knowledge to the individuals involved.

Portal Travel: According to some accounts, the Anshar possess the ability to create portals or wormholes that allow them to travel instantaneously between their cities and certain locations on the surface. These portals are said to be used for both observation and interaction, enabling the Anshar to monitor human activities and, when necessary, intervene in critical situations.

Guiding Global Transformation: A central theme in the Anshar narrative is the idea that these beings are preparing to assist humanity during a period of global transformation, often referred to as "The Great Awakening" or "The Shift." In this context, the Anshar are seen as benevolent guides who will help humanity navigate the challenges of this transition, leading to a more harmonious and enlightened future.

The Broader Context of Inner Earth and Hollow Earth Theories

The Anshar narrative fits within a larger tradition of Inner Earth and Hollow Earth theories, which propose that the Earth is either partially or entirely hollow and inhabited by advanced civilizations. These theories have been popularized in various forms, from the mythological realms of Agartha and Shambhala to more modern concepts of hidden alien bases and secret government projects.

The idea of advanced beings living beneath the Earth's surface has captivated the imagination of many, offering a vision of a world where ancient knowledge and advanced technology are preserved, waiting to be revealed to humanity when the time is right. The Anshar, with their blend of spiritual wisdom and technological prowess, represent a modern interpretation of these ancient myths, adapted to fit contemporary concerns about global transformation, extraterrestrial contact, and the evolution of human consciousness.

Skepticism and Criticism

As with many aspects of ufology and esotericism, the Anshar narrative has been met with skepticism and criticism. Mainstream scientists and skeptics argue that there is no credible evidence to support the existence of advanced civilizations living within the Earth, and they view the stories of the Anshar as speculative fiction rather than fact.

Critics also point out that the accounts of the Anshar, like those of other Inner Earth beings, rely heavily on anecdotal evidence and the testimony of a few individuals, making it difficult to verify the claims. Some suggest that the Anshar narrative may be influenced by psychological or cultural factors, including the human tendency to imagine hidden worlds and powerful beings as a way of coping with the challenges of modern life.

Despite these criticisms, the idea of the Anshar continues to resonate with those who are drawn to alternative explanations for the mysteries of existence and the potential for human evolution. For many, the Anshar represent a source of hope and inspiration, embodying the possibility of a future where humanity is guided by wisdom, compassion, and advanced knowledge.

The Anshar, as described in modern esoteric and ufological narratives, represent a fascinating blend of ancient myth and contemporary spiritual thought. Whether viewed as literal beings, symbolic archetypes, or a modern reimagining of Inner Earth legends, the Anshar offer a vision of a world where advanced civilizations live in harmony with the Earth and possess the knowledge to guide humanity through a period of profound transformation.

While the existence of the Anshar and their subterranean cities remains unproven, the narrative surrounding them continues to inspire those who are seeking answers to the deeper questions of life, consciousness, and the future of humanity. In a world often characterized by uncertainty and division, the Anshar provide a hopeful vision of a more enlightened and connected existence, one in which humanity is not alone but is part of a larger cosmic community.

As with many elements of esoteric thought and ufology, the Anshar narrative challenges us to expand our understanding of reality and to consider the possibility that there are realms and beings beyond our current awareness. Whether or not the Anshar are real, the ideas they represent continue to captivate the imagination and encourage exploration of the mysteries that lie beneath the surface of our world and within the depths of our consciousness.

The Ant People: Indigenous Lore Meets Extraterrestrial Theory

The concept of the "Ant People" is a fascinating blend of indigenous lore and modern extraterrestrial theory, merging ancient myths with contemporary ideas about alien contact and influence. The Ant People are beings described in the oral traditions of several Native American tribes, most notably the Hopi of the Southwestern United States. These beings are said to have played a crucial role in the survival of these tribes during times of great hardship, such as cataclysmic events or periods of environmental collapse. In recent years, some researchers and theorists have interpreted the Ant People as potential extraterrestrial beings, suggesting that these ancient stories may be accounts of contact with otherworldly visitors. This chapter explores the origins and significance of the Ant People in indigenous lore, the connection to extraterrestrial theory, and the broader implications of this intersection of ancient and modern narratives.

The Ant People in Indigenous Lore

The Hopi, one of the oldest Native American tribes in the Southwestern United States, have a rich oral tradition that includes stories of the Ant People, or "Anu Sinom" in the Hopi language. According to Hopi legend, the Ant People were benevolent beings who helped the Hopi survive two cataclysmic events, referred to as the destruction of the First and Second Worlds. These events, described as massive natural disasters, forced the Hopi to seek refuge underground.

The Ant People are said to have guided the Hopi to their subterranean dwellings and provided them with food, water, and protection during these times of crisis. The Hopi describe the Ant People as being small, with slender bodies, large heads, and elongated limbs—an appearance that some have noted bears a resemblance to the "Grey" aliens commonly reported in modern UFO encounters.

In Hopi tradition, the Ant People are revered as wise and compassionate beings who played a crucial role in the preservation of their ancestors. The Hopi continue to honor these beings through ceremonies and oral storytelling, passing down the knowledge of their ancestors' survival with the help of the Ant People.

Connection to Extraterrestrial Theory

In recent decades, some researchers and theorists have proposed that the stories of the Ant People may be interpreted as accounts of contact with extraterrestrial beings. This interpretation suggests that the Ant People were not merely mythological figures or symbolic representations, but rather actual visitors from another world who interacted with the Hopi and other indigenous tribes.

Proponents of this theory point to several aspects of the Hopi description of the Ant People that align with modern depictions of extraterrestrials. The physical characteristics of the Ant People—such as their large heads, small bodies, and elongated limbs—are often compared to the stereotypical image of the Greys, a type of alien frequently reported in UFO encounters.

Additionally, the idea of these beings living underground and possessing advanced knowledge and technology resonates with other narratives of extraterrestrial contact, particularly those involving hidden or subterranean alien bases. Some theorists suggest that the Ant People may have been part of a broader program of extraterrestrial assistance or experimentation, in which these beings intervened during times of crisis to guide and protect human populations. This idea fits within the larger context of ancient astronaut theories, which propose that extraterrestrial beings have played a significant role in human history, often posing as gods, angels, or other supernatural entities.

Interpretations and Implications

The interpretation of the Ant People as extraterrestrial beings raises several intriguing questions and possibilities. For one, it challenges the conventional understanding of indigenous myths and legends, suggesting that these stories may contain elements of historical truth, albeit interpreted through a cultural lens that framed these beings as spiritual or supernatural. If the Ant People were indeed extraterrestrials, it implies that contact between humans and otherworldly beings may have occurred long before the modern era, influencing the development of human cultures and societies in profound ways. This interpretation also suggests that ancient indigenous knowledge, often dismissed as mere myth or superstition, could hold valuable insights into the history of human-extraterrestrial interactions. On the other hand, it is important to consider the cultural context in which the stories of the Ant People originated. For the Hopi and other indigenous tribes, these stories are deeply embedded in their spiritual and cultural identity, serving as a way to explain the survival of their ancestors and the continuity of their traditions. The Ant People, in this context, are not just physical beings but also symbolic representations of resilience, cooperation, and the interconnectedness of life. For many indigenous people, the reduction of these spiritual beings to mere extraterrestrial visitors can be seen as a form of cultural appropriation or a misunderstanding of the deeper meanings behind their myths. It is essential to approach these stories with respect for the cultural context in which they were created, recognizing that they may carry multiple layers of meaning—both as literal accounts and as symbolic narratives.

Broader Cultural Impact

The idea of the Ant People as extraterrestrial beings has found its way into popular culture, particularly within the realms of ufology, ancient astronaut theories, and speculative fiction. The blending of indigenous lore with modern extraterrestrial narratives has created a rich tapestry of ideas that continues to capture the imagination of those interested in the mysteries of human history and the possibility of life beyond Earth. This intersection of ancient and modern narratives also highlights the ways in which different cultures and belief systems can interact and influence one another. As people seek to understand their place in the universe, they often draw on both ancient wisdom and contemporary science, creating new stories that resonate with the complexities of the modern world.

The Ant People have thus become a symbol of the enduring mystery of human origins and the possibility that our history may be far more complex and interconnected than previously understood. Whether seen as literal beings, symbolic figures, or a combination of both, the Ant People represent the idea that humanity's past is filled with encounters—both physical and spiritual—that continue to shape our present and future. The Ant People, as described in Hopi and other indigenous traditions, offer a fascinating glimpse into the rich and complex worldviews of ancient cultures. Whether interpreted as mythological beings, symbolic representations, or extraterrestrial visitors, the Ant People hold a significant place in the stories that explain the survival and continuity of these cultures. The modern interpretation of the Ant People as potential extraterrestrial beings reflects a broader trend of re-examining ancient myths and legends through the lens of contemporary ufology and ancient astronaut theories. While this interpretation opens up intriguing possibilities about the history of human-extraterrestrial contact, it also raises important questions about the respect and understanding of indigenous cultures and their sacred traditions. Ultimately, the story of the Ant People serves as a reminder that the mysteries of our past are still unfolding and that the search for answers often leads us to unexpected intersections between the ancient and the modern, the spiritual and the physical. Whether one views the Ant People as myth, history, or something in between, their story continues to inspire curiosity, reflection, and a deeper appreciation for the diverse ways in which humanity has sought to understand its place in the cosmos.

Indrid Cold: The Smiling Man

Indrid Cold, often referred to as "The Smiling Man," is one of the more enigmatic and unsettling figures in the realm of ufology and paranormal lore. His story, which involves eerie encounters with a seemingly otherworldly being who exudes an unnatural, persistent smile, has become a staple of American folklore, particularly in relation to UFO sightings and high strangeness. The tale of Indrid Cold is closely associated with the Mothman phenomenon in Point Pleasant, West Virginia, but it also stands alone as a mysterious case that has intrigued and puzzled researchers for decades. This chapter explores the origins of the Indrid Cold story, the details of the encounters, the theories about his nature and purpose, and the lasting impact of this figure on popular culture and paranormal investigation.

The Origins of Indrid Cold: The Encounter of Woodrow Derenberger

The story of Indrid Cold began on the evening of November 2, 1966, near Parkersburg, West Virginia. Woodrow Derenberger, a local salesman, was driving home after a business trip when he had an encounter that would change his life. As Derenberger later recounted, he was driving along Interstate 77 when a strange, elongated craft suddenly appeared in front of his vehicle, causing him to pull over to the side of the road.

The craft, which Derenberger described as looking like a "kerosene lamp chimney" turned on its side, hovered above the ground before a figure emerged from it. This figure walked toward Derenberger's truck with an unsettlingly broad smile on his face. The being, who introduced himself telepathically as "Indrid Cold," was described as having a human-like appearance, with slicked-back hair, a shiny, metallic-looking suit, and a demeanor that was both friendly and unnerving.

During their brief conversation, Cold communicated telepathically, assuring Derenberger that he meant no harm and was simply a "searcher" who wished to learn more about humans. Cold asked Derenberger a series of benign questions, such as what the nearby town was called and what people did there. After a short exchange, Cold returned to his craft, which then ascended into the sky and disappeared.

Derenberger, deeply shaken by the encounter, reported the incident to local authorities and soon found himself at the center of a media frenzy. His story, along with the appearance of Indrid Cold, became a sensation, attracting the attention of UFO researchers and the curious public alike. Over the years, Derenberger claimed to have had multiple encounters with Cold, during which he learned more about Cold's origins and mission.

Theories about Indrid Cold

The mysterious nature of Indrid Cold has given rise to a variety of theories about who—or what—he might be. Some of the most prominent theories include:

Extraterrestrial Visitor: The most straightforward interpretation of Indrid Cold is that he is an extraterrestrial being, possibly a member of an alien race conducting research on Earth. His strange craft, telepathic communication, and otherworldly appearance all suggest that he might come from another planet or dimension. In this view, Cold's encounters with Derenberger were part of a broader effort to study human behavior and culture.

Interdimensional Being: Another theory posits that Indrid Cold is an interdimensional being, capable of crossing between different planes of existence. This would explain his ability to appear and disappear in unusual ways and his seeming lack of understanding about certain aspects of human life. In this context, Cold could be a traveler from a parallel dimension, where the rules of reality differ from those in our own world.

MIB (Men in Black): Some researchers have speculated that Indrid Cold might be connected to the Men in Black, mysterious figures who reportedly appear after UFO sightings or paranormal events to intimidate witnesses and suppress information. While Cold's demeanor is generally described as friendly, his strange appearance and behavior bear some resemblance to other reports of MIB encounters. If Cold is indeed a member of this shadowy group, his role may be to gather information or manipulate witnesses for unknown purposes.

Psychological Phenomenon: Sceptics argue that Indrid Cold might be a psychological or hallucinatory phenomenon, possibly induced by stress, sleep deprivation, or other factors. In this view, Derenberger's encounter with Cold could have been a product of his own mind, perhaps influenced by the growing public interest in UFOs and paranormal activity during the 1960s. This theory suggests that Cold is not a physical being but rather a manifestation of Derenberger's subconscious fears or desires.

The Mothman Connection

Indrid Cold's story is often linked with the broader Mothman phenomenon, which occurred in Point Pleasant, West Virginia, around the same time as Derenberger's initial encounter. The Mothman is described as a large, winged creature with glowing red eyes, whose sightings were often accompanied by reports of strange lights, UFOs, and other paranormal activity.

Some researchers believe that Indrid Cold may have been connected to the Mothman sightings, either as a fellow entity or as part of a broader pattern of high strangeness that affected the region during that period. The appearance of both Indrid Cold and the Mothman within a short span of time has led to speculation that these beings may share a common origin or purpose.

John Keel, a journalist and paranormal investigator who chronicled the Mothman events in his book *The Mothman Prophecies*, explored the possibility that Indrid Cold was one of many strange entities operating in the area. Keel suggested that Cold, the Mothman, and other phenomena might be part of a larger, more complex web of interdimensional activity, with the Point Pleasant region serving as a focal point for these encounters.

Cultural Impact and Legacy

Indrid Cold, with his eerie smile and mysterious origins, has become an enduring figure in American folklore and paranormal lore. His story has been featured in books, documentaries, and films, often as a symbol of the unknown and the unsettling. The image of the "Smiling Man" has been interpreted in various ways, from a benign visitor to a harbinger of doom, depending on the context and interpretation.

The story of Indrid Cold has also influenced the broader narrative of UFOs and extraterrestrial contact, contributing to the idea that encounters with otherworldly beings are not always straightforward or easily categorized. Cold's ambiguous nature—both friendly and unsettling, familiar yet strange—reflects the complexities and uncertainties inherent in the study of the paranormal.

In popular culture, Indrid Cold has appeared as a character in various fictional works, often portrayed as a mysterious figure with unclear motives. His presence in these stories underscores the ongoing fascination with the idea of otherworldly visitors who defy easy explanation.

Indrid Cold, the Smiling Man, remains one of the most enigmatic figures in the world of ufology and the paranormal. His encounters with Woodrow Derenberger and the broader context of the Mothman phenomenon have left a lasting impact on the study of unexplained phenomena, blending elements of extraterrestrial theory, interdimensional speculation, and psychological mystery.

Whether Indrid Cold is viewed as an alien visitor, an interdimensional traveler, a member of the Men in Black, or a figment of the imagination, his story continues to captivate those interested in the unknown. His persistent smile and strange demeanor serve as a reminder that the universe may hold secrets that are beyond our current understanding, and that the line between reality and the paranormal is often blurred.

As with many aspects of the paranormal, the true nature of Indrid Cold may never be fully understood, but his story endures as a compelling example of the mysteries that lie at the edges of human experience. Whether real or imagined, Indrid Cold invites us to consider the possibility that we are not alone—and that the beings who share our world may be far stranger than we can imagine.

The Chupacabra: Alien Creature or Cryptid?

The Chupacabra, often referred to as "The Goat-Sucker," is one of the most infamous and mysterious creatures in modern cryptozoology. First reported in the 1990s in Puerto Rico, the Chupacabra quickly gained notoriety for its gruesome method of attacking livestock, particularly goats, by draining their blood through small puncture wounds. The creature's elusive nature, strange physical descriptions, and association with blood-sucking attacks have led to widespread speculation about its origins. Some believe the Chupacabra to be a cryptid—a creature whose existence is suggested but not scientifically proven—while others propose it might be an extraterrestrial entity or the result of secret government experiments. This chapter explores the origins of the Chupacabra legend, various theories about its nature, and its impact on popular culture and cryptozoology.

Origins of the Chupacabra Legend

The first widely publicized Chupacabra sightings occurred in Puerto Rico in 1995, following a series of mysterious livestock deaths. Farmers reported finding their animals—mostly goats, sheep, and chickens—dead with puncture wounds on their necks, drained of blood but otherwise untouched. These attacks were unlike those of known predators, which typically leave behind evidence of feeding or struggle. The lack of blood around the carcasses and the precision of the wounds fueled speculation that something unusual was responsible.

The creature itself was first described by a Puerto Rican woman named Madelyne Tolentino, who claimed to have seen a strange, bipedal being near her home in Canóvanas. According to Tolentino, the Chupacabra had a reptilian appearance, with large, glowing red eyes, sharp spines or quills along its back, and a row of spikes from its head down to its tail. It was about the size of a small bear, with leathery or scaly skin, and it moved with an unnatural gait.

Tolentino's description spread quickly, and soon similar reports began to surface from other parts of Puerto Rico and eventually across Latin America and the southern United States. The name "Chupacabra," derived from the Spanish words "chupar" (to suck) and "cabra" (goat), was coined to describe the creature's reported behavior of draining livestock blood.

Theories about the Chupacabra

The mysterious nature of the Chupacabra has given rise to a wide range of theories about its origins and identity. These theories can be broadly categorized into three main groups: cryptid, extraterrestrial, and natural explanations.

The Chupacabra as a Cryptid

Many cryptozoologists believe that the Chupacabra is a cryptid—a previously unknown animal species that has yet to be scientifically documented. This theory posits that the Chupacabra could be a surviving remnant of an ancient or undiscovered species that has evolved to survive in remote regions. Some have suggested that it might be a relative of the mythical vampire bat or a new species of reptilian predator.

The cryptid theory is supported by the consistency of certain physical descriptions, particularly those involving the Chupacabra's spines, bipedal movement, and predatory behavior. Proponents argue that the creature's elusive nature and the difficulty in capturing or observing it directly could explain why it has remained undocumented by science.

The Chupacabra as an Extraterrestrial Being

Another popular theory is that the Chupacabra is not of this Earth but is instead an extraterrestrial entity. This idea is partly based on the strange, otherworldly descriptions of the creature, which some witnesses have likened to classic depictions of alien beings. The Chupacabra's reported ability to drain blood in a manner reminiscent of surgical precision has also led to speculation that it might be part of an alien experiment or a biological weapon sent to Earth for unknown purposes.

Supporters of the extraterrestrial theory point to the timing of the first sightings in the 1990s, a period of heightened interest in UFOs and alien encounters. Some suggest that the Chupacabra could be a creature accidentally or deliberately released on Earth by extraterrestrial visitors, possibly as part of a larger agenda involving genetic experimentation or interspecies interaction.

The Chupacabra as a Misidentified Natural Animal

Skeptics of the cryptid and extraterrestrial theories often propose that the Chupacabra is not a new or alien species at all but rather a misidentified, known animal. In many cases, animals such as coyotes, dogs, or raccoons suffering from severe mange—a skin disease caused by parasitic mites—have been identified as the culprits in supposed Chupacabra sightings. These animals, emaciated and hairless due to mange, can appear drastically different from their healthy counterparts, leading to confusion and fear.

The blood-sucking behavior attributed to the Chupacabra is also explained by natural causes. Predators may target the neck area of livestock, leaving behind puncture wounds that resemble the bite marks attributed to the Chupacabra. In some cases, the absence of blood around the carcasses can be explained by natural processes, such as coagulation or post-mortem drainage.

This natural explanation is supported by scientific investigations, which have often identified the remains of animals thought to be Chupacabras as known species with severe health conditions. However, this theory does not account for the more bizarre and consistent elements of the original Chupacabra descriptions, such as its spiny back and bipedal movement.

The Chupacabra in Popular Culture

The Chupacabra quickly became a cultural phenomenon, particularly in Latin America and the southern United States, where it has been featured in various forms of media, including television shows, movies, and books. The creature's notoriety grew as it became a symbol of the unknown and the unexplained, representing the fear and fascination surrounding the idea of cryptids and otherworldly beings.

In the years since the first sightings, the Chupacabra has appeared in numerous fictional works, often depicted as a monstrous predator or a subject of cryptozoological investigation. The creature has been featured in episodes of popular television shows such as *The X-Files* and *Supernatural*, where it is portrayed as a dangerous and mysterious entity.

The Chupacabra has also been the subject of documentaries and news reports, often focusing on the ongoing debate about its existence and the various theories that attempt to explain the phenomenon. The creature's popularity has even extended to merchandise, with Chupacabra-themed toys, clothing, and other products becoming widely available.

The Impact on Cryptozoology and Public Perception

The Chupacabra legend has had a significant impact on the field of cryptozoology, inspiring both professional and amateur researchers to investigate reports of the creature and to explore the broader questions surrounding the existence of undiscovered species. The creature has become one of the most famous examples of a modern cryptid, alongside others such as Bigfoot and the Loch Ness Monster.

The debate over the Chupacabra also highlights the challenges faced by cryptozoologists in distinguishing between genuine unknown species and misidentified or mythologized animals. The creature's case has become a touchstone for discussions about the reliability of eyewitness testimony, the role of media in shaping public perception, and the ways in which cultural factors influence the interpretation of mysterious phenomena.

For the general public, the Chupacabra represents the enduring allure of the unknown and the possibility that there are still mysteries in the natural world waiting to be discovered. The creature's legend taps into deep-seated fears of predation, blood loss, and the presence of something unnatural lurking in the dark, making it a potent symbol of the unexplained.

The Chupacabra, whether viewed as a cryptid, an alien creature, or a misidentified animal, remains one of the most intriguing and enduring mysteries of modern folklore. Its story encapsulates the tension between scientific skepticism and the human desire to believe in the extraordinary, as well as the ways in which cultural narratives evolve in response to fear and uncertainty.

As with many cryptids, the true nature of the Chupacabra may never be fully resolved. While scientific investigations have provided plausible explanations for many sightings, the creature's original descriptions and the widespread belief in its existence continue to fuel speculation and interest. The Chupacabra's legend serves as a reminder of the power of myth and the enduring appeal of the unknown, inviting us to question what lies beyond the edges of our understanding and to consider the possibility that some mysteries may never be fully explained.

Whether a product of nature, the result of extraterrestrial involvement, or simply a figment of the imagination, the Chupacabra has secured its place in the pantheon of cryptids and continues to captivate the imagination of those who seek to uncover the secrets of the world around us.

The Flat Earth Connection: Fringe Theories and Aliens

The Flat Earth theory, a belief that the Earth is not a globe but a flat disc, has seen a resurgence in recent years, largely due to the influence of social media and online communities. While the idea of a flat Earth might seem archaic and scientifically debunked, it has managed to persist as a fringe theory, often intersecting with other conspiracy theories, including those involving extraterrestrials. The connection between Flat Earth theories and alien conspiracies reveals a broader pattern of distrust in mainstream science and government institutions, as well as a fascination with alternative explanations for the nature of our world. This chapter explores the origins of the Flat Earth theory, its resurgence in modern times, and its intersection with alien-related conspiracies.

The Origins of the Flat Earth Theory

The belief in a flat Earth dates back to ancient civilizations, where early cosmologies often depicted the world as a flat disc or plane. These views were based on observational experiences and mythological interpretations, as there was no advanced understanding of astronomy or the Earth's place in the cosmos.

In Western history, the idea of a spherical Earth began to take hold in the classical period, with Greek philosophers such as Pythagoras and Aristotle providing early evidence for a round Earth based on observations of the stars, the horizon, and lunar eclipses. By the time of the Middle Ages, the spherical Earth model was widely accepted among educated people in Europe and the Islamic world.

However, the notion of a flat Earth persisted in various forms, often tied to religious or cultural beliefs. It wasn't until the Age of Exploration and the scientific advancements of the Renaissance that the round Earth model became firmly established as the consensus view, supported by empirical evidence from circumnavigation and astronomical observations.

The Resurgence of the Flat Earth Theory

The modern Flat Earth movement began to reemerge in the 19th century, largely as a reaction against the increasing dominance of scientific explanations for natural phenomena. Key figures such as Samuel Rowbotham, an English writer and inventor, promoted the idea of a flat Earth through his work "Zetetic Astronomy," which argued that the Earth was a flat plane based on what he claimed were observational experiments.

Despite the overwhelming evidence supporting a spherical Earth, the Flat Earth theory never entirely disappeared, and it experienced a significant revival in the 21st century, fueled by the rise of the internet and social media. Online platforms allowed proponents of the Flat Earth theory to share ideas, create communities, and challenge mainstream scientific views without the constraints of traditional academic or media gatekeepers.

The modern Flat Earth movement often intersects with other conspiracy theories, such as those involving NASA faking space missions, the Illuminati controlling world governments, or the existence of hidden lands beyond the known Earth. This convergence of ideas reflects a broader skepticism toward established knowledge and institutions, with Flat Earth believers frequently questioning the legitimacy of scientific authorities and promoting the idea that the truth is being deliberately hidden from the public.

The Intersection with Alien Conspiracies

One of the more intriguing aspects of the modern Flat Earth movement is its intersection with theories about extraterrestrial life and alien conspiracies. While the connection between Flat Earth and alien theories might seem contradictory—given that the concept of outer space is central to most alien narratives—several strands of thought have emerged that attempt to reconcile or combine these ideas.

The Dome Theory and Extraterrestrial Beings

A significant portion of the Flat Earth community subscribes to the idea that the Earth is enclosed by a dome or firmament, sometimes described as a vast, impenetrable structure that separates the Earth from whatever lies beyond. This dome is often depicted as being made of a transparent, crystalline substance and is said to contain the Sun, Moon, stars, and other celestial bodies, which are all much closer to the Earth than in the traditional spherical model.

Within this framework, some Flat Earth theorists propose that extraterrestrial beings could be either inhabitants of this enclosed system or entities that exist beyond the dome. These beings might be capable of entering and exiting the dome through portals or other means, allowing them to interact with humans or manipulate events on Earth. In this context, UFO sightings and alien encounters are sometimes interpreted as evidence of these beings interacting with the dome or entering the Earth's enclosed system.

The Hidden Lands Theory

Another strand of thought within the Flat Earth community suggests that there are hidden lands or realms beyond the known Earth, possibly existing beyond the Antarctic ice wall, which some Flat Earthers believe marks the edge of the known world. These hidden lands could be home to advanced civilizations, including extraterrestrial beings, who remain hidden from humanity by the powers that control the Earth.

Proponents of this theory argue that the existence of these hidden lands is being kept secret by a global conspiracy involving governments, scientists, and space agencies. They suggest that these extraterrestrial beings may have influenced human history or continue to do so, either as benevolent overseers or as manipulative forces with their own agendas.

Alien Deception and the Flat Earth

A more conspiratorial viewpoint within the Flat Earth community posits that the entire concept of space, extraterrestrial life, and alien contact is part of a grand deception orchestrated by powerful elites to keep humanity ignorant of the true nature of the Earth. According to this theory, the idea of a round Earth and the existence of outer space are fabrications designed to distract people from the reality of the flat Earth and to maintain control over the population.

In this scenario, any evidence of extraterrestrial life—such as UFO sightings, alien abductions, or government disclosures—is seen as part of the deception, aimed at reinforcing the false narrative of a spherical Earth within a vast universe. The ultimate goal of this deception, according to some proponents, is to prevent humanity from discovering the truth about the flat Earth and the potential for other hidden realities.

Criticism and Skepticism

The Flat Earth theory and its associated ideas have been widely criticized by scientists, educators, and skeptics, who argue that the theory is based on outdated or misunderstood information and lacks empirical support. The overwhelming consensus among scientists is that the Earth is a sphere, a conclusion supported by centuries of evidence from astronomy, geology, physics, and space exploration.

Critics of the Flat Earth theory also point out that the movement often relies on cherry-picking data, misinterpreting scientific concepts, and promoting a distrust of experts and institutions. The intersection of Flat Earth ideas with alien conspiracies further complicates the matter, as it involves combining multiple layers of fringe theories, each with its own set of unsupported claims.

Despite these criticisms, the Flat Earth movement continues to attract followers, driven by a combination of skepticism, curiosity, and a desire to challenge established narratives. For some, the theory represents a form of resistance against what they perceive as a corrupt and deceptive system, even if the ideas themselves are scientifically unfounded.

Cultural Impact and Popularity

The resurgence of the Flat Earth theory has had a significant cultural impact, particularly in the age of social media, where fringe ideas can spread rapidly and gain traction among like-minded individuals. The movement has been the subject of numerous documentaries, news reports, and debates, often highlighting the tension between scientific evidence and alternative beliefs.

The connection between Flat Earth and alien theories has also contributed to the broader landscape of conspiracy culture, where various ideas—ranging from UFOs and secret space programs to hidden civilizations and global conspiracies—often intersect and reinforce one another. This convergence of ideas reflects a growing trend toward questioning established knowledge and exploring alternative explanations for the nature of reality.

In popular culture, the Flat Earth theory has been both mocked and examined as a phenomenon that challenges conventional wisdom. It has been featured in films, television shows, and podcasts, often as a symbol of the persistence of fringe beliefs in the face of overwhelming evidence to the contrary.

The Flat Earth theory, despite its scientific implausibility, continues to captivate the imagination of a segment of the population, intersecting with other fringe theories, including those involving extraterrestrial life. This connection between Flat Earth ideas and alien conspiracies highlights the broader pattern of skepticism toward established knowledge and the appeal of alternative explanations for the nature of our world.

While the Flat Earth theory and its associated ideas are widely debunked by science, their persistence serves as a reminder of the complex relationship between belief, evidence, and trust in authority. For those who subscribe to these theories, the Flat Earth represents not just a challenge to scientific consensus but also a broader questioning of the narratives that shape our understanding of reality.

As the Flat Earth movement continues to evolve and intersect with other conspiracy theories, it reflects the ongoing tension between mainstream science and alternative worldviews, as well as the human desire to explore the boundaries of knowledge—no matter how unconventional the path may be. Whether viewed as a symbol of resistance or a cautionary tale about the spread of misinformation, the Flat Earth theory remains a potent and controversial part of the modern landscape of fringe beliefs.

Implants: Alien Technology in the Human Body

The phenomenon of alien implants—tiny, mysterious objects believed to be placed in the human body by extraterrestrial beings—has been a topic of intense interest and debate within the UFO community and among paranormal researchers. These implants are often described as small, metallic or biological devices that are inserted into the body during an alleged alien abduction. Proponents of the alien implant theory suggest that these objects serve various purposes, ranging from monitoring and tracking to influencing human behavior or physiology. This chapter delves into the history and characteristics of reported alien implants, the theories surrounding their purpose, and the challenges faced in verifying their existence.

The History of Alien Implant Reports

Reports of alien implants began to emerge in the late 20th century, coinciding with the increasing number of alien abduction accounts. Many of these reports involved individuals who claimed to have been abducted by extraterrestrial beings and later discovered unusual objects embedded in their bodies. These objects were often detected during medical examinations, X-rays, or MRIs, leading to speculation that they were not of terrestrial origin.

One of the most prominent figures in the study of alien implants is Dr. Roger Leir, a podiatrist who became known for his work in extracting and analyzing these mysterious objects. Dr. Leir claimed to have removed several implants from individuals who believed they had been abducted by aliens. According to Leir, these implants exhibited unusual properties, such as being composed of rare or unknown materials, emitting electromagnetic radiation, or being encapsulated in biological tissue that was resistant to the body's immune response.

Leir's work brought significant attention to the concept of alien implants, and he became a central figure in the UFO and alien abduction communities. His findings were featured in documentaries, books, and television shows, contributing to the broader narrative of extraterrestrial intervention in human affairs.

Characteristics of Alleged Alien Implants

The reported characteristics of alien implants vary widely, but there are several common features described by those who claim to have encountered them:

Size and Shape: Alien implants are typically described as being small, often no larger than a grain of rice. They are usually oval, cylindrical, or spherical in shape, though some reports describe irregular or complex geometries.

Material Composition: Some implants are said to be composed of metallic substances, while others are described as organic or biological in nature. Dr. Leir and other researchers have claimed that the metallic implants they examined contained elements or isotopes not typically found on Earth, though these claims are disputed by mainstream scientists.

Encapsulation: A distinctive feature of many reported implants is that they are often encapsulated in a tough, fibrous membrane that resists removal. This membrane is said to prevent the body from rejecting the implant, allowing it to remain in place without causing inflammation or infection.

Electromagnetic Properties: Some individuals and researchers have reported that alien implants emit electromagnetic radiation or other signals, which are sometimes detected by electronic devices. This has led to speculation that the implants may serve as tracking devices or communication relays.

Movement: In some cases, individuals have reported that the implants moved or changed position within their bodies, either spontaneously or in response to external stimuli. This characteristic has been interpreted as evidence of the implants' advanced technology or autonomous function.

Theories about the Purpose of Alien Implants

Theories about the purpose of alien implants are diverse, reflecting the broader range of beliefs about extraterrestrial intentions and capabilities. Some of the most common theories include:

Monitoring and Tracking: One of the most widely accepted theories within the UFO community is that alien implants are used to monitor and track individuals who have been abducted. The implants may collect data on the individual's physiology, behavior, or environment, which is then transmitted to the extraterrestrials for analysis. This theory suggests that the implants serve as a means of maintaining contact with abductees or keeping track of their whereabouts.

Behavioral Influence: Another theory proposes that alien implants are used to influence the thoughts, emotions, or actions of the individuals who carry them. This could involve the implant emitting signals that affect brain function or releasing substances that alter mood or perception. Proponents of this theory suggest that extraterrestrials might use implants to control or manipulate humans for unknown purposes.

Biological Experimentation: Some researchers believe that alien implants are part of a larger program of biological experimentation. The implants may be used to modify human DNA, monitor the effects of certain conditions or environments, or even prepare the human body for future interactions with extraterrestrial beings. This theory aligns with broader narratives about alien abductions involving genetic manipulation or hybridization.

Communication Devices: A less common but intriguing theory is that alien implants function as communication devices, allowing extraterrestrials to communicate directly with the implanted individual, either through telepathic means or via encoded signals. This could explain why some abductees report receiving messages or experiencing telepathic contact during their encounters.

Surveillance and Control: In more conspiratorial circles, it is suggested that alien implants are part of a larger agenda of surveillance and control, possibly in collaboration with human governments or secret organizations. This theory posits that the implants are used to monitor large segments of the population or to maintain control over key individuals who are of interest to the extraterrestrials or their human collaborators.

Skepticism and Scientific Challenges

The idea of alien implants has been met with significant skepticism from the scientific community, which generally views these claims as lacking credible evidence. Critics argue that the alleged implants could be explained by more mundane phenomena, such as foreign objects accidentally embedded in the body, misidentification of natural biological structures, or psychosomatic conditions.

Several challenges face the verification of alien implants:

Lack of Peer-Reviewed Research: Most of the research on alien implants has been conducted outside of mainstream scientific institutions, with little to no peer-reviewed studies supporting the claims. This lack of rigorous scientific scrutiny makes it difficult to evaluate the validity of the findings.

Possible Terrestrial Origins: Many objects identified as alien implants could have terrestrial origins, such as fragments of metal, glass, or organic material that entered the body through injury or medical procedures. Without definitive evidence showing that these objects are of non-terrestrial origin, the alien implant hypothesis remains speculative.

Psychological Explanations: Some psychologists suggest that the belief in alien implants may be related to psychological conditions, such as delusional disorders, sleep paralysis, or body dysmorphic disorder. In these cases, individuals may perceive normal sensations or foreign objects as evidence of extraterrestrial intervention, even in the absence of physical proof.

Technological Ambiguities: Claims about the advanced technological properties of alien implants, such as their electromagnetic emissions or resistance to removal, have not been conclusively demonstrated in controlled laboratory settings. Skeptics argue that these properties could be misinterpretations or exaggerations of more ordinary phenomena.

Cultural Impact and Popularity

Despite the skepticism, the concept of alien implants has become deeply ingrained in popular culture and the broader UFO narrative. Stories of implants are frequently featured in books, movies, television shows, and documentaries, often presented as evidence of extraterrestrial meddling in human affairs. The idea of alien implants taps into a range of fears and fascinations, including concerns about bodily autonomy, surveillance, and the unknown.

In the realm of fiction, alien implants are often portrayed as sinister devices used by malevolent beings to control or monitor humans. These narratives reflect broader anxieties about technology, government surveillance, and the loss of personal freedom. The persistence of the alien implant theme in popular culture underscores the enduring appeal of these ideas, even in the face of scientific skepticism.

The phenomenon of alien implants remains one of the more enigmatic and controversial aspects of the UFO and alien abduction narrative. While there is little concrete evidence to support the existence of extraterrestrial implants, the reports and theories surrounding them continue to captivate those who believe in the possibility of alien contact and intervention.

For many, the idea of alien implants represents a tangible connection between humans and extraterrestrials, a physical manifestation of the otherwise elusive phenomena associated with UFO encounters. Whether viewed as real objects, psychological symbols, or cultural artifacts, alien implants play a significant role in the ongoing exploration of the unknown.

The debate over alien implants highlights the challenges of studying phenomena that exist at the fringes of scientific inquiry. It raises important questions about the nature of evidence, the limits of human perception, and the ways in which extraordinary claims are investigated and understood. As long as the mystery of alien implants remains unresolved, they will continue to provoke curiosity, debate, and speculation about the true nature of our relationship with the cosmos.

The Starseed Phenomenon: Alien Souls on Earth

The Starseed phenomenon is a captivating and deeply spiritual concept that has gained significant traction within New Age and metaphysical communities. Starseeds are believed to be individuals on Earth who possess alien or extraterrestrial origins, either through their soul's lineage or their spiritual evolution. These beings are thought to have incarnated on Earth from other planets, star systems, or dimensions with the purpose of assisting humanity in its spiritual awakening and the transition to a higher state of consciousness. This chapter delves into the origins of the Starseed phenomenon, the characteristics often attributed to Starseeds, the roles they are believed to play on Earth, and the broader implications of this idea for those who resonate with it.

Origins of the Starseed Phenomenon

The concept of Starseeds has its roots in various spiritual and metaphysical traditions, but it gained prominence in the late 20th century, particularly through the work of authors and channelers within the New Age movement. The idea builds on earlier notions of reincarnation, spiritual evolution, and the belief that souls can originate from places beyond Earth.

One of the earliest and most influential proponents of the Starseed concept was Brad Steiger, an American author and paranormal researcher. In his 1976 book *Gods of Aquarius*, Steiger introduced the idea that certain individuals on Earth possess a cosmic origin, having been "seeded" from other star systems. Steiger's work was instrumental in popularizing the notion that these extraterrestrial souls had a special mission on Earth.

As the New Age movement evolved, the concept of Starseeds became intertwined with other spiritual ideas, such as the belief in ascension, the awakening of human consciousness, and the existence of higher dimensions. Channelers and spiritual teachers began to receive messages from purported extraterrestrial beings, who claimed that many humans were Starseeds with a specific purpose to fulfill during a period of global transformation.

Characteristics of Starseeds

Starseeds are often described as having certain characteristics that set them apart from other people. While not every Starseed exhibits all of these traits, many who identify as Starseeds report experiencing a combination of the following:

A Strong Sense of Purpose: Starseeds often feel a deep inner knowing that they are here on Earth for a specific reason. They may have an intense desire to help others, promote peace, and contribute to the betterment of the world. This sense of purpose can manifest as a calling to work in areas such as healing, teaching, environmentalism, or social justice.

A Feeling of Being Different or Out of Place: Many Starseeds report feeling like they don't quite belong on Earth or that they are different from those around them. This can lead to a sense of isolation or alienation, as well as a longing for a place they cannot remember. This feeling is often interpreted as a sign of their extraterrestrial origins.

Spiritual Awareness and Psychic Abilities: Starseeds are often highly intuitive and spiritually aware, with a natural inclination toward metaphysical practices such as meditation, energy healing, and psychic development. They may have vivid dreams, out-of-body experiences, or memories of past lives in other worlds.

A Deep Connection to the Cosmos: Starseeds frequently feel a strong connection to the stars, planets, and the universe as a whole. They may be drawn to astronomy, astrology, or the exploration of ancient civilizations that were believed to have connections with extraterrestrial beings. This connection is often accompanied by a sense of homesickness or nostalgia for the cosmos.

Empathy and Sensitivity: Starseeds are typically highly empathetic and sensitive to the emotions and energies of others. This can make them compassionate and caring, but also prone to feeling overwhelmed or drained by negative environments. Their empathy often extends to animals, plants, and the Earth itself, leading them to become advocates for environmental and humanitarian causes.

A Desire for Knowledge and Truth: Starseeds are usually seekers of knowledge, truth, and wisdom. They are drawn to spiritual teachings, ancient mysteries, and the exploration of consciousness. This quest for understanding often leads them to question mainstream narratives and to seek out alternative perspectives on reality.

The Role of Starseeds on Earth

Starseeds are believed to have incarnated on Earth with a specific mission: to assist in the spiritual awakening of humanity and to help guide the planet through a period of transformation known as the "Ascension." This transition is often described as a shift from the third dimension (associated with material existence and duality) to the fifth dimension (associated with spiritual enlightenment, unity, and love).

Some of the roles that Starseeds are believed to play include:

Lightworkers: Many Starseeds identify as Lightworkers, individuals who work to bring light and positive energy to the world. This can take the form of healing, teaching, or spreading messages of love, compassion, and spiritual awakening. Lightworkers are seen as catalysts for change, helping to raise the vibration of the planet and support the evolution of consciousness.

Bringers of New Knowledge: Starseeds are often viewed as bringers of new knowledge and wisdom, particularly in areas related to spirituality, science, and technology. They are believed to carry memories or insights from their home star systems that can help humanity develop new ways of living and understanding the universe.

Guides and Mentors: Starseeds are thought to serve as guides and mentors for those who are awakening to their own spiritual potential. They may offer support, guidance, and encouragement to others who are on the path of self-discovery and personal transformation. In this role, Starseeds help to create a network of awakened souls who can work together to bring about positive change.

Bridges between Worlds: Some Starseeds see themselves as bridges between different dimensions, star systems, or realities. They may feel a deep connection to both Earth and their cosmic origins, and they work to integrate these energies within themselves and share them with others. This bridging role is essential for helping humanity navigate the challenges of the Ascension process.

The Broader Implications of the Starseed Phenomenon

The Starseed phenomenon has profound implications for those who resonate with it, offering a sense of identity, purpose, and connection to a larger cosmic community. For many, identifying as a Starseed provides a framework for understanding their spiritual experiences and the feelings of being different or out of place that they may have struggled with throughout their lives.

The idea of Starseeds also reflects broader themes within the New Age movement, including the belief in the interconnectedness of all life, the evolution of consciousness, and the possibility of contact with higher-dimensional beings. It emphasizes the idea that humanity is part of a much larger, cosmic story, one that involves not only Earth but the entire universe.

Critics of the Starseed phenomenon, however, often view it as a form of escapism or a way of coping with feelings of alienation and disconnection. Some psychologists suggest that the Starseed identity may serve as a means of explaining and validating personal experiences that are difficult to reconcile with mainstream beliefs. Others argue that the focus on extraterrestrial origins could distract from more immediate, Earth-centered forms of spiritual and personal growth.

Despite these critiques, the Starseed phenomenon continues to resonate with a growing number of people, particularly those who are drawn to metaphysical and esoteric teachings. It offers a sense of belonging to something greater than oneself and a purpose that extends beyond the mundane concerns of everyday life.

The Starseed phenomenon is a fascinating blend of spiritual, metaphysical, and extraterrestrial ideas that has captured the imagination of many within the New Age and spiritual communities. For those who identify as Starseeds, this concept provides a powerful narrative that explains their sense of purpose, their spiritual experiences, and their connection to the cosmos.

Whether viewed as a literal truth, a symbolic framework, or a psychological coping mechanism, the Starseed phenomenon reflects the human desire to understand our place in the universe and to find meaning in our lives. It speaks to the longing for connection, the quest for knowledge, and the hope for a brighter, more enlightened future.

As humanity continues to explore the mysteries of consciousness and the cosmos, the Starseed phenomenon will likely remain an important part of the spiritual landscape, offering a vision of a world where Earth is not just a solitary planet but a vital part of a vast, interconnected universe filled with diverse and intelligent beings, all working together to create a better reality.

Crop Circles: Messages from Beyond

Crop circles, the intricate patterns that mysteriously appear overnight in fields of crops, have captivated the public imagination for decades. These often elaborate designs, which range from simple geometric shapes to complex pictograms, are typically found in fields of wheat, barley, corn, and other crops. The phenomenon has sparked a wide array of theories, from human-made hoaxes to messages from extraterrestrial beings or interdimensional entities. This chapter explores the history of crop circles, the various interpretations of their meaning, the evidence for and against their extraterrestrial origins, and the cultural impact they have had on the global consciousness.

The History of Crop Circles

The modern crop circle phenomenon began to gain widespread attention in the late 1970s and early 1980s, primarily in the United Kingdom. Early reports typically described simple circular patterns, often found in fields of wheat or barley. These circles were sometimes associated with strange lights or unexplained sounds, leading to speculation about their origins.

However, reports of crop circles—or similar phenomena—can be traced back much further. Historical records from as early as the 17th century include descriptions of mysterious circles appearing in fields. One of the most famous early references is the "Mowing Devil" woodcut from 1678, which depicts a creature cutting circular patterns into a field. While this depiction is often cited in discussions of crop circles, it is more likely an example of folklore rather than evidence of the modern phenomenon.

As crop circles began to appear with greater frequency in the late 20th century, their designs grew increasingly complex. What started as simple circles soon evolved into intricate geometric patterns, some of which spanned hundreds of feet and incorporated sophisticated mathematical concepts such as fractals and the Golden Ratio. These more elaborate formations fueled speculation that they were not the work of human pranksters but rather of advanced, possibly extraterrestrial, intelligence.

Theories about the Origins of Crop Circles

The mystery of crop circles has given rise to a number of theories about their origins. These theories can be broadly categorized into three main groups: human-made, natural phenomena, and extraterrestrial or paranormal.

Human-Made Hoaxes

One of the most widely accepted explanations for crop circles is that they are the work of human pranksters or artists. In 1991, two British men, Doug Bower and Dave Chorley, famously confessed to having created many of the early crop circles in England using simple tools such as planks, ropes, and surveyors' tape. Their admission was accompanied by demonstrations of how they made the circles, leading many to conclude that crop circles were nothing more than elaborate hoaxes.

Since Bower and Chorley's confession, numerous other groups and individuals have claimed responsibility for creating crop circles, often as a form of artistic expression or as part of organized competitions. These crop circle makers, sometimes referred to as "circlemakers," have produced increasingly complex designs, pushing the boundaries of what can be achieved using simple tools and careful planning.

Despite the prevalence of hoaxes, some crop circle enthusiasts argue that not all formations can be easily explained as human-made. They point to the precision and scale of certain patterns, as well as the short timeframes in which they appear, as evidence that something more mysterious may be at work.

Natural Phenomena

Another theory posits that crop circles could be the result of natural phenomena, such as meteorological events or geomagnetic forces. Some researchers have suggested that wind vortices, known as "plasma vortices" or "vortex rings," could create the circular patterns by pressing down the crops in a swirling motion. However, this explanation struggles to account for the more complex and detailed formations that have appeared over the years.

Others have proposed that crop circles might be related to underground water sources or geological fault lines, with changes in the Earth's electromagnetic field influencing the growth patterns of the crops. This theory suggests that crop circles could be a type of natural imprint caused by environmental factors that we do not yet fully understand.

Extraterrestrial or Paranormal Origins

The most intriguing and controversial theory is that crop circles are messages from extraterrestrial beings or other paranormal entities. Proponents of this theory argue that the complexity and symbolism of many crop circle formations suggest an intelligence beyond human capabilities. They view crop circles as a form of communication, possibly intended to convey messages to humanity or to demonstrate the presence of an advanced civilization.

Some who subscribe to the extraterrestrial theory point to instances where crop circles have appeared in conjunction with UFO sightings, strange lights, or other unexplained phenomena. In these cases, witnesses have reported seeing glowing orbs, beams of light, or even unidentified flying objects near the sites of crop circles, leading to speculation that these entities are responsible for creating the patterns.

The idea of crop circles as messages from beyond has been bolstered by the interpretation of certain designs as containing mathematical or astronomical information. For example, some crop circles have been decoded as representing complex mathematical equations, star maps, or even DNA sequences. These interpretations are often presented as evidence that the creators of the crop circles possess advanced knowledge and are trying to share it with humanity.

The Evidence and Controversies

While the extraterrestrial theory has a strong following, it is also met with considerable skepticism. The lack of concrete evidence—such as physical traces of alien technology or clear, unambiguous communication—leads many scientists and researchers to dismiss the idea that crop circles are of non-human origin.

Critics argue that all crop circles can be explained as the work of humans, either as deliberate hoaxes or as part of an evolving art form. They point out that the tools and techniques used by circlemakers are capable of producing highly intricate designs, often under the cover of night and with remarkable precision. The rapid development of crop circle-making as an art form, particularly since the 1990s, has led some to suggest that the phenomenon is primarily a cultural and artistic movement rather than a paranormal one.

In response, crop circle enthusiasts often cite the peculiarities observed in some formations, such as unusual alterations to the crops themselves. These anomalies include bent, rather than broken, stalks; changes in the cellular structure of the plants; and the presence of microscopic spheres or magnetic particles within the soil. Some researchers claim that these features are difficult to replicate through mechanical means and may suggest the involvement of an unknown force.

The debate over crop circles is further complicated by the role of the media, which has often sensationalized the phenomenon and contributed to the spread of misinformation. Documentaries, books, and online content have all played a part in shaping public perception of crop circles, sometimes blurring the line between genuine inquiry and entertainment.

Cultural Impact and Popularity

Regardless of their origins, crop circles have become a significant cultural phenomenon, inspiring a wide range of artistic, spiritual, and philosophical interpretations. The patterns themselves are often regarded as beautiful and mysterious, attracting tourists, researchers, and curious onlookers to the fields where they appear.

Crop circles have also influenced various forms of media, including literature, film, and television. They have been featured in movies such as *Signs* (2002), which depicted crop circles as a precursor to an alien invasion, and in numerous television shows exploring the paranormal and unexplained phenomena. The imagery of crop circles has been used in advertising, music videos, and even fashion, further embedding the concept into popular culture.

In the spiritual community, crop circles are often seen as symbols of higher consciousness, divine intervention, or cosmic harmony. Some believe that meditating within a crop circle can enhance spiritual experiences or facilitate contact with other dimensions. Workshops and conferences dedicated to crop circles are held annually, where enthusiasts and researchers gather to discuss the latest formations and share their interpretations.

The mystery of crop circles continues to intrigue and divide, with no definitive answer as to their origins or meaning. Whether they are the work of skilled artists, the result of natural forces, or messages from extraterrestrial beings, crop circles have undeniably captured the imagination of people around the world. For those who believe in the paranormal or extraterrestrial explanation, crop circles represent a profound and ongoing attempt at communication from beyond our world. They are seen as a call to awaken to a greater reality, to recognize the interconnectedness of all life, and to explore the mysteries of the universe with an open mind.

For sceptics and scientists, crop circles are a fascinating example of human creativity and the power of suggestion. They highlight the ways in which culture, art, and belief intersect, creating phenomena that can be both beautiful and bewildering, even without a supernatural cause. As long as crop circles continue to appear, the debate over their meaning and origin will persist, inviting us to ponder the limits of human knowledge and the possibilities of the unknown. Whether viewed as art, anomaly, or alien message, crop circles remain one of the most enigmatic and visually striking mysteries of our time, encouraging us to look beyond the ordinary and consider the extraordinary.

The Council of Nine: Divine Extraterrestrial Beings

The Council of Nine is one of the more esoteric and intriguing concepts within the realms of New Age spirituality, ufology, and conspiracy theory. Often described as a group of divine extraterrestrial beings or interdimensional entities, the Council of Nine is believed by some to be a guiding force behind human evolution and spiritual development. Proponents of this concept claim that the Council of Nine has been in communication with humanity for thousands of years, offering wisdom, guidance, and insight into the nature of reality and the cosmos. This chapter explores the origins of the Council of Nine, the beliefs and teachings associated with them, their influence on New Age thought, and the controversies surrounding their existence.

Origins of the Council of Nine

The concept of the Council of Nine first gained prominence in the 1950s and 1960s through the work of Dr. Andrija Puharich, a parapsychologist and medical researcher who was deeply involved in the study of the paranormal. Puharich, who had an interest in telepathy, psychic phenomena, and channeling, encountered the idea of the Council of Nine during his research into mediumistic communications.

Puharich's work with an Indian mystic named Dr. D.G. Vinod in the early 1950s led to a series of channeling sessions in which Vinod purportedly communicated with a group of entities who identified themselves as the "Nine Principles." These beings claimed to be ancient and wise extraterrestrial entities who had been involved in guiding humanity for millennia. The communications suggested that the Nine were responsible for overseeing the spiritual and evolutionary progress of humanity, acting as a kind of cosmic council or governing body.

The idea of the Council of Nine was further popularized in the 1970s by Gene Roddenberry, the creator of *Star Trek*, who became involved in channeling sessions with the Nine through the medium Phyllis Schlemmer. These sessions, documented in the book *The Only Planet of Choice* by Schlemmer, portrayed the Council of Nine as benevolent beings who were concerned with the fate of humanity and the Earth. Roddenberry's involvement lent a certain degree of credibility and intrigue to the concept, particularly within the New Age and science fiction communities.

Beliefs and Teachings of the Council of Nine

The teachings associated with the Council of Nine are diverse and often complex, reflecting a blend of spiritual, metaphysical, and extraterrestrial themes. Some of the key beliefs and ideas attributed to the Council of Nine include:

Divine Guidance: The Council of Nine is often described as a group of divine or semi-divine beings who exist in higher dimensions or on other planes of reality. They are believed to have been involved in the creation of the Earth and humanity, acting as guardians or overseers of human evolution. Their primary role is to guide humanity toward greater spiritual awareness, unity, and enlightenment.

The Evolution of Consciousness: One of the central teachings of the Council of Nine is the idea that humanity is on a path of spiritual evolution. This evolution involves the awakening of higher consciousness, the recognition of the interconnectedness of all life, and the development of a more harmonious and peaceful global society. The Nine are said to be assisting humanity in this process, providing guidance and support to those who are open to their messages.

Channeling and Communication: The Council of Nine is believed to communicate with humanity through chosen mediums or channelers. These individuals are said to be receptive to the Nine's messages, which are transmitted telepathically or through other forms of non-physical communication. The messages often emphasize themes of love, unity, and the need for humanity to transcend materialism and ego-driven behavior.

Interdimensional and Extraterrestrial Influence: The Nine are sometimes described as interdimensional beings who have the ability to influence events on Earth from their higher plane of existence. They are also linked to the broader concept of extraterrestrial involvement in human affairs, with some suggesting that the Nine are part of a larger cosmic federation or alliance of advanced civilizations working to guide and protect humanity.

The Role of Free Will: According to the teachings of the Council of Nine, humanity possesses free will and the ability to shape its own destiny. The Nine do not interfere directly in human affairs but instead offer guidance and support to help humanity make choices that align with higher principles and the greater good. The emphasis is on self-responsibility, personal growth, and the collective evolution of consciousness.

Influence on New Age Thought

The concept of the Council of Nine has had a significant impact on New Age thought, particularly in the areas of channeling, spiritual evolution, and extraterrestrial contact. The idea of a benevolent group of higher beings guiding humanity resonates with broader New Age themes, such as the belief in ascended masters, spiritual hierarchies, and the interconnectedness of all life.

The Council of Nine is often cited in discussions about the role of extraterrestrials in human history and spiritual development. Their teachings have been compared to those of other channeled entities, such as the Pleiadians, the Arcturians, and the Ashtar Command, all of whom are believed by some to be involved in assisting humanity during a period of global transformation.

The emphasis on unity, love, and the evolution of consciousness has also made the Council of Nine a popular subject in New Age literature, workshops, and spiritual gatherings. Many people who resonate with the teachings of the Nine see them as a source of inspiration and guidance, offering a vision of a more enlightened and harmonious future.

Controversies and Skepticism

As with many concepts in the realm of the paranormal and New Age spirituality, the idea of the Council of Nine has been met with skepticism and controversy. Critics argue that the concept lacks empirical evidence and is based on the subjective experiences of a small number of individuals. The fact that the Nine's messages are often conveyed through channeling, a practice that is difficult to verify or validate scientifically, has led some to dismiss the concept as a form of pseudoscience or fantasy.

Some sceptics also point out that the teachings of the Council of Nine bear similarities to older spiritual and religious ideas, raising questions about whether the Nine are truly extraterrestrial beings or simply a modern reinterpretation of traditional beliefs. The involvement of figures like Gene Roddenberry, who was known for his creative and imaginative work in science fiction, further complicates the matter, leading some to speculate that the concept of the Nine may have been influenced by fiction rather than fact.

Despite these criticisms, the concept of the Council of Nine continues to have a dedicated following among those who are drawn to its teachings. For believers, the Nine represent a source of wisdom and guidance that transcends the limitations of the material world, offering insights into the deeper mysteries of existence and the potential for human evolution.

The Council of Nine remains one of the more enigmatic and compelling concepts within the intersection of New Age spirituality, ufology, and metaphysical thought. Whether viewed as divine extraterrestrial beings, interdimensional entities, or symbolic representations of higher consciousness, the Nine offer a vision of a world guided by love, unity, and spiritual evolution.

For those who resonate with the teachings of the Council of Nine, these beings represent a source of guidance and support during a time of profound change and transformation. Their messages emphasize the importance of personal growth, the interconnectedness of all life, and the potential for humanity to achieve a higher state of consciousness.

While the existence of the Council of Nine remains a matter of belief rather than empirical proof, their influence on New Age thought and the broader cultural discourse around extraterrestrial contact and spiritual evolution is undeniable. The concept of the Nine invites us to consider the possibility that humanity is part of a much larger cosmic drama, one in which we are not alone but are guided by beings who have a deep understanding of the universe and a genuine concern for our well-being.

As with many aspects of the paranormal and spiritual realms, the true nature of the Council of Nine may never be fully understood, but their teachings continue to inspire and challenge those who seek to explore the mysteries of existence and the potential for a more enlightened future. Whether as a literal council of extraterrestrial beings or as a metaphor for higher wisdom, the Council of Nine remains a powerful symbol of humanity's quest for meaning and connection in a vast and mysterious cosmos.

MJ-12: Secret Government and Alien Affairs

MJ-12, or Majestic 12, is one of the most enduring and controversial topics within the realm of UFO conspiracy theories. Allegedly a secret government group formed in the aftermath of the Roswell incident in 1947, MJ-12 is said to have been tasked with investigating and managing matters related to extraterrestrial technology, alien encounters, and possibly even direct communication with extraterrestrial beings. The existence of MJ-12 is widely debated, with some viewing it as undeniable proof of a government cover-up regarding UFOs, while others see it as an elaborate hoax or disinformation campaign. This chapter explores the origins of the MJ-12 story, the documents and claims associated with it, the theories about its purpose and activities, and the broader implications for our understanding of government secrecy and extraterrestrial contact.

The Origins of MJ-12

The story of MJ-12 first surfaced in 1984, when a roll of film containing images of documents labeled "TOP SECRET/MAJIC" was received by a UFO researcher named Jaime Shandera. These documents, known as the "Majestic 12 documents," purportedly detailed the formation of a secret group called Majestic 12, or MJ-12, by President Harry S. Truman in 1947. The group's primary mission was said to be the investigation and management of all aspects related to UFOs and extraterrestrial technology, particularly following the alleged crash of an alien spacecraft near Roswell, New Mexico, in July 1947.

The documents listed twelve members of the MJ-12 group, including prominent military and scientific figures of the time, such as Admiral Roscoe H. Hillenkoetter, the first director of the CIA; Dr. Vannevar Bush, a key scientific advisor during World War II; and General Nathan Twining, who later became Chairman of the Joint Chiefs of Staff. The documents suggested that these individuals were entrusted with the highest level of secrecy and were responsible for overseeing the recovery and reverse-engineering of alien technology, as well as managing the public narrative regarding UFOs.

The release of the MJ-12 documents sparked immediate controversy and debate within the UFO community and beyond. While some researchers hailed the documents as explosive evidence of a government cover-up, others questioned their authenticity, pointing out inconsistencies and possible signs of forgery.

The MJ-12 Documents: Authenticity and Controversy

The MJ-12 documents have been the subject of intense scrutiny since their release. Supporters of the MJ-12 theory argue that the documents are genuine and provide a rare glimpse into the inner workings of a top-secret government group dealing with extraterrestrial matters. They point to the detailed nature of the documents and the involvement of high-ranking officials as evidence that MJ-12 was a real entity.

However, many sceptics and researchers have raised serious doubts about the authenticity of the documents. Critics argue that the documents contain numerous anachronisms, inconsistencies, and errors that suggest they are not genuine. For example, the use of certain typefaces, language, and document formats in the MJ-12 papers has been cited as being inconsistent with government documents from the 1940s and 1950s. Additionally, some of the historical facts presented in the documents have been called into question, leading some to believe that the documents were created as part of a hoax or disinformation campaign.

The U.S. government has officially denied the existence of MJ-12, with agencies such as the FBI concluding that the documents are likely fraudulent. Despite these denials, the debate over the authenticity of the MJ-12 documents continues, with some researchers continuing to investigate the possibility that the group existed and played a significant role in managing UFO-related activities.

Theories about MJ-12's Purpose and Activities

Assuming that MJ-12 or a similar group did exist, theories about its purpose and activities vary widely. Some of the most common theories include:

Management of Alien Technology: One of the primary tasks attributed to MJ-12 is the recovery and reverse-engineering of alien technology. This theory suggests that the group was responsible for retrieving crashed UFOs, such as the one allegedly found near Roswell, and attempting to understand and replicate the advanced technology found within these craft. Proponents of this theory argue that breakthroughs in modern technology, particularly in the fields of aerospace, electronics, and materials science, may have been influenced by the study of alien artifacts.

Control of Extraterrestrial Contact: Another theory is that MJ-12 was tasked with managing and controlling contact between humans and extraterrestrial beings. This could involve everything from direct communication with alien species to the negotiation of treaties or agreements. Some believe that MJ-12 was involved in establishing secret bases where humans and aliens could interact, such as the alleged underground facility at Dulce, New Mexico.

Public Perception and Disinformation: MJ-12 is also believed to have played a role in shaping public perception of UFOs and extraterrestrial encounters. This could involve the deliberate dissemination of disinformation to obscure the truth about alien contact, as well as the suppression of credible UFO sightings and encounters. The group may have been responsible for influencing the media, government agencies, and even the scientific community to dismiss or ridicule reports of UFOs, thereby maintaining secrecy around the true nature of extraterrestrial activities.

Monitoring and Security: Some theories suggest that MJ-12 was involved in monitoring and securing sensitive information related to UFOs and alien encounters. This could include the surveillance of UFO researchers, witnesses, and whistle-blowers, as well as the enforcement of strict security measures to prevent leaks or unauthorized disclosures. The group's role may have extended to coordinating with other government agencies, such as the CIA or NSA, to protect national security interests related to extraterrestrial matters.

MJ-12 in Popular Culture and Conspiracy Theory

The concept of MJ-12 has had a profound impact on popular culture and the development of UFO conspiracy theories. The idea of a secret government group managing extraterrestrial affairs has been featured in numerous books, documentaries, and fictional works, often serving as a central plot device in stories about government cover-ups and alien encounters.

In the 1990s, MJ-12 became a key element in the mythology of *The X-Files*, a popular television series that explored themes of government secrecy, paranormal phenomena, and extraterrestrial life. The show depicted MJ-12 as a shadowy organization involved in a vast conspiracy to hide the truth about alien contact from the public, reflecting the broader cultural fascination with the idea of a secret government cabal controlling information about UFOs.

MJ-12 has also been referenced in various other media, including films, video games, and novels, further cementing its place in the lexicon of conspiracy theory and popular culture. The group's alleged activities have been the subject of countless debates, discussions, and investigations within the UFO community, with some researchers dedicating their careers to uncovering the truth about MJ-12.

Skepticism and Criticism

Despite its enduring popularity, the MJ-12 narrative has faced significant criticism from skeptics, historians, and government officials. Many argue that the entire concept of MJ-12 is based on a combination of forged documents, misinterpretations, and speculative theories rather than hard evidence.

One of the main criticisms is the lack of corroborating documentation or testimony from credible sources. While the MJ-12 documents provide a tantalizing glimpse into the possibility of a secret government group, there has been little to no concrete evidence to support the existence of such an organization. Additionally, many of the individuals named in the documents, including the supposed members of MJ-12, have not been linked to any activities that would suggest involvement in a secret extraterrestrial task force.

Furthermore, the MJ-12 narrative is often seen as a product of the Cold War era, when fears of government secrecy, nuclear threats, and technological competition were at their peak. The idea of a powerful, hidden group controlling information about extraterrestrial life may reflect broader societal anxieties about power, control, and the unknown rather than a genuine historical reality.

MJ-12 remains one of the most enigmatic and controversial topics in the world of UFO conspiracy theories. Whether viewed as a genuine secret government group or as an elaborate hoax, the story of MJ-12 has captivated the imaginations of countless individuals, fueling speculation about the true extent of government involvement in extraterrestrial affairs.

For those who believe in the existence of MJ-12, the group represents the ultimate proof of a government cover-up regarding UFOs and alien contact. The idea that a select group of individuals could hold the keys to humanity's most profound mysteries—our place in the universe and our relationship with other intelligent beings—is both thrilling and unsettling.

For sceptics, MJ-12 serves as a cautionary tale about the dangers of accepting unverified information and the power of conspiracy theories to shape public perception. The persistence of the MJ-12 narrative, despite the lack of concrete evidence, highlights the allure of secret knowledge and the human tendency to seek explanations for the unknown, even when those explanations may be based more on imagination than reality.

As long as questions about UFOs, government secrecy, and the possibility of extraterrestrial life remain unanswered, the legend of MJ-12 will continue to intrigue, inspire, and provoke debate. Whether real or fictional, MJ-12 has become a symbol of the enduring mystery that surrounds the UFO phenomenon and the search for truth in a world where much remains hidden from view.

The Dulce Base: Underground War with Aliens

The Dulce Base, often described as a secret underground facility located beneath Archuleta Mesa in Dulce, New Mexico, is one of the most infamous and controversial topics in UFO conspiracy theory. Allegedly, this base is not only a top-secret government installation but also the site of an ongoing, covert war between humans and extraterrestrials. The story of the Dulce Base combines elements of government secrecy, advanced technology, genetic experimentation, and interspecies conflict, making it a focal point for those who believe in deep, hidden alliances between humans and aliens. This chapter explores the origins of the Dulce Base legend, the various claims about what takes place there, the evidence supporting or refuting its existence, and the broader implications for our understanding of extraterrestrial involvement in human affairs.

Origins of the Dulce Base Legend

The legend of the Dulce Base began to take shape in the late 1970s and early 1980s, with reports and rumours circulating within the UFO community about a secret underground facility in New Mexico. The story gained significant traction thanks to the claims of Paul Bennewitz, an Albuquerque businessman and physicist who became convinced that he was receiving signals from extraterrestrial craft operating near Kirtland Air Force Base.

Bennewitz's suspicions led him to believe that there was a hidden base in the Dulce area where the U.S. government was conducting experiments involving extraterrestrial technology and even collaborating with alien beings. He began to publicize his findings, warning of an alien presence and a secret underground war being waged beneath the surface of the Earth.

Bennewitz's claims were later expanded upon by other figures in the UFO and conspiracy theory communities, including Bill Cooper, John Lear, and Phil Schneider. Schneider, in particular, became a central figure in the Dulce Base narrative after he publicly claimed to have been involved in the construction of several underground bases, including Dulce. He described horrific battles between humans and aliens in the deep underground tunnels, resulting in the deaths of numerous military personnel.

Claims and Theories About the Dulce Base

The Dulce Base is often described as a massive, multi-level facility extending several miles underground. According to various accounts, the base is home to a variety of advanced technologies, including anti-gravity devices, energy weapons, and genetic laboratories. It is also said to be the site of ongoing experimentation involving both human and extraterrestrial subjects.

Some of the most common claims and theories about the Dulce Base include:

Human-Alien Collaboration: One of the most pervasive theories is that the Dulce Base is a joint operation between the U.S. government and various extraterrestrial species, particularly the Greys and Reptilians. Proponents of this theory believe that these aliens have provided advanced technology to the government in exchange for access to human subjects for experimentation. This alleged collaboration is said to involve everything from genetic manipulation to mind control techniques.

Genetic Experimentation: Many of the stories surrounding Dulce involve gruesome and unethical genetic experiments being conducted on both humans and extraterrestrials. Some accounts describe hybrid beings—part human, part alien—being created in the base's laboratories. Others speak of horrific genetic mutations, with the goal of creating a new, more advanced species or even developing biological weapons.

Underground War: Perhaps the most dramatic aspect of the Dulce Base legend is the claim that a secret war is being fought beneath the Earth's surface between humans and extraterrestrials.

According to these accounts, tensions between the government and the alien beings escalated into open conflict, resulting in bloody battles within the base's tunnels. Phil Schneider's accounts of his experiences in these battles, where he claimed to have personally killed alien beings and been gravely injured, have been a significant part of this narrative.

Advanced Technology: The Dulce Base is also said to house some of the most advanced technology known to humankind, much of it derived from extraterrestrial sources. This includes propulsion systems for spacecraft, advanced weaponry, and even time manipulation devices. The base is purportedly a testing ground for technology far beyond what is publicly acknowledged, with implications for both military and civilian applications.

Mind Control and Psychological Experimentation: Another element of the Dulce Base legend involves the use of advanced mind control techniques on both human and alien subjects. These experiments are said to explore the limits of human consciousness, memory manipulation, and the development of psychological warfare tactics. Some believe that individuals who have been subjected to these experiments have been brainwashed or had their memories altered to prevent them from revealing what they know.

Evidence and Skepticism

As with many conspiracy theories, the story of the Dulce Base is supported primarily by anecdotal evidence, testimony from a few key individuals, and the interpretation of circumstantial evidence. The lack of concrete, verifiable proof has led many to dismiss the Dulce Base narrative as a hoax, a case of mistaken identity, or a disinformation campaign.

Critics of the Dulce Base story point out several key issues:

Lack of Physical Evidence: Despite the dramatic claims of battles and advanced technology, there is no physical evidence to support the existence of the Dulce Base or the events that supposedly occurred there. No photographs, documents, or credible scientific studies have been produced that confirm the base's existence.

Inconsistent Testimony: The accounts of individuals like Phil Schneider and Paul Bennewitz have been criticized for their inconsistencies and lack of corroboration. Schneider's claims, in particular, have been questioned due to the lack of supporting evidence and the sensational nature of his stories. Bennewitz's experiences have been interpreted by some as the result of psychological issues or even deliberate misinformation fed to him by government agencies.

Disinformation and Hoaxes: Some researchers believe that the Dulce Base story may have been a deliberate disinformation campaign designed to distract or confuse the UFO community. The idea of secret underground bases and alien wars is an attractive and sensational narrative, but it may have been used to cover up more mundane but sensitive government activities, such as military testing or classified projects.

Geological Improbabilities: Geologists and engineers have pointed out the practical difficulties and enormous costs associated with constructing a massive underground facility like the one described in the Dulce Base narrative. The logistics of digging and maintaining such a base in the remote and geologically complex region of Archuleta Mesa would be extremely challenging, if not impossible, without leaving some trace or evidence.

Cultural Impact and Popularity

Despite the skepticism, the story of the Dulce Base has had a significant impact on popular culture and the UFO conspiracy community. It has been featured in numerous books, documentaries, and online forums, where it continues to captivate the imaginations of those interested in government secrecy, extraterrestrial life, and the potential for hidden truths beneath the surface of our world.

The Dulce Base has become a touchstone for discussions about the extent of government knowledge and involvement in UFO phenomena. It represents the darker side of the UFO narrative, where advanced technology and secret knowledge are intertwined with themes of manipulation, conflict, and the exploitation of both humans and extraterrestrials.

The idea of an underground base housing advanced technology and engaged in secret wars with aliens has also inspired various works of fiction, from novels and films to video games. The narrative's blend of science fiction and horror elements appeals to those fascinated by the possibility that our world is far stranger and more complex than we might imagine.

The Dulce Base story is a potent mix of conspiracy theory, urban legend, and modern myth. Whether viewed as a genuine secret installation, a disinformation campaign, or a collective fantasy, the Dulce Base narrative continues to intrigue and provoke discussion within the UFO community and beyond.

For believers, Dulce represents the ultimate example of government secrecy and the hidden depths of human-alien interaction. The idea that advanced technology, genetic experimentation, and interspecies conflict are being conducted beneath our feet is both thrilling and terrifying, offering a dramatic alternative to the more benign narratives of extraterrestrial contact.

For sceptics, the Dulce Base story serves as a cautionary tale about the power of rumor, the dangers of misinformation, and the complexities of interpreting anecdotal evidence. The persistence of the Dulce legend, despite the lack of concrete proof, highlights the challenges of separating fact from fiction in the world of conspiracy theories and paranormal claims.

As long as questions about extraterrestrial life, government secrecy, and the possibility of hidden bases remain unanswered, the legend of the Dulce Base will continue to inspire curiosity, debate, and speculation. Whether real or imagined, Dulce stands as a symbol of the enduring mystery and fascination that surrounds the UFO phenomenon and the search for truth in a world filled with shadows and secrets.

The Montauk Project: Time Travel and Aliens

The Montauk Project is one of the most intricate and widely discussed conspiracy theories, blending elements of time travel, mind control, and extraterrestrial involvement into a narrative that has captivated the imaginations of conspiracy theorists, paranormal enthusiasts, and pop culture creators alike. Allegedly taking place at Camp Hero, a decommissioned military base in Montauk, New York, the Montauk Project is said to have been a series of secret government experiments conducted during the late 20th century. These experiments purportedly explored advanced technologies, including time travel, teleportation, and contact with extraterrestrial beings. This chapter delves into the origins of the Montauk Project story, the key claims associated with it, the evidence and skepticism surrounding the theory, and its impact on popular culture.

Origins of the Montauk Project

The Montauk Project narrative first gained widespread attention in the 1980s and 1990s, largely through the work of Preston Nichols and Peter Moon, who co-authored a series of books detailing the alleged events at Camp Hero. The most notable of these books, *The Montauk Project: Experiments in Time* (1992), lays out the basic premise of the conspiracy, claiming that the U.S. government conducted a series of highly classified experiments at the Montauk Air Force Station, with the aim of exploring the limits of human consciousness, time travel, and contact with extraterrestrial life.

According to Nichols and Moon, the Montauk Project was an extension or continuation of the infamous Philadelphia Experiment, a supposed World War II-era experiment in which the U.S. Navy attempted to render the USS Eldridge, a naval destroyer escort, invisible. The Philadelphia Experiment, as the story goes, inadvertently opened a rift in space-time, leading to disastrous consequences for the crew and setting the stage for further research into time travel and other advanced technologies.

The Montauk Project is said to have been initiated in response to the findings of the Philadelphia Experiment, with the goal of mastering time travel, teleportation, and mind control. The project allegedly involved a wide range of experiments, many of which were conducted on unwitting subjects, including children and military personnel. These experiments supposedly took place in secret underground facilities beneath Camp Hero, with the iconic radar tower at the base serving as a key component of the technology used in the project.

Key Claims of the Montauk Project

The Montauk Project encompasses a wide array of claims, many of which are highly speculative and often fantastical in nature. Some of the most significant and recurring elements of the Montauk Project narrative include:

Time Travel and the Montauk Chair: One of the most central claims of the Montauk Project is the development and use of time travel technology. According to Nichols and other proponents, the project utilized a device known as the "Montauk Chair," which was allegedly capable of amplifying psychic abilities and manipulating time. The chair was said to be connected to a sophisticated array of computers and the base's radar equipment, allowing operators to open portals to different times and places. Subjects seated in the chair could reportedly project their consciousness through time, enabling them to experience past and future events or even alter the course of history.

Mind Control and Psychic Warfare: The Montauk Project is also heavily associated with experiments in mind control and psychic warfare. It is claimed that the project sought to develop techniques for controlling the minds of individuals and entire populations, using a combination of electromagnetic fields, drugs, and psychological manipulation. The Montauk Chair was allegedly used to enhance the psychic abilities of certain subjects, enabling them to influence the thoughts and behaviors of others or even create physical manifestations through sheer willpower.

Extraterrestrial Involvement: Another key aspect of the Montauk Project narrative is the involvement of extraterrestrial beings. Various accounts suggest that the project established contact with alien civilizations, who provided advanced technology and knowledge in exchange for certain concessions or agreements. Some versions of the story claim that alien entities were directly involved in the experiments at Montauk, either as collaborators or as subjects themselves. These interactions are said to have had profound implications for human technology and the future of humanity.

The Montauk Monster and Genetic Experimentation: The Montauk Project is sometimes linked to reports of genetic experimentation and the creation of hybrid creatures. The most famous of these is the so-called "Montauk Monster," a mysterious creature that washed ashore near Montauk in 2008, sparking speculation that it was the result of secret experiments conducted at Camp Hero. While the creature was later identified as a decomposed raccoon, the story fueled existing rumors about the project's involvement in genetic manipulation and the creation of bizarre life forms.

The Philadelphia Experiment Connection: As mentioned earlier, the Montauk Project is often described as a continuation of the Philadelphia Experiment. Proponents claim that the time travel and teleportation research conducted at Montauk was a direct outgrowth of the discoveries made during the Philadelphia Experiment, with some even suggesting that a time portal opened during the experiment led to the Montauk base being used as a hub for interdimensional travel.

The Montauk Boys: Another disturbing aspect of the Montauk Project narrative is the alleged abduction and experimentation on young boys, known as the "Montauk Boys." According to this theory, these boys were subjected to brutal mind control experiments designed to create "Manchurian Candidate" style super soldiers—individuals who could be programmed to carry out missions without their conscious knowledge. The Montauk Boys were supposedly taken from orphanages, foster homes, or off the streets, and many of them were said to have never returned.

Evidence and Skepticism

The claims surrounding the Montauk Project are widely regarded as speculative and lack solid evidence. Critics and sceptics point out several key issues that cast doubt on the veracity of the story:

Lack of Verifiable Evidence: Despite the detailed and dramatic nature of the claims, there is little to no verifiable evidence to support the existence of the Montauk Project or the experiments it allegedly conducted. No official documents, photographs, or credible eyewitness testimony have emerged that confirm the existence of such a program. The primary sources for the Montauk narrative are the books written by Nichols and Moon, as well as the testimony of a few individuals with questionable credibility.

Questionable Sources: The primary proponents of the Montauk Project, including Preston Nichols, have been criticized for their lack of credentials and for promoting theories that are difficult to substantiate. Critics argue that the story may have been fabricated or exaggerated for the purpose of selling books and generating interest in their ideas.

Confusion with Science Fiction: Some elements of the Montauk Project narrative closely resemble plots from science fiction literature and films. For example, the concept of time travel and mind control through advanced technology is a common trope in science fiction. This has led some to speculate that the Montauk Project story may have been influenced by or even directly copied from fictional sources.

Psychological Explanations: Some sceptics suggest that the Montauk Project narrative may be the result of psychological phenomena, such as false memories, confabulation, or delusions. Given the highly unusual and often contradictory nature of the claims, it is possible that some individuals who believe they were involved in the project are misinterpreting their experiences or are influenced by suggestion and group dynamics.

Impact on Popular Culture

Despite the skepticism, the Montauk Project has had a significant impact on popular culture, inspiring numerous works of fiction, documentaries, and discussions in conspiracy theory circles. The story has been referenced in television shows, books, and films, often as a cautionary tale about the dangers of unchecked government experimentation and the potential for science to cross ethical boundaries.

One of the most notable examples of the Montauk Project's influence is the popular Netflix series *Stranger Things*. The show, originally titled *Montauk*, features a plot involving government experiments, psychic abilities, and interdimensional travel—elements that closely parallel the Montauk Project narrative. While the creators of *Stranger Things* have stated that the show was inspired by various conspiracy theories and urban legends, the connections to the Montauk Project are clear and have been widely discussed by fans and researchers alike.

The Montauk Project has also inspired a number of books, both fictional and non-fictional, that explore similar themes of government secrecy, time travel, and extraterrestrial contact. The enduring popularity of these ideas reflects a broader cultural fascination with the possibility that there are hidden truths and technologies that remain beyond our current understanding.

The Montauk Project remains one of the most elaborate and controversial conspiracy theories in the realms of UFOlogy, paranormal investigation, and government secrecy. Whether viewed as a genuine secret program, a hoax, or a modern myth, the story continues to captivate the imagination of those who are drawn to the idea of hidden knowledge and the potential for advanced technology to unlock the mysteries of time and space. For believers, the Montauk Project represents a tantalizing glimpse into a world of secret experiments, time travel, and extraterrestrial contact, offering a dramatic narrative that challenges our conventional understanding of reality. The story serves as a warning about the potential dangers of unchecked scientific experimentation and the ethical dilemmas that arise when humans seek to manipulate the very fabric of existence.

For sceptics, the Montauk Project is a cautionary tale about the power of conspiracy theories to capture the public imagination and the challenges of separating fact from fiction in the world of paranormal and government secrecy. The lack of concrete evidence and the fantastical nature of the claims make it difficult to take the Montauk Project seriously as a historical reality, but its impact on culture and thought is undeniable. As with many conspiracy theories, the Montauk Project reflects deeper cultural anxieties about power, control, and the unknown. It challenges us to consider the limits of human knowledge and the ethical implications of scientific exploration, while also reminding us of the enduring appeal of mystery and the possibility that there is more to reality than meets the eye

Secret Space Programs: Beyond the Public Eye

The concept of Secret Space Programs (SSPs) refers to the belief that governments, particularly the United States, and powerful private organizations have been operating advanced space exploration and defense initiatives far beyond what is publicly acknowledged. These programs are said to involve highly advanced technology, including faster-than-light spacecraft, bases on the Moon and Mars, and even contact and collaboration with extraterrestrial civilizations. Proponents of SSP theories argue that humanity's capabilities in space are far more advanced than what has been disclosed to the public, and that a hidden elite is using this technology for purposes that remain largely unknown. This chapter explores the origins of SSP theories, the key claims made by advocates, the evidence and skepticism surrounding these ideas, and the broader implications for our understanding of space exploration and government secrecy.

Origins of Secret Space Program Theories

The idea of Secret Space Programs has roots in the broader context of UFOlogy, conspiracy theories, and Cold War-era speculation about advanced military technology. The notion that governments might be hiding the true extent of their technological capabilities, particularly in the realm of space exploration, has been a recurring theme in conspiracy circles for decades.

One of the earliest influences on SSP theories was the space race between the United States and the Soviet Union during the 1950s and 1960s. As both superpowers competed for dominance in space, there were widespread rumours and fears that one side might develop technology that could be used for military purposes or that could surpass what was publicly known. These fears were exacerbated by the secrecy surrounding many aspects of space exploration and military research during this period.

The emergence of the UFO phenomenon in the mid-20th century also played a significant role in shaping SSP theories. As reports of unidentified flying objects and alleged alien encounters became more widespread, some researchers and conspiracy theorists began to speculate that these phenomena were linked to secret government projects, possibly involving reverse-engineered extraterrestrial technology. The idea that governments might be hiding advanced spacecraft and alien technologies became a central theme in many UFO-related conspiracy theories.

In the late 20th and early 21st centuries, the concept of SSPs gained further traction through the testimonies of alleged whistle-blowers and insiders, who claimed to have firsthand knowledge of these programs. These individuals, often operating under pseudonyms or with their identities obscured, provided detailed accounts of secret missions, advanced spacecraft, and covert operations in space. Their stories, though often difficult to verify, resonated with those who were already skeptical of official narratives about space exploration.

Key Claims of Secret Space Programs

The claims associated with Secret Space Programs are varied and often elaborate, encompassing a wide range of technologies, missions, and objectives. Some of the most common elements of SSP theories include:

Advanced Spacecraft: One of the central claims of SSP theories is that governments and private organizations possess spacecraft far more advanced than anything publicly acknowledged. These spacecraft are said to be capable of faster-than-light travel, anti-gravity propulsion, and stealth capabilities, allowing them to operate covertly in space.

Proponents of SSP theories often point to sightings of mysterious craft or anomalous objects in space as evidence of these secret technologies.

Bases on the Moon, Mars, and Beyond: Another common claim is that secret bases have been established on the Moon, Mars, and other celestial bodies. These bases are purportedly used for a variety of purposes, including military operations, scientific research, and diplomatic relations with extraterrestrial beings. Some SSP theorists believe that these bases are part of a broader effort to colonize space and establish a breakaway civilization that operates independently of Earth's governments.

Collaboration with Extraterrestrials: A significant aspect of many SSP theories is the belief that governments have established contact with extraterrestrial civilizations and are working with them in secret. This collaboration is said to involve the exchange of technology, knowledge, and even genetic material, with the goal of advancing humanity's capabilities or pursuing mutual interests in space. Some SSP proponents argue that these alliances are kept hidden from the public to prevent panic or disruption to the existing world order.

Space Warfare and Defense: SSP theories often include the idea that space is a contested domain, with various factions, both human and extraterrestrial, vying for control. Secret space programs are said to be engaged in covert warfare, defending Earth from hostile alien forces or rival human groups. This narrative suggests that the true nature of space exploration is far more militarized than the peaceful exploration often portrayed in public space programs like NASA.

Breakaway Civilizations: Some SSP theorists propose that a "breakaway civilization" has emerged, consisting of a highly advanced elite with access to secret space technologies and extraterrestrial knowledge. This group is believed to operate independently of the rest of humanity, pursuing its own goals in space and possibly planning for a future where they will no longer be dependent on Earth. The idea of a breakaway civilization adds a layer of intrigue and fear to SSP theories, suggesting that humanity's future is being shaped by a hidden power.

Time Travel and Temporal Manipulation: In some versions of SSP theories, secret programs are said to have developed time travel technology or the ability to manipulate timelines. This idea often intersects with other conspiracy theories about government experiments and black projects, such as the Montauk Project. Proponents of this theory argue that time travel could be used to alter history, prevent disasters, or gain strategic advantages in space.

Evidence and Scepticism

The claims surrounding Secret Space Programs are highly controversial and often lack concrete evidence. Critics and sceptics of SSP theories point to several key issues that challenge the plausibility of these ideas:

Lack of Verifiable Evidence: One of the most significant criticisms of SSP theories is the lack of verifiable evidence to support the existence of such programs. While there are numerous testimonies, anecdotes, and speculative interpretations of various events, there is little to no hard evidence—such as official documents, photographs, or physical artifacts—that definitively prove the existence of SSPs. The secrecy surrounding military and space programs does make it difficult to access information, but sceptics argue that extraordinary claims require extraordinary evidence, which is currently lacking.

Questionable Whistle-blower Testimonies: Much of the SSP narrative is based on the testimonies of alleged whistle-blowers or insiders, who claim to have firsthand knowledge of these programs. However, these individuals often operate under pseudonyms, have limited or unverifiable credentials, or present stories that are difficult to substantiate. Critics argue that these testimonies should be treated with caution, as they may be influenced by psychological factors, personal motivations, or even deliberate disinformation.

Technological and Logistical Challenges: The advanced technologies described in SSP theories, such as faster-than-light travel, anti-gravity propulsion, and time travel, present significant scientific and logistical challenges. While there is ongoing research into these areas, mainstream science considers them to be speculative or theoretical at best. The development and deployment of such technologies would likely require immense resources and breakthroughs that are currently beyond known human capabilities.

Confusion with Science Fiction: Some elements of SSP theories closely resemble plots from science fiction literature and films. The idea of secret bases on the Moon or Mars, advanced spacecraft, and collaboration with extraterrestrials are common tropes in science fiction. This overlap has led some sceptics to suggest that SSP theories may be influenced by or derived from fictional sources rather than actual events.

Secrecy vs. Leaks: While the idea of a highly secretive space program is central to SSP theories, sceptics point out that it would be extremely difficult to maintain such a large-scale conspiracy over decades without significant leaks or whistle-blowers coming forward with credible, verifiable evidence. The fact that no irrefutable proof has emerged despite the purported scale and scope of these programs raises questions about their plausibility.

Cultural Impact and Popularity

Despite the skepticism, the concept of Secret Space Programs has had a profound impact on popular culture and conspiracy theory communities. SSP narratives resonate with broader themes of government secrecy, technological advancement, and the potential for hidden knowledge that could transform human civilization.

The idea of SSPs has been explored in numerous books, documentaries, and online forums, where proponents share their theories, analyze potential evidence, and discuss the implications of these programs. The SSP narrative appeals to those who are skeptical of official narratives, as well as those who are fascinated by the possibility of advanced technology and extraterrestrial contact.

In recent years, SSP theories have gained additional visibility through the disclosure movement, which advocates for the release of government-held information about UFOs, extraterrestrials, and related topics. Some disclosure advocates believe that revealing the truth about SSPs could lead to a new era of technological and spiritual advancement for humanity.

SSP theories have also influenced science fiction and entertainment, with films, television shows, and video games drawing on the idea of secret space missions, advanced technology, and hidden extraterrestrial alliances. These narratives often explore the ethical dilemmas and power struggles that might arise from such programs, reflecting the fears and hopes of a society grappling with rapid technological change and the unknown.

The concept of Secret Space Programs is a complex and controversial topic that sits at the intersection of conspiracy theory, UFOlogy, and speculative science. Whether viewed as a genuine hidden reality, a modern myth, or a combination of both, SSP theories continue to captivate the imagination of those who are drawn to the idea of advanced technology, extraterrestrial contact, and the potential for a hidden world beyond the public eye.

For believers, SSPs represent the ultimate example of government secrecy and the possibility that humanity's true capabilities in space far exceed what is publicly known. The idea that we may already be exploring the stars, collaborating with extraterrestrial beings, and developing technologies that could revolutionize our understanding of the universe is both thrilling and inspiring.

For sceptics, SSP theories serve as a reminder of the challenges of verifying extraordinary claims and the power of narrative to shape our perceptions of reality. The lack of verifiable evidence and the reliance on anecdotal testimonies and speculative interpretations make it difficult to accept SSP theories as factual. However, these theories also highlight the human tendency to question authority, seek out hidden truths, and imagine possibilities beyond the constraints of our current understanding.

Broader Implications of Secret Space Programs

The debate over Secret Space Programs touches on several important themes that extend beyond the specifics of the conspiracy itself. These include:

Government Secrecy and Transparency: The idea of SSPs raises broader questions about government secrecy, particularly in the realms of defense and space exploration. How much do governments actually know about extraterrestrial life, advanced technology, and the potential for space colonization? If SSPs exist, what are the implications for democratic accountability and public oversight? The secrecy surrounding national security and space exploration programs often fuels speculation and mistrust, leading to the proliferation of conspiracy theories.

Human Potential and Technological Advancement: SSP theories tap into the human fascination with technological progress and the idea that there may be untapped potential for innovation that could radically transform society. Whether through faster-than-light travel, anti-gravity propulsion, or other advanced technologies, SSP narratives suggest that humanity may be on the cusp of breakthroughs that could change the course of history. This raises questions about how such technologies should be developed, controlled, and shared, as well as the ethical considerations involved.

Extraterrestrial Contact and the Future of Humanity: The idea that SSPs involve collaboration with extraterrestrial beings speaks to a broader curiosity about our place in the universe and the potential for contact with other intelligent civilizations. If such contact has already occurred, what does it mean for our understanding of life, consciousness, and the future of humanity? SSP theories often posit that extraterrestrial knowledge could offer solutions to some of the most pressing challenges facing humanity, from environmental degradation to global conflict.

The Role of Fiction in Shaping Belief: The overlap between SSP theories and science fiction highlights the powerful role that fiction can play in shaping our beliefs and expectations about the future.

Science fiction has long explored themes of space exploration, advanced technology, and extraterrestrial contact, often blurring the lines between imagination and possibility. SSP theories can be seen as a reflection of this cultural influence, as well as a way for individuals to make sense of a rapidly changing world.

The Future of Secret Space Program Theories

As interest in space exploration and the search for extraterrestrial life continues to grow, SSP theories are likely to remain a prominent topic of discussion. Advances in space technology, including the privatization of space exploration through companies like SpaceX, Blue Origin, and others, may further fuel speculation about what is being kept hidden from the public.

Additionally, ongoing efforts to disclose government-held information about UFOs and other related phenomena may shed new light on the validity of SSP theories. In recent years, there has been a growing movement within the UFO community and among some politicians to push for greater transparency and the release of classified documents related to unidentified aerial phenomena (UAPs) and potential extraterrestrial encounters.

However, even with increased transparency, the nature of SSP theories—rooted in secrecy, speculation, and the unknown—means that they will likely continue to evolve and adapt to new developments. Whether they are ultimately proven, debunked, or remain in the realm of speculation, SSP theories offer a fascinating glimpse into the ways in which humans grapple with the mysteries of the cosmos and the possibilities of a future that is still largely beyond our reach.

Secret Space Programs, as a concept, encapsulate the tension between what is known and what is imagined, between the official narrative and the potential for hidden truths. These theories reflect deep-seated anxieties about government secrecy, technological advancement, and the unknown, while also offering a sense of wonder and possibility about humanity's future in space.

For some, SSPs are a testament to the idea that there is more to reality than what we are told, that there are hidden forces at work shaping the destiny of humanity. For others, they serve as a reminder of the importance of critical thinking, skepticism, and the need for evidence in evaluating extraordinary claims.

As humanity continues to explore the stars and push the boundaries of our technological capabilities, the allure of Secret Space Programs will likely persist, challenging us to consider the limits of our knowledge and the possibilities that lie beyond the horizon. Whether these programs are real, fictional, or somewhere in between, they remain a powerful symbol of our quest to understand the universe and our place within it.

The Cattle Mutilations: Alien Experiments on Earth

The phenomenon of cattle mutilations, which involves the mysterious and often gruesome deaths of livestock, has been a subject of intrigue, fear, and speculation for decades. These incidents are typically characterized by the removal of specific organs and tissues, seemingly with surgical precision, and the absence of blood or signs of struggle. While there are various theories attempting to explain cattle mutilations, one of the most persistent and controversial is the idea that they are the result of alien experiments on Earth. This chapter delves into the history of cattle mutilations, the key features of these incidents, the range of theories proposed to explain them, and the broader implications for our understanding of extraterrestrial involvement on our planet.

The History of Cattle Mutilations

Reports of cattle mutilations began to surface in the United States in the 1960s, particularly in the western and mid-western states. However, similar incidents have been reported around the world, including in South America, Europe, and Australia. The first widely publicized case occurred in 1967 near Alamosa, Colorado, when a horse named "Lady" (initially misidentified as "Snippy" in news reports) was found dead under mysterious circumstances. The horse's flesh had been removed from its head and neck with what appeared to be surgical precision, and there were no signs of blood or struggle.

Throughout the 1970s and 1980s, reports of cattle mutilations increased, with ranchers and farmers discovering their livestock dead with similar injuries: cleanly excised organs, missing eyes, tongues, and reproductive organs, and an eerie absence of blood. In many cases, the mutilations were accompanied by reports of strange lights in the sky, unidentified flying objects (UFOs), and other unexplained phenomena.

As the reports grew in number, law enforcement agencies, veterinarians, and even the FBI became involved in investigations. Despite extensive efforts, no definitive explanation was found, and the cases were often left unresolved. The lack of clear answers fueled speculation and led to the rise of various theories about the cause of these mutilations.

Key Features of Cattle Mutilations

Cattle mutilation cases tend to share several common characteristics, which have made them particularly perplexing:

Surgical Precision: The removal of organs and tissues in cattle mutilations is often described as being done with surgical precision. The cuts are typically clean and exact, with no ragged edges or tearing, leading some investigators to conclude that advanced tools or techniques were used. In some cases, the excision of organs is so precise that it seems beyond the capability of known predators or even standard veterinary instruments.

Lack of Blood: One of the most puzzling aspects of cattle mutilations is the absence of blood at the scene. Despite the extensive wounds, there is often little to no blood found around the animal or in its body. This has led to speculation that the blood may have been drained or removed by some unknown means, contributing to the idea that the mutilations are the work of an intelligent and technologically advanced force.

Specific Organs Targeted: The organs and tissues most commonly removed in cattle mutilations include the eyes, tongue, udders, reproductive organs, and rectum. The fact that the same body parts are repeatedly targeted has led some to believe that the mutilations are not random acts of violence but are carried out for a specific purpose, possibly related to scientific experimentation or biological sampling.

No Signs of Struggle: In many cases, the mutilated animals show no signs of a struggle or defensive behavior, such as broken limbs or disturbed surroundings. The absence of tracks or footprints around the carcass is also commonly reported, leading to the suggestion that the animals may have been killed elsewhere and then placed back at the scene, or that they were somehow incapacitated before the mutilations took place.

Strange Lights and UFO Sightings: Reports of strange lights in the sky or sightings of unidentified flying objects (UFOs) are frequently associated with cattle mutilations. Witnesses often describe seeing bright lights or strange craft near the location of a mutilation either before or after the incident, reinforcing the theory that extraterrestrial beings may be involved.

Theories about Cattle Mutilations

Over the years, a variety of theories have been proposed to explain cattle mutilations, ranging from the mundane to the extraordinary. The most prominent theories include:

Extraterrestrial Involvement

One of the most popular and controversial explanations is that cattle mutilations are the result of experiments conducted by extraterrestrial beings. Proponents of this theory argue that the surgical precision of the mutilations, the specific organs targeted, and the associated UFO sightings all point to the involvement of an advanced non-human intelligence.

According to this theory, aliens may be conducting biological experiments on Earth, using cattle as test subjects to study terrestrial biology, harvest genetic material, or monitor the effects of environmental changes. Some suggest that the mutilations could be part of a broader alien agenda, possibly involving hybridization programs or the study of Earth's ecosystems.

Government or Military Experiments

Another theory posits that cattle mutilations are the result of secret government or military experiments. This could involve testing biological or chemical weapons, studying the effects of radiation, or conducting genetic research. The precision of the mutilations and the secrecy surrounding them could be explained by the use of advanced technology, possibly developed in collaboration with extraterrestrials or as part of classified projects.

Some researchers believe that the mutilations are related to the monitoring of environmental contamination, such as the effects of nuclear fallout or industrial pollutants. The government, according to this theory, may be using cattle as a convenient way to sample the environment without alarming the public.

Cult Activity

Some investigators have suggested that cattle mutilations are the work of cults or religious groups engaged in ritualistic practices. The specific organs targeted and the bloodless nature of the mutilations have been interpreted by some as evidence of sacrificial rites or ceremonies. However, this theory has been criticized for its lack of concrete evidence and for failing to account for the widespread geographic distribution of the incidents.

Predatory Animals and Scavengers

Skeptics often argue that cattle mutilations can be explained by natural causes, such as predatory animals or scavengers. According to this theory, the clean cuts and missing organs could result from the actions of predators, such as coyotes, birds, or insects, feeding on the carcass. The lack of blood could be attributed to natural coagulation processes or post-mortem blood loss, and the absence of tracks might be due to environmental factors like wind or rain.

While this theory accounts for some aspects of cattle mutilations, it does not fully explain the more unusual features, such as the precise excision of organs or the reports of associated UFO activity. As a result, it is often considered a partial explanation rather than a definitive one.

Hoaxes and Human Interference

Some researchers believe that at least some cases of cattle mutilation may be the result of hoaxes or human interference. This could involve individuals seeking attention, playing pranks, or attempting to spread fear in rural communities. In some cases, insurance fraud has also been suggested as a motive, with farmers or ranchers mutilating their own animals to claim compensation.

However, the scale and consistency of the mutilation reports, as well as the associated phenomena, make it unlikely that all cases can be attributed to hoaxes or human interference.

Cultural Impact and Popularity

Cattle mutilations have had a significant impact on popular culture, particularly within the UFO and paranormal communities. The eerie and unexplained nature of these incidents has made them a staple of conspiracy theories, documentaries, books, and television shows. The idea of aliens conducting secret experiments on Earth resonates with broader themes of government cover-ups, the unknown, and humanity's vulnerability in the face of advanced technology.

Cattle mutilations have also been featured in numerous fictional works, where they are often used to create an atmosphere of fear and mystery. Films, television series, and novels exploring themes of extraterrestrial contact frequently incorporate elements of cattle mutilations, reflecting the enduring fascination with the phenomenon.

In rural communities where mutilations have occurred, the events have sometimes led to fear and suspicion, with locals speculating about the involvement of aliens, secret government programs, or other malevolent forces. The lack of clear answers has only heightened the sense of unease, making cattle mutilations a symbol of the unknown and the unexplained.

The phenomenon of cattle mutilations remains one of the most enduring and enigmatic mysteries in the realms of UFOlogy and paranormal investigation. Whether viewed as evidence of extraterrestrial experimentation, secret government projects, or natural predation, cattle mutilations challenge our understanding of the world and the forces that may be at play behind the scenes.

For believers in the extraterrestrial theory, cattle mutilations represent a disturbing example of alien intervention on Earth, suggesting that humanity is being observed, studied, or manipulated by beings from beyond our planet. The precision of the mutilations, the specific organs targeted, and the association with UFO sightings all point to the involvement of a technologically advanced and possibly malevolent intelligence.

For sceptics, cattle mutilations serve as a reminder of the complexities of interpreting unexplained phenomena and the need for critical thinking in the face of sensational claims. While some cases may be explained by natural causes or human interference, the persistence of the phenomenon and the lack of definitive answers continue to fuel speculation and debate.

As with many paranormal and conspiracy theories, the truth behind cattle mutilations may never be fully known. However, the phenomenon continues to captivate the imagination of those who are drawn to the mysteries of the unknown, challenging us to consider the possibility that there are forces at work in our world that remain beyond our current understanding. Whether the result of alien experiments, secret government activities, or something else entirely, cattle mutilations remain a powerful symbol of the unexplained.

Reverse Engineering: From Roswell to Modern Technology

The concept of reverse engineering alien technology has been a cornerstone of UFO conspiracy theories for decades. It is widely believed among UFO enthusiasts that the U.S. government, particularly following the alleged crash of a UFO in Roswell, New Mexico, in 1947, has secretly recovered and reverse-engineered advanced extraterrestrial technology. This technology, according to the theory, has been the source of many modern technological advancements, including developments in aerospace, computing, and materials science. This chapter explores the origins of the reverse engineering narrative, the key claims associated with it, the evidence and skepticism surrounding these ideas, and the broader implications for our understanding of technological progress and government secrecy.

Origins of the Reverse Engineering Narrative

The idea that modern technology might be derived from extraterrestrial sources first gained widespread attention in the wake of the Roswell incident. In July 1947, a rancher named Mac Brazel discovered unusual debris on his property near Roswell, New Mexico. The U.S. military initially announced that a "flying disc" had been recovered, but this statement was quickly retracted, and the debris was identified as part of a weather balloon. This abrupt change in narrative fueled speculation that the government was hiding the truth.

The Roswell incident soon became a focal point for UFO enthusiasts, who believed that the debris recovered was not from a weather balloon but from an alien spacecraft. Over the following decades, numerous witnesses and alleged insiders came forward with claims that the U.S. government had recovered not only the remains of a crashed UFO but also the bodies of its extraterrestrial occupants. These claims often included assertions that the government had reverse-engineered the alien technology, leading to significant advancements in various scientific fields.

The narrative gained further traction in the 1980s and 1990s, particularly through the work of individuals like Philip Corso, whose book *The Day After Roswell* (1997) claimed that much of the technology we use today—such as fiber optics, lasers, and integrated circuits—was derived from alien artifacts recovered at Roswell. Corso's claims, though controversial and lacking substantial evidence, resonated with those who were already inclined to believe in government cover-ups and the existence of extraterrestrial technology.

Key Claims of Reverse Engineering

The reverse engineering narrative is built on several key claims, each of which ties modern technological advancements to the recovery of alien technology:

Roswell and Alien Artifacts: The central claim of the reverse engineering theory is that the U.S. government recovered alien technology from the Roswell crash site and subsequently used it as a basis for significant technological advancements. Proponents argue that the debris recovered included materials and devices far beyond the capabilities of 1940s technology, including advanced alloys, microprocessors, and energy systems.

Advancements in Aerospace Technology: One of the most commonly cited areas of reverse-engineered technology is aerospace. Some UFO theorists believe that many of the advancements in aviation, such as stealth technology, anti-gravity propulsion systems, and high-performance aircraft like the SR-71 Blackbird and the B-2 Spirit stealth bomber, were derived from alien spacecraft. These technologies are often said to be the result of decades of secret research conducted at facilities like Area 51.

Computing and Microelectronics: Another major area of alleged reverse-engineered technology is computing. Proponents claim that breakthroughs in microelectronics, including the development of transistors, integrated circuits, and modern computing devices, were made possible by the study of alien technology. The rapid pace of advancement in computing from the 1950s onward is often pointed to as evidence that humanity had help from an extraterrestrial source.

Materials Science: The development of new materials, such as Kevlar, advanced composites, and memory metals, is also frequently attributed to reverse engineering. According to some theories, these materials were first encountered in the wreckage of alien craft and were subsequently reproduced and adapted for human use. The ability of these materials to withstand extreme conditions or exhibit unusual properties is often cited as evidence of their extraterrestrial origin.

Energy and Propulsion Systems: The reverse engineering narrative also encompasses advancements in energy and propulsion systems, particularly those related to alternative or exotic energy sources. Some theorists believe that the study of alien power sources, such as zero-point energy or advanced nuclear systems, has led to the development of technologies that are still largely classified but have the potential to revolutionize energy production and space travel.

Evidence and Skepticism

The claims surrounding reverse engineering of alien technology are among the most controversial and widely debated within the UFO community. While the idea is compelling, it is also fraught with challenges and skepticism:

Lack of Concrete Evidence: One of the primary criticisms of the reverse engineering theory is the lack of concrete evidence to support it. While there are numerous claims and anecdotal accounts, there is no definitive proof that alien technology has been recovered and reverse-engineered. The evidence that does exist is often circumstantial or based on the testimony of individuals whose credibility is difficult to assess.

Historical Context: Skeptics argue that many of the technological advancements attributed to reverse engineering can be explained by human ingenuity and the natural progression of scientific research. The development of transistors, for example, was the result of decades of work by scientists and engineers, with clear documentation of the research process. Similarly, advancements in aerospace and materials science can be traced to specific research programs and technological breakthroughs that have well-documented origins.

Alternative Explanations: Some researchers suggest that the idea of reverse engineering alien technology may be a convenient way to explain the rapid pace of technological progress in the 20th century, particularly during the Cold War. The competition between the United States and the Soviet Union drove massive investment in research and development, leading to significant technological advancements. The reverse engineering narrative may also reflect broader anxieties about government secrecy and the unknown.

Disinformation and Hoaxes: There is also the possibility that some of the claims about reverse engineering are the result of disinformation or deliberate hoaxes. Governments, particularly during the Cold War, had a vested interest in controlling the narrative around advanced technology and may have spread rumours or disinformation to confuse or mislead adversaries. Additionally, some individuals may have fabricated stories about reverse engineering for personal gain or attention.

The Burden of Proof: The extraordinary nature of the claims associated with reverse engineering places a high burden of proof on those who advocate for it. While the idea is intriguing, the lack of verifiable evidence means that it remains in the realm of speculation rather than established fact. Without definitive proof, such as declassified documents, physical artifacts, or corroborated insider testimony, the reverse engineering narrative is difficult to substantiate.

Cultural Impact and Popularity

Despite the skepticism, the concept of reverse engineering alien technology has had a significant impact on popular culture and the UFO community. The idea that many of the technologies we use today could have extraterrestrial origins is a compelling narrative that has been explored in numerous books, films, and television shows. In fiction, the theme of reverse-engineered alien technology is often used to create stories about government cover-ups, secret wars, and the hidden potential of humanity. Films like *Independence Day* and *Stargate* explore the idea that ancient or alien technologies could be the key to understanding our place in the universe and defending against extraterrestrial threats.

In the UFO community, the reverse engineering narrative is often seen as a crucial piece of the puzzle in understanding the broader phenomenon of alien contact and government secrecy. For many, it represents the possibility that humanity is not alone in the universe and that we may already be benefiting from the knowledge and technology of other civilizations. The idea also resonates with broader cultural themes about the limits of human knowledge, the potential for technological progress, and the ethical implications of using technology that we do not fully understand. It raises questions about the responsibilities of those who hold such knowledge and the potential consequences of keeping it hidden from the public.

The concept of reverse engineering alien technology, particularly in the context of the Roswell incident and subsequent technological advancements, remains one of the most enduring and intriguing aspects of UFO conspiracy theories. Whether viewed as a plausible explanation for the rapid pace of technological progress or as a speculative narrative rooted in the mysteries of the unknown, the idea continues to captivate the imagination of those who are curious about the potential for extraterrestrial influence on human history.

For believers, the reverse engineering narrative offers a tantalizing glimpse into a hidden world of advanced technology and secret knowledge. It suggests that humanity may have already made contact with extraterrestrial civilizations and that we are using their technology to push the boundaries of what is possible. For sceptics, the reverse engineering theory serves as a reminder of the importance of evidence and critical thinking in evaluating extraordinary claims. While the idea is fascinating, the lack of concrete proof means that it remains in the realm of speculation rather than established fact.

As long as questions about the origins of modern technology and the possibility of extraterrestrial contact remain unanswered, the idea of reverse engineering will continue to inspire debate, curiosity, and speculation. Whether true or not, it challenges us to consider the limits of our knowledge and the potential for discovery in a universe that is vast, mysterious, and full of possibilities.

Contactees vs. Abductees: Differing Experiences

The phenomenon of human-alien encounters has long fascinated both believers and skeptics alike. Within this broad spectrum of encounters, two distinct groups have emerged: contactees and abductees. While both claim to have experienced interactions with extraterrestrial beings, the nature of these encounters, the narratives they create, and the implications of these experiences differ significantly. Contactees often describe their interactions with aliens as positive, enlightening, and voluntary, while abductees typically recount their experiences as frightening, invasive, and non-consensual. This chapter explores the histories, characteristics, and differing experiences of contactees and abductees, as well as the cultural and psychological implications of these divergent narratives.

The Contactee Movement: Positive Encounters and Cosmic Messages

The contactee movement began in the 1950s, during a time of heightened interest in UFOs and the possibility of extraterrestrial life. Contactees are individuals who claim to have had direct, often repeated, interactions with benevolent extraterrestrial beings. These beings are typically depicted as wise, peaceful, and spiritually advanced, coming from distant planets or star systems with a message of goodwill and enlightenment for humanity.

Origins and Early Figures

The contactee movement is closely associated with several prominent figures who came forward during the 1950s with claims of extraterrestrial contact. One of the earliest and most famous contactees was George Adamski, who claimed to have met with "Nordic" aliens from Venus. Adamski described these beings as tall, blonde, and human-like, with a deep concern for the future of Earth and humanity. He recounted traveling aboard their spacecraft and receiving messages urging humans to abandon nuclear weapons and embrace a more spiritual way of life.

Other notable contactees include George Van Tassel, who claimed to have communicated with extraterrestrials from Venus through telepathy and to have received instructions for building a device called the "Integratron," which he believed could rejuvenate human cells and extend life. Similarly, Howard Menger and Daniel Fry reported their own encounters with benevolent aliens who imparted similar messages of peace and universal brotherhood.

Common Themes and Experiences

Contactees often describe their experiences as deeply transformative, leading them to adopt new spiritual beliefs and practices. The encounters are usually framed as part of a cosmic mission, with the contactee chosen by the extraterrestrials to spread their message to humanity. Common themes in contactee narratives include:

Spiritual Enlightenment: Contactees frequently report that their encounters with extraterrestrials have led to a greater understanding of the universe and humanity's place within it. They often adopt new spiritual or metaphysical beliefs, viewing themselves as messengers or intermediaries between the aliens and humanity.

Benevolent Aliens: The extraterrestrial beings described by contactees are typically portrayed as peaceful, wise, and concerned with the welfare of Earth. These beings often come from advanced civilizations that have overcome the challenges facing humanity, such as war, environmental destruction, and social inequality.

Warnings and Prophecies: Contactees often receive warnings from the aliens about the dangers of nuclear weapons, environmental degradation, and moral decay. These warnings are usually accompanied by prophecies of potential disasters if humanity does not change its ways, as well as promises of a brighter future if we follow the aliens' guidance.

Voluntary and Positive Encounters: Unlike abductees, contactees generally describe their encounters as voluntary and positive. They often express a sense of honor or privilege at being chosen for contact and report feeling a deep connection to the extraterrestrial beings they meet.

The Abductee Experience: Fearful Encounters and Trauma

In contrast to the contactee movement, the phenomenon of alien abduction emerged in the 1960s and 1970s and is characterized by reports of involuntary and often traumatic encounters with extraterrestrials. Abductees are individuals who claim to have been taken against their will by alien beings, subjected to invasive medical procedures, and returned to Earth with little or no memory of the experience.

Origins and Early Cases

One of the earliest and most well-known cases of alien abduction is that of Betty and Barney Hill, a married couple who reported being abducted by extraterrestrials in 1961 while driving through New Hampshire. The Hills' account, which was later detailed in the book *Interrupted Journey* by John G. Fuller, described their abduction by small, grey-skinned beings who conducted medical examinations on them aboard a spacecraft. The Hills' story is often cited as the first widely publicized case of alien abduction and set the template for many subsequent reports.

Another influential case is that of Travis Walton, who claimed to have been abducted by aliens in 1975 while working as a logger in Arizona. Walton's account, which was later dramatized in the film *Fire in the Sky* (1993), described being taken aboard a spacecraft, subjected to painful medical procedures, and later returned to Earth with no memory of the intervening days.

Common Themes and Experiences

Abductees often report experiences that are markedly different from those of contactees. While contactees describe their encounters as positive and enlightening, abductees frequently recount their experiences as terrifying, invasive, and psychologically damaging. Common themes in abductee narratives include:

Involuntary and Traumatic Encounters: Abductees typically describe their experiences as non-consensual and deeply traumatic. They often report being paralyzed, restrained, or otherwise unable to resist the aliens during the abduction. The experience is frequently accompanied by feelings of fear, helplessness, and violation.

Medical Examinations: A common feature of abduction accounts is the description of invasive medical procedures performed by the aliens. These procedures often involve the extraction of bodily fluids, the implantation of devices, or the examination of reproductive organs. Abductees sometimes report experiencing pain or discomfort during these procedures, and many describe feeling like they are being treated as test subjects or specimens.

Memory Loss and Missing Time: Many abductees report gaps in their memory or "missing time" following the abduction. They may have only vague or fragmented memories of the experience, which can lead to confusion, anxiety, and a sense of unreality. Some abductees recover memories of their experiences through hypnosis or other forms of therapy, though the accuracy and reliability of such memories are often debated.

Physical and Psychological Aftereffects: Abductees frequently report physical symptoms, such as unexplained scars, burns, or marks on their bodies, following the abduction. They may also experience psychological aftereffects, including anxiety, depression, nightmares, and post-traumatic stress disorder (PTSD). The traumatic nature of the experience can have a profound impact on an abductee's life, relationships, and sense of self.

Differing Interpretations and Theories

The contrasting experiences of contactees and abductees have led to a variety of interpretations and theories about the nature of alien encounters. These interpretations often reflect broader cultural, psychological, and philosophical perspectives:

Spiritual and Metaphysical Interpretations: Some researchers view the contactee phenomenon as a manifestation of spiritual or metaphysical experiences, with the extraterrestrials representing higher-dimensional beings or archetypal figures. From this perspective, the contactee's encounters are seen as symbolic or transformative experiences that reflect humanity's evolving consciousness and spiritual development.

Psychological Explanations: Many skeptics and psychologists interpret both contactee and abductee experiences as products of psychological processes, such as sleep paralysis, hallucinations, or dissociative states. In the case of abductees, the traumatic nature of the experience may be linked to repressed memories, unresolved trauma, or suggestibility during hypnosis. Some researchers suggest that the differing narratives of contactees and abductees may reflect individual differences in personality, belief systems, and coping mechanisms.

Cultural Influences: The narratives of contactees and abductees are often influenced by broader cultural factors, including science fiction literature, films, and media portrayals of extraterrestrial encounters. The contactee movement emerged during a time of optimism and interest in space exploration, while the abduction phenomenon gained prominence in a period of growing anxiety about government secrecy, technological advances, and the unknown. These cultural influences may shape the way individuals interpret and narrate their experiences.

Multiple Types of Aliens: Some UFO researchers propose that the differing experiences of contactees and abductees may be explained by the involvement of multiple types of extraterrestrial beings with different agendas. For example, contactees might be interacting with benevolent, spiritually advanced beings (such as the Nordics), while abductees might be encountering more malevolent or indifferent entities (such as the Greys or Reptilians). This theory suggests that the nature of the encounter depends on the specific type of extraterrestrial involved.

Cultural Impact and Popularity

The contrasting narratives of contactees and abductees have had a significant impact on popular culture, shaping public perceptions of extraterrestrial encounters and influencing how these experiences are portrayed in literature, film, and television. The contactee movement, with its themes of spiritual enlightenment and cosmic brotherhood, has inspired a range of science fiction works that explore the idea of benevolent aliens guiding humanity toward a better future. In contrast, the abduction phenomenon has fueled darker, more dystopian narratives that focus on the fear and trauma of encountering an unknown and potentially hostile force.

The experiences of contactees and abductees have also contributed to ongoing debates within the UFO and paranormal communities about the nature of extraterrestrial contact. Some researchers argue that both groups are experiencing real encounters with alien beings, while others believe that the experiences are purely psychological or symbolic in nature. The differing interpretations reflect broader questions about the limits of human perception, the nature of reality, and the potential for contact with other forms of intelligence.

The phenomena of contactees and abductees represent two distinct but related aspects of the broader narrative of human-alien encounters. While contactees describe their interactions with extraterrestrial beings as positive, enlightening, and often voluntary, abductees recount their experiences as frightening, invasive, and traumatic. These differing experiences reflect not only the individual perceptions and interpretations of those involved but also broader cultural, psychological, and spiritual factors that shape how we understand and narrate encounters with the unknown.

For contactees, their experiences are often seen as a call to higher consciousness, a mission to spread messages of peace, and a connection to a greater cosmic community. The positive and voluntary nature of their encounters allows them to view extraterrestrial beings as benevolent guides or protectors who are concerned with humanity's spiritual and moral development. These experiences often lead to personal transformation, a sense of purpose, and a deepened understanding of the universe.

In contrast, abductees typically describe their encounters with extraterrestrials as invasive, non-consensual, and traumatic. The fear, helplessness, and psychological distress associated with these experiences contribute to a narrative of victimization and violation. The abduction phenomenon raises troubling questions about the potential motives of extraterrestrial beings, the nature of consent, and the impact of such experiences on an individual's mental health and well-being.

The Divergence between Contactees and Abductees

The divergence between the experiences of contactees and abductees can be interpreted in several ways:

Psychological and Perceptual Differences: One explanation for the differences in these experiences is rooted in psychology. Contactees and abductees may have different psychological profiles, belief systems, and expectations that influence how they perceive and interpret their encounters. Contactees might be more inclined to interpret strange experiences in a positive light due to their spiritual beliefs or optimistic outlook, while abductees may have a more fearful or suspicious disposition, leading them to perceive their experiences as threatening.

Cultural Narratives and Influences: The narratives of contactees and abductees are also shaped by cultural influences. Contactees emerged during a time of post-war optimism, the rise of the space age, and a fascination with utopian futures. In contrast, abductees' experiences gained prominence during a period of Cold War anxiety, distrust in government institutions, and a growing awareness of the darker side of technological progress. These cultural contexts have likely influenced how individuals frame and understand their encounters.

Multiple Types of Encounters: Another perspective is that contactees and abductees are genuinely experiencing different types of encounters with different entities. This theory suggests that there could be a variety of extraterrestrial or interdimensional beings with differing intentions toward humanity. Some may be benevolent and seeking to guide us, while others may be indifferent or even hostile, engaging in activities that humans perceive as invasive or harmful.

Symbolic and Archetypal Interpretations: Some researchers and psychologists view both contactee and abductee experiences as symbolic or archetypal in nature, reflecting deep-seated human fears, desires, and spiritual longings. From this perspective, the experiences are not necessarily literal encounters with extraterrestrials but rather manifestations of the unconscious mind, processing complex emotions and existential questions through the lens of alien contact.

Implications for Our Understanding of Alien Contact

The differing experiences of contactees and abductees have significant implications for how we understand the phenomenon of alien contact and its impact on individuals and society:

The Complexity of Human Experience: The stark contrast between contactee and abductee narratives highlights the complexity of human experience and the ways in which perception, belief, and culture shape our understanding of the world. These differences challenge us to consider the possibility that alien encounters may not be a singular, objective phenomenon but rather a multifaceted one that varies according to individual and collective consciousness.

The Role of Fear and Hope: The contactee and abductee phenomena illustrate the dual role of fear and hope in our relationship with the unknown. Contactees embody the hope that humanity is part of a larger, benevolent cosmic order, while abductees reflect the fear that we are vulnerable to forces beyond our control. These themes resonate deeply in human psychology and culture, influencing how we interpret and respond to the idea of extraterrestrial life.

The Potential for Alien Contact: The narratives of contactees and abductees also raise important questions about the potential nature of extraterrestrial contact. If these encounters are real, what do they tell us about the intentions and ethics of the beings involved? Are we dealing with multiple types of entities, each with its own agenda, or are these experiences the result of psychological or cultural factors? The answers to these questions have profound implications for our understanding of humanity's place in the cosmos and the future of interspecies relations.

The experiences of contactees and abductees represent two sides of the same coin in the broader narrative of human-alien encounters. While contactees offer a vision of hope, spiritual awakening, and cosmic unity, abductees present a darker, more troubling narrative of fear, trauma, and violation. Together, these narratives paint a complex and multifaceted picture of how humans interact with the unknown, whether through the lens of extraterrestrial contact, psychological processes, or cultural influences.

As our understanding of these phenomena continues to evolve, the stories of contactees and abductees will likely remain a source of fascination, debate, and reflection. They challenge us to explore the limits of human perception, the boundaries of reality, and the potential for contact with other forms of intelligence. Whether these experiences are real encounters with extraterrestrial beings, manifestations of the unconscious mind, or a blend of both, they offer a profound insight into the human condition and our quest to understand the mysteries of the universe.

Alien Abduction Syndromes: Psychological or Real?

Alien abduction syndromes represent one of the most perplexing and debated phenomena in both psychology and UFOlogy. Individuals who claim to have been abducted by extraterrestrial beings often describe vivid and detailed experiences that include being taken aboard alien spacecraft, subjected to invasive medical procedures, and encountering strange beings. These accounts are often accompanied by physical symptoms, psychological distress, and, in some cases, profound changes in belief systems and personal identity. The central question surrounding alien abduction syndromes is whether these experiences are psychological in nature—perhaps the result of sleep disorders, trauma, or cultural influences—or whether they represent real encounters with extraterrestrial entities. This chapter explores the characteristics of alien abduction syndromes, the various psychological and physical explanations proposed by researchers, and the ongoing debate over the reality of these experiences.

Characteristics of Alien Abduction Syndromes

Individuals who report alien abductions often describe their experiences with a striking degree of consistency, despite cultural and geographical differences. Some of the most common features of alien abduction syndromes include:

Sleep Paralysis and Hypnagogic States: Many abduction experiences begin when the individual is in bed, either falling asleep or waking up. They may feel paralyzed, unable to move or speak, and experience a sense of terror as they perceive beings entering their room. These beings are often described as small, gray-skinned entities with large heads and eyes—commonly known as "Greys." The individual may feel a sense of floating or being lifted from their bed, followed by the sensation of being transported to an unknown location.

Invasive Medical Procedures: A hallmark of alien abduction experiences is the description of medical examinations performed by the extraterrestrials. These procedures often involve the removal of bodily fluids, the insertion of instruments into the body, and the implantation of devices. Abductees frequently report feelings of pain, fear, and helplessness during these procedures, and may have vague memories of being on a table in a sterile, brightly lit environment.

Missing Time: Abductees often report episodes of "missing time," where they are unable to account for hours or even days following the experience. This missing time is usually filled in later through hypnosis or other memory-retrieval techniques, revealing detailed accounts of the abduction experience. The phenomenon of missing time adds to the sense of unreality and disorientation that many abductees feel.

Post-Abduction Symptoms: After the experience, many abductees report physical symptoms such as unexplained scars, bruises, burns, or marks on their bodies. They may also experience psychological symptoms, including anxiety, depression, nightmares, and flashbacks. These symptoms can persist for years and may significantly impact the individual's quality of life.

Profound Belief Changes: Some abductees undergo profound changes in their belief systems following their experiences. They may come to believe in the existence of extraterrestrial life, adopt new spiritual or metaphysical beliefs, or feel a sense of mission or purpose related to their abduction. In some cases, the experience leads to a sense of connection with the extraterrestrials or a belief that they are part of a larger cosmic plan.

Psychological Explanations for Alien Abduction Syndromes

Skeptics and many psychologists propose that alien abduction syndromes can be explained by a variety of psychological and neurological factors. These explanations suggest that the experiences are not literal encounters with extraterrestrials, but rather manifestations of the mind under certain conditions.

Sleep Paralysis and Hypnagogic Hallucinations: One of the most widely accepted psychological explanations for alien abduction experiences is sleep paralysis. Sleep paralysis occurs when an individual is in a state between wakefulness and sleep, during which they are conscious but unable to move. This condition is often accompanied by hypnagogic hallucinations—vivid and sometimes terrifying images or sensations that can include the perception of beings in the room. The combination of paralysis and hallucinations can create a powerful and convincing experience that feels real to the individual, leading them to interpret it as an alien abduction.

False Memory Syndrome: Another explanation is that the memories of abduction are false memories, created through suggestion, hypnosis, or the influence of popular culture. False memory syndrome refers to the phenomenon where individuals come to believe in memories that are not based on actual events, often as a result of suggestive questioning or therapeutic techniques. The detailed narratives of alien abductions may be constructed from a combination of media influences, personal anxieties, and the brain's natural tendency to fill in gaps in memory.

Trauma and Dissociation: Some researchers suggest that alien abduction experiences may be linked to past trauma, particularly childhood abuse. In this view, the abduction narrative serves as a dissociative coping mechanism, allowing the individual to process or distance themselves from traumatic memories. The experience of being "abducted" by aliens can be seen as a symbolic representation of the individual's feelings of powerlessness, violation, or betrayal.

Cultural Influence and Mass Hysteria: The role of cultural influence in shaping alien abduction experiences cannot be overlooked. The prevalence of UFO stories, science fiction media, and reports of alien encounters in popular culture may prime individuals to interpret certain experiences—such as sleep paralysis or anxiety attacks—as alien abductions. This cultural backdrop, combined with the spread of abduction narratives through books, films, and the internet, may contribute to a form of mass hysteria or collective delusion.

Physical Explanations and Skepticism

In addition to psychological explanations, some researchers propose that physical or environmental factors may contribute to the experiences reported by abductees. These explanations often focus on the possibility of misinterpreting natural phenomena or the influence of external stimuli.

Environmental Factors: Some abduction experiences may be triggered by environmental factors such as electromagnetic fields, infrasound, or changes in atmospheric pressure. These stimuli can affect the brain's functioning, leading to altered states of consciousness, hallucinations, or feelings of unease. In areas where UFO sightings and abduction reports are common, unusual environmental conditions may contribute to the experiences described by witnesses.

Medical Conditions: Certain medical conditions, such as temporal lobe epilepsy, migraines, or sleep disorders, can cause hallucinations, altered perceptions, and other symptoms that might be interpreted as alien encounters. Individuals with these conditions may be more prone to experiencing vivid and disturbing visions or sensations, which they may then attribute to extraterrestrial activity.

Skepticism and the Burden of Proof: Skeptics argue that extraordinary claims—such as those involving alien abduction—require extraordinary evidence. The lack of concrete physical evidence, such as clear documentation, biological samples, or corroborated third-party testimony, makes it difficult to accept abduction stories as literal truth. Instead, skeptics contend that the experiences are better understood as psychological phenomena shaped by a combination of individual factors and cultural influences.

The Case for the Reality of Alien Abductions

Despite the skepticism, a significant number of researchers, experiencers, and UFO enthusiasts believe that alien abductions are real, physical events involving encounters with extraterrestrial beings. Several arguments are put forward in support of this perspective:

Consistency of Reports: Proponents of the reality of alien abductions point to the consistency of abduction reports across different cultures, geographical locations, and time periods. Many abductees describe similar beings, procedures, and experiences, even when they have no prior knowledge of each other's stories. This consistency is seen as evidence that the phenomenon is not merely a product of imagination or cultural influence.

Physical Evidence: Some abductees report physical evidence of their encounters, such as scars, implants, or radiation burns. While the evidence is often difficult to verify and remains controversial, these physical anomalies are cited as proof that the experiences have a tangible, real-world basis.

Hypnotic Regression: Hypnotic regression is often used to recover memories of abduction experiences that are not consciously accessible. Advocates argue that the detailed and emotionally intense memories retrieved through hypnosis suggest that the experiences are real. However, it should be noted that the reliability of memories recovered through hypnosis is highly debated, with many psychologists warning that hypnosis can create or reinforce false memories.

Impact on Experiencers: The profound impact that abduction experiences have on the lives of those who report them is also cited as evidence of their reality. Many abductees describe significant changes in their beliefs, behaviors, and identities following their experiences. They often become involved in UFO research, adopt new spiritual or metaphysical perspectives, and sometimes even form support groups with others who have had similar experiences. The depth of these changes suggests that the experiences, whether real or psychological, are deeply meaningful to those who have them.

Cultural and Psychological Implications

The debate over whether alien abduction syndromes are psychological or real has broader implications for our understanding of human experience, consciousness, and the nature of reality. Regardless of their origin, these experiences challenge our assumptions about the limits of human perception and the boundaries between the physical and the psychological.

The Nature of Reality: Alien abduction syndromes raise fundamental questions about the nature of reality and the reliability of human perception. If the experiences are psychological, they reveal the incredible power of the mind to create vivid, immersive, and convincing alternate realities. If they are real, they suggest that our understanding of the universe is incomplete and that we may be interacting with other forms of intelligence in ways that defy conventional explanation.

The Role of Culture and Belief: The influence of culture and belief on the interpretation of abduction experiences highlights the complex interplay between individual psychology and collective narratives. The way we frame and understand anomalous experiences is deeply shaped by the cultural context in which they occur, as well as by our personal beliefs and expectations. This interplay can create powerful narratives that resonate with broader societal anxieties, hopes, and fears

.

The Impact of Trauma and Memory: The exploration of alien abduction syndromes also delves into the impact of trauma and the nature of memory. Whether the experiences are real or psychological, they often have profound effects on individuals, sometimes triggering symptoms similar to post-traumatic stress disorder (PTSD). The phenomenon also raises important questions about the reliability of memory, particularly in cases where hypnotic regression is used to recover supposed memories of abduction. The human mind's capacity to generate or alter memories under certain conditions is a key area of study that challenges our understanding of truth and reality.

The Search for Meaning: Alien abduction syndromes, like many extraordinary experiences, can be understood as part of humanity's broader search for meaning. For some abductees, the experience leads to a profound personal transformation, offering a sense of purpose or connection to something greater than themselves. Whether viewed as real encounters with extraterrestrials or as symbolic experiences, these narratives often provide individuals with a framework for understanding their place in the universe and addressing existential questions about life, identity, and the unknown.

The Stigma of Reporting Abduction Experiences: The social and psychological stigma associated with reporting alien abduction experiences is significant. Many abductees face ridicule, disbelief, and ostracism when they share their stories, which can exacerbate feelings of isolation and distress. This stigma can deter individuals from seeking support or sharing their experiences, further complicating efforts to understand and study the phenomenon. The reluctance to openly discuss such experiences also contributes to the secrecy and mystery surrounding alien abduction syndromes.

The Ongoing Debate

The debate over whether alien abduction syndromes are psychological or real remains unresolved, with compelling arguments on both sides. On one hand, the psychological explanations offer plausible and scientifically grounded accounts of how these experiences might arise without the need for extraterrestrial intervention. On the other hand, the consistency, intensity, and impact of abduction reports, along with the physical evidence claimed by some abductees, keep the possibility of a more literal interpretation alive in the minds of many researchers and experiencers.

This debate reflects broader tensions between skepticism and belief, science and the unknown, and the search for empirical truth versus the acceptance of subjective experience. As our understanding of the human mind and the universe continues to evolve, so too will the discourse around alien abduction syndromes.

Alien abduction syndromes occupy a unique and controversial space at the intersection of psychology, culture, and the paranormal. Whether these experiences are the product of psychological phenomena such as sleep paralysis, false memories, or trauma, or whether they represent real encounters with extraterrestrial beings, they challenge our understanding of the mind, reality, and the boundaries of human experience. For those who report abduction experiences, the events are often deeply transformative, affecting their beliefs, behaviors, and sense of identity. These experiences, regardless of their origins, demand serious consideration and compassionate understanding, both from researchers and from society at large. As we continue to explore the mysteries of consciousness, memory, and perception, the phenomenon of alien abduction syndromes will likely remain a fascinating and provocative subject of study. Whether viewed as a psychological anomaly, a cultural artifact, or a genuine encounter with the unknown, it offers valuable insights into the complexities of the human experience and our enduring quest to understand the world around us. Ultimately, the exploration of alien abduction syndromes invites us to reflect on the limits of our knowledge, the power of belief, and the nature of reality itself. It challenges us to remain open to the possibilities that lie beyond our current understanding while also applying rigorous scientific inquiry to the mysteries that continue to captivate our imagination.

Exopolitics: Governments and Extraterrestrial Relations

Exopolitics, a term that has gained traction in UFO and extraterrestrial studies, refers to the political implications and potential diplomatic relations between humanity and extraterrestrial civilizations. It explores the idea that governments, particularly those of major world powers, may already be in contact with extraterrestrial beings or are preparing for such contact in the future. Exopolitics examines the role of secrecy, the possibility of hidden treaties or agreements, the influence of extraterrestrial intelligence on global affairs, and the broader impact on society if these interactions were to become public knowledge. This chapter delves into the origins of exopolitics, its key concepts, the evidence supporting or challenging the idea, and the implications for humanity's future.

Origins of Exopolitics

The concept of exopolitics emerged in the late 20th and early 21st centuries as a natural extension of UFOlogy and the increasing speculation about government secrecy regarding extraterrestrial encounters. The term "exopolitics" was popularized by Dr. Michael Salla, a scholar in international politics who became one of the leading figures in the field. In his book *Exopolitics: Political Implications of the Extraterrestrial Presence* (2004), Salla argued that governments may be involved in covert interactions with extraterrestrial civilizations and that understanding these interactions is crucial for shaping humanity's future.

Exopolitics draws on a variety of sources, including alleged whistleblower testimonies, declassified government documents, and the broader UFO phenomenon, to build a framework for understanding the potential political and diplomatic dynamics between humans and extraterrestrials. While mainstream political science has largely ignored or dismissed exopolitics, it has gained a following among UFO researchers, conspiracy theorists, and those interested in the possibility of extraterrestrial life.

Key Concepts of Exopolitics

Exopolitics encompasses a range of ideas and theories about the nature of extraterrestrial contact and its implications for global politics. Some of the key concepts include:

Government Secrecy and Disclosure: A central tenet of exopolitics is the belief that governments, particularly the United States, have been in contact with extraterrestrial beings for decades but have kept this information secret from the public. Proponents argue that the secrecy is maintained to prevent widespread panic, protect technological advantages, or preserve the existing power structures. The disclosure movement, which advocates for the release of classified information about UFOs and extraterrestrial contact, is a significant aspect of exopolitics. Disclosure advocates believe that revealing the truth about extraterrestrial presence would have profound implications for global society and governance.

Extraterrestrial Influence on Global Affairs: Exopolitics explores the idea that extraterrestrial civilizations may be influencing or guiding human affairs, either overtly or covertly. This influence could take many forms, from providing advanced technology to shaping geopolitical events or even intervening in conflicts. Some theories suggest that extraterrestrial beings may be working with specific governments or global elites to steer humanity's development in certain directions, often for their own purposes or to ensure stability on Earth.

Hidden Treaties and Agreements: Another key concept in exopolitics is the possibility that secret treaties or agreements exist between human governments and extraterrestrial civilizations. These agreements might involve the exchange of technology, resources, or information in return for certain concessions, such as allowing abductions or experimentation on humans. The idea of secret pacts with extraterrestrials is often linked to alleged incidents like the Roswell crash or the establishment of bases like Area 51, where these agreements are supposedly managed.

Galactic Diplomacy: Exopolitics envisions a future where humanity is integrated into a larger galactic community and must navigate the complexities of interstellar diplomacy. This includes establishing communication protocols, forming alliances, and negotiating with multiple extraterrestrial species with different cultures, interests, and levels of technological advancement. Galactic diplomacy also raises questions about the role of existing international institutions, such as the United Nations, in managing extraterrestrial relations and the potential for new global governance structures to emerge.

Ethical and Legal Considerations: The ethical and legal implications of extraterrestrial contact are a significant area of focus in exopolitics. This includes debates over the rights of extraterrestrial beings, the ethical treatment of any entities involved in abductions or experiments, and the legal status of extraterrestrial technology or resources. Exopolitics also examines the potential impact on human rights, sovereignty, and the rule of law if extraterrestrial influence is confirmed.

Evidence and Debate

The evidence supporting exopolitics is a mix of alleged insider testimonies, declassified documents, and the interpretation of UFO sightings and encounters. However, much of this evidence is contested and remains speculative, leading to ongoing debate within both the UFO community and mainstream academia.

Whistle-blower Testimonies: A significant portion of exopolitical discourse relies on the testimonies of alleged whistle-blowers who claim to have direct knowledge of government interactions with extraterrestrials. These individuals often describe working on secret projects, witnessing alien technology, or being involved in negotiations with extraterrestrial beings. While these testimonies are compelling to some, they are also difficult to verify, and skeptics often question the credibility of the sources.

Declassified Documents: Some exopolitics researchers point to declassified government documents as evidence of extraterrestrial involvement in global affairs. These documents often reference UFO sightings, military encounters with unidentified aerial phenomena (UAPs), and the formation of task forces to study these incidents. While the existence of such documents is undisputed, their interpretation varies widely. Some see them as proof of extraterrestrial presence, while others argue that they reflect more mundane concerns, such as foreign technology or psychological operations.

UFO Sightings and Encounters: The global phenomenon of UFO sightings is another pillar of exopolitics. Proponents argue that the sheer number and consistency of reports, coupled with the occasional involvement of credible witnesses (such as pilots or military personnel), suggest that something beyond conventional explanation is occurring. However, the lack of definitive physical evidence, such as extraterrestrial artifacts or clear, unambiguous footage, makes it challenging to draw firm conclusions.

Skepticism and Alternative Explanations: Mainstream scholars and skeptics often argue that exopolitics is based on speculation, conspiracy theories, and misinterpretations of evidence. They suggest that the phenomena attributed to extraterrestrial influence could be explained by human psychology, government secrecy related to advanced military technology, or the influence of popular culture. The lack of peer-reviewed research and rigorous scientific methodology in exopolitics further complicates its acceptance in academic circles.

Implications for Humanity

If the ideas proposed by exopolitics were to be validated, the implications for humanity would be profound and far-reaching:

Global Governance and Power Structures: Confirmation of extraterrestrial contact would likely lead to significant changes in global governance. Existing institutions might need to adapt or be replaced by new structures capable of managing interstellar relations. The balance of power among nations could shift dramatically, depending on which countries have access to extraterrestrial technology or alliances. Questions about sovereignty, the role of multinational corporations, and the influence of global elites would also come to the forefront.

Technological Advancement and Societal Change: Access to extraterrestrial technology could trigger a new era of rapid technological advancement, with the potential to solve many of humanity's most pressing problems, such as energy scarcity, environmental degradation, and disease. However, it could also exacerbate existing inequalities, lead to new forms of warfare, or create unforeseen ethical dilemmas. The societal impact of such advancements would likely be profound, reshaping everything from the economy to education to individual lifestyles.

Cultural and Religious Repercussions: The confirmation of extraterrestrial civilizations would challenge many of humanity's cultural and religious beliefs. It could lead to a re-examination of humanity's place in the universe, the origins of life, and the nature of consciousness. Religious institutions might need to reconcile their teachings with the existence of extraterrestrial beings, potentially leading to new interpretations or even the emergence of new belief systems.

Human Identity and Purpose: On a more personal level, the knowledge that humanity is not alone in the universe could lead to profound shifts in how individuals perceive themselves and their purpose. It could foster a sense of unity and collective identity among humans, as well as a greater emphasis on planetary stewardship and the protection of Earth. Alternatively, it could also lead to existential anxiety or a sense of insignificance in the face of a vast, populated cosmos.

Ethical and Moral Challenges: The interaction with extraterrestrial civilizations would raise complex ethical and moral questions. How should humanity treat extraterrestrial beings? What rights should they have? How should humans handle the potential dangers of advanced technology? The answers to these questions would have significant implications for international law, human rights, and the ethical frameworks that guide human behavior.

Exopolitics represents a bold and speculative attempt to grapple with the potential reality of extraterrestrial contact and its implications for global politics, society, and humanity's future. While the field remains controversial and largely outside the mainstream, it raises important questions about government secrecy, the possibility of hidden knowledge, and the future of human civilization in a potentially populated universe.

For proponents of exopolitics, the field offers a framework for understanding and preparing for the challenges and opportunities that extraterrestrial contact could bring. It calls for greater transparency, the development of new diplomatic and governance structures, and a rethinking of humanity's place in the cosmos.

For sceptics, exopolitics serves as a reminder of the need for critical thinking, evidence-based research, and caution in interpreting extraordinary claims. The lack of concrete proof and the speculative nature of many exopolitical theories underscore the challenges of separating fact from fiction in the realm of UFOs and extraterrestrial life.

As humanity continues to explore the universe and search for signs of extraterrestrial life, the questions raised by exopolitics will likely remain relevant. Whether or not there is truth to the claims of government contact with alien civilizations, the field encourages us to consider the broader implications of such an encounter. It challenges us to think about how humanity would respond to the discovery of intelligent life beyond Earth, how our political and social systems might need to adapt, and what it would mean for our understanding of ourselves and our place in the cosmos.

The Future of Exopolitics

As we move further into the 21st century, the field of exopolitics may continue to evolve, influenced by new discoveries in space exploration, advancements in technology, and changes in global geopolitics. Several potential developments could shape the future of exopolitics:

Space Exploration and Discoveries: Ongoing space missions, such as those conducted by NASA, ESA, and private space companies like SpaceX, could provide new data that either supports or challenges the claims made by exopolitics. The discovery of microbial life on Mars, the detection of bio-signatures in the atmospheres of exoplanets, or even direct evidence of extraterrestrial technology would have profound implications for the field. Such discoveries could lend credibility to exopolitical theories or force a re-evaluation of existing assumptions.

Advancements in Communication and Technology: As technology continues to advance, new tools and methods for detecting extraterrestrial signals or analyzing unexplained phenomena may emerge. These advancements could lead to breakthroughs in our understanding of potential extraterrestrial contacts. Additionally, the development of artificial intelligence and quantum computing could open up new possibilities for simulating and understanding the dynamics of interstellar diplomacy and communication.

Global Political and Social Change: The changing landscape of global politics, particularly in response to challenges like climate change, pandemics, and economic inequality, could influence the discourse around exopolitics. As nations and international organizations grapple with these issues, the idea of extraterrestrial contact might be viewed through the lens of global cooperation and collective problem-solving. A shift towards more transparent governance and a greater emphasis on global unity could also create a more favorable environment for the disclosure of any hidden extraterrestrial knowledge.

Cultural Shifts and Public Perception: Public interest in UFOs and extraterrestrial life has been growing, fueled in part by recent disclosures and declassifications of UAP-related information by governments around the world. As this interest continues to rise, exopolitics could gain greater visibility and legitimacy as a field of study. The increasing acceptance of the possibility of extraterrestrial life in popular culture may also lead to a more open-minded approach to exopolitical theories.

Academic and Interdisciplinary Engagement: While exopolitics is currently on the fringes of mainstream academia, there is potential for greater interdisciplinary engagement. Scholars from fields such as political science, international relations, sociology, and anthropology could contribute valuable insights into the potential implications of extraterrestrial contact. By applying rigorous methodologies and theoretical frameworks, these disciplines could help bridge the gap between speculation and evidence, providing a more grounded approach to exopolitics.

Exopolitics, with its focus on the potential political and diplomatic implications of extraterrestrial contact, offers a unique perspective on some of the most profound questions facing humanity. While it remains a speculative and controversial field, its exploration of government secrecy, extraterrestrial influence, and the future of global governance challenges us to think critically about our place in the universe and the potential for interactions with other intelligent beings.

As our understanding of the cosmos continues to expand, and as humanity's technological capabilities grow, the questions raised by exopolitics will likely become increasingly relevant. Whether or not extraterrestrial contact has already occurred, the possibility of such an event in the future compels us to consider the ethical, legal, and societal implications of engaging with civilizations beyond our own.

Exopolitics encourages us to envision a future where humanity is not alone in the universe, where the boundaries of international relations extend beyond Earth, and where the challenges of diplomacy, ethics, and governance take on a truly cosmic dimension. It invites us to prepare for the unknown, to remain open to the possibilities that lie beyond our current understanding, and to approach the future with both caution and curiosity.

In the end, the exploration of exopolitics is not just about extraterrestrial life; it is about the potential evolution of humanity itself, as we confront the mysteries of the cosmos and our place within it. Whether through the lens of skepticism or belief, exopolitics offers a compelling framework for thinking about the future of our species and the profound changes that could come with the discovery of life beyond Earth.

The Vatican's Role: Secrets in Religion and Alien Life

The intersection of religion and the possibility of extraterrestrial life has long been a topic of intrigue and speculation, and within this realm, the Vatican's role has drawn significant attention. As one of the most influential religious institutions in the world, the Vatican has a unique position in the discussion about the implications of discovering intelligent life beyond Earth. The idea that the Vatican might possess secret knowledge regarding extraterrestrial life or be preparing for such a revelation touches on both religious doctrine and the broader question of how humanity would reconcile its spiritual beliefs with the existence of alien civilizations. This chapter explores the Vatican's historical and contemporary stance on extraterrestrial life, the role of religion in the broader UFO discourse, and the implications of potential Vatican involvement in the secrecy surrounding alien encounters.

Historical Context: The Vatican and the Cosmos

The Catholic Church has a long history of engagement with astronomy and the study of the cosmos. The Vatican Observatory, one of the oldest astronomical research institutions in the world, was established in the 16th century. The Church's interest in astronomy dates back even further, to the medieval period, when scholars within the Church sought to understand the heavens as a way of exploring God's creation. This historical involvement in astronomy has laid the groundwork for the Vatican's modern engagement with the possibility of extraterrestrial life. The Church has, over the centuries, navigated the complex relationship between science and faith, often adapting its teachings in response to new scientific discoveries. This adaptability suggests that the Vatican could play a significant role in framing the theological implications of discovering intelligent life beyond Earth.

The Vatican's Official Stance on Extraterrestrial Life

In recent years, several high-ranking officials within the Vatican have spoken openly about the possibility of extraterrestrial life. This marks a shift from earlier eras, when such discussions might have been considered heretical or speculative.

Statements from Vatican Officials: In 2008, the Vatican's chief astronomer, Father José Gabriel Funes, made headlines when he stated that the existence of extraterrestrial life would not contradict Catholic doctrine. He suggested that God's creation could extend to other intelligent beings and that such beings, if they exist, would be part of the same divine plan as humanity. Funes' statements reflected a growing openness within the Church to consider the possibility that life could exist elsewhere in the universe.

Theological Considerations: The Vatican has also considered the theological implications of extraterrestrial life. If intelligent beings exist on other planets, questions arise about their relationship with God, their understanding of morality and sin, and whether they, like humans, are in need of salvation. Some theologians within the Church have speculated that extraterrestrial beings might have their own unique relationship with God, independent of humanity's narrative of sin and redemption. This line of thought allows for the possibility that different forms of intelligent life might have their own religious experiences and beliefs.

Preparation for Disclosure?: The Vatican's engagement with the topic of extraterrestrial life has led some to speculate that the Church might be preparing for a future disclosure event, in which the existence of extraterrestrial civilizations is publicly confirmed. The idea that the Vatican might possess secret knowledge about extraterrestrial life, possibly held in the vast archives of the Vatican Library, has fueled numerous conspiracy theories.

These theories suggest that the Church could be involved in a broader effort to manage the public reaction to such a revelation, ensuring that it aligns with religious and ethical principles.

The Vatican and UFOs: Secrecy and Speculation

Beyond the official statements and theological considerations, there are more speculative theories about the Vatican's role in the secrecy surrounding UFOs and alien encounters. These theories often intersect with broader conspiracy narratives about government cover-ups and the involvement of religious institutions in controlling information.

The Vatican Archives: The Vatican Secret Archives, now known as the Vatican Apostolic Archives, have long been a source of fascination and speculation. These archives contain centuries' worth of documents, including correspondence, manuscripts, and records that are not accessible to the general public. Some theorists speculate that these archives might contain evidence of extraterrestrial contact, hidden knowledge about the cosmos, or even records of ancient alien encounters described in religious texts. While there is no concrete evidence to support these claims, the mystery surrounding the archives fuels ongoing speculation.

Biblical References and Ancient Aliens: Some researchers and theorists argue that certain passages in the Bible and other religious texts could be interpreted as references to extraterrestrial beings or encounters. For example, the descriptions of "angels" or "heavenly beings" descending from the sky, or the visions of prophets like Ezekiel, have been reinterpreted by some as potential accounts of ancient alien contact. Proponents of this theory suggest that the Vatican may be aware of these interpretations and is either suppressing or preparing to reveal this knowledge.

Religious Influence on Disclosure: If extraterrestrial life were to be confirmed, the Vatican's role in shaping the narrative could be significant. The Church's moral and ethical authority, particularly among the world's 1.3 billion Catholics, means that it could play a key role in guiding how humanity understands and responds to the discovery. The Vatican could potentially work with other global institutions to ensure that the disclosure of extraterrestrial life is framed in a way that supports global stability, ethical considerations, and religious continuity.

Implications of Vatican Involvement in Extraterrestrial Disclosure

If the Vatican were to be involved in the disclosure of extraterrestrial life, the implications would be profound, not only for the Catholic Church but for global society as a whole:

Religious Adaptation and Unity: The Vatican's involvement could help to bridge the gap between religious beliefs and the scientific reality of extraterrestrial life. The Church's ability to adapt its teachings to new scientific discoveries could serve as a model for other religious institutions, promoting a sense of unity and continuity in the face of potentially disruptive revelations. The Vatican's framing of extraterrestrial life as part of God's creation could help to mitigate fear and promote a positive, inclusive understanding of humanity's place in the universe.

Ethical Leadership: The Vatican's longstanding focus on ethics and morality could position it as a leader in the global conversation about how to interact with extraterrestrial civilizations. Questions about the rights of extraterrestrial beings, the ethical use of alien technology, and the potential impact on human society would require thoughtful, principled leadership. The Vatican's influence could help to ensure that these discussions are grounded in a moral framework that prioritizes the dignity of all life.

Potential Challenges to Doctrine: While the Vatican has shown a willingness to engage with the possibility of extraterrestrial life, such a revelation could still pose challenges to certain aspects of Catholic doctrine. For example, the question of original sin and the need for salvation might need to be reinterpreted in light of the existence of other intelligent beings. Additionally, the discovery of civilizations with their own religious or spiritual practices could lead to a re-examination of the universality of Christian teachings. These challenges would require the Church to navigate a delicate balance between tradition and innovation.

Global Influence and Perception: The Vatican's involvement in extraterrestrial disclosure could enhance its global influence, positioning the Church as a key player in one of the most significant events in human history. However, it could also lead to increased scrutiny and criticism, particularly if the Church is perceived as withholding information or being part of a larger cover-up. The way in which the Vatican handles its role in this potential scenario could have lasting effects on its reputation and its relationship with both believers and non-believers.

The Vatican's role in the discussion of extraterrestrial life is a fascinating intersection of religion, science, and speculation. As one of the most influential religious institutions in the world, the Vatican has a unique capacity to shape how humanity understands the potential discovery of intelligent life beyond Earth. Whether through its official statements, theological reflections, or its more mysterious and secretive aspects, the Vatican is poised to play a significant role in the unfolding narrative of extraterrestrial contact.

For believers, the Vatican's engagement with the possibility of extraterrestrial life offers reassurance that their faith can coexist with scientific discoveries. For sceptics and conspiracy theorists, the Vatican's involvement raises questions about secrecy, control, and the hidden knowledge that might lie within its archives. As humanity continues to explore the cosmos and search for signs of life beyond our planet, the Vatican's role in this quest will likely remain a topic of interest and debate.

Whether as a moral guide, a source of ethical leadership, or a guardian of ancient secrets, the Vatican's influence on the discussion of extraterrestrial life will shape how we reconcile our spiritual beliefs with the vast possibilities of the universe. The discovery of alien life, if it occurs, will be one of the most profound events in human history, and the Vatican's response to such a revelation could help to define the future of religion, ethics, and global unity in a rapidly changing world.

Time Travelers or Extraterrestrials?

The question of whether mysterious visitors to Earth might be time travelers from our own future or extraterrestrial beings from distant planets presents a fascinating intersection of science fiction, physics, and UFOlogy. While the idea of time travel has long been a staple of science fiction, advances in theoretical physics have made the concept at least plausible, albeit highly speculative.

This has led some researchers and enthusiasts to propose that what we perceive as encounters with extraterrestrial beings might, in fact, be interactions with humans from the future, traveling back in time to study or observe their own history. Conversely, the traditional view holds that these visitors are aliens from other star systems, traversing vast distances through space. This chapter explores the theories and evidence supporting both possibilities, the implications of each, and how these ideas challenge our understanding of time, space, and reality itself.

The Concept of Time Travel

Time travel, while a popular concept in fiction, is rooted in complex scientific theories, particularly those related to general relativity. According to Einstein's theory of general relativity, time and space are interconnected, forming a four-dimensional fabric known as spacetime. Massive objects, such as planets and stars, cause spacetime to curve, and this curvature affects the flow of time. In theory, if one could manipulate spacetime—perhaps by traveling at speeds close to the speed of light or by navigating through a wormhole—it might be possible to travel forward or backward in time.

Physicists have speculated about various mechanisms that could allow time travel, such as:

Wormholes: Wormholes, also known as Einstein-Rosen bridges, are hypothetical tunnels in spacetime that could connect distant points in space and time. If a stable wormhole could be created or discovered, it might allow for travel between different times or locations in the universe. However, the existence of wormholes remains theoretical, and even if they do exist, they might be extremely unstable or impossible to traverse.

Time Dilation: Time dilation, a consequence of Einstein's theory of relativity, occurs when an object approaches the speed of light. Time for the object slows down relative to an observer at rest. This means that, in theory, a spaceship traveling close to the speed of light could experience time much more slowly than on Earth, allowing its occupants to "travel" into the future. However, this does not allow for travel into the past.

Closed Timelike Curves: Some solutions to the equations of general relativity suggest the possibility of closed timelike curves—paths through spacetime that loop back on themselves, theoretically allowing for time travel to the past. These ideas remain speculative and face numerous paradoxes and challenges, such as the famous "grandfather paradox," which questions what would happen if a time traveler were to alter the past in such a way that it prevents their own existence.

Time Travelers as an Explanation for UFOs

The theory that UFOs might be piloted by time travelers rather than extraterrestrials offers a unique perspective on the phenomenon. Proponents of this idea suggest that what we interpret as encounters with aliens might actually be interactions with humans from a distant future, who have developed the technology to travel back in time.

Advanced Human Evolution: One argument in favor of the time traveler theory is that the beings often described in UFO encounters—small, large-headed, and humanoid—could be future humans who have undergone significant evolutionary changes.

The large heads and small bodies could reflect adaptations to a future environment, possibly one where intelligence has increased, and physical strength is less important.

Studying the Past: Time travelers from the future might be visiting our era to study historical events, observe human behavior, or gather data about their own ancestors. This would explain why UFO sightings often seem to focus on specific locations or events, such as nuclear facilities, where significant technological or historical activities are occurring.

Non-Interference Policy: The idea of a "prime directive" similar to the one in *Star Trek*—a policy of non-interference in past events—might explain why time travelers do not make open contact with humanity. They might be avoiding actions that could alter the timeline or create paradoxes that would affect their own existence.

Temporal Paradoxes: The time traveler theory raises interesting questions about the potential for paradoxes. For example, what if a time traveler's actions in our time inadvertently cause significant changes to the future? Theoretical physicists debate whether such paradoxes could occur, with some suggesting that the universe might prevent paradoxes through mechanisms we do not yet understand, while others propose that time travel might lead to the creation of alternate timelines or parallel universes.

Extraterrestrials as an Explanation for UFOs

The more traditional interpretation of UFO encounters is that they involve beings from other star systems, traveling across vast distances through space to visit Earth. This theory, while also speculative, is grounded in the vastness of the universe and the possibility that intelligent life might exist elsewhere.

Interstellar Travel: The concept of extraterrestrials visiting Earth hinges on the idea that these beings have developed technology capable of interstellar travel. This could involve faster-than-light travel, the use of wormholes, or other advanced propulsion systems that are currently beyond human capabilities. The distances involved are immense, but given the age and scale of the universe, it is conceivable that civilizations far older and more advanced than ours might have found ways to overcome these challenges.

Diverse Biological Forms: Unlike the time traveler theory, which assumes that UFO occupants are human, the extraterrestrial hypothesis allows for a wide variety of biological forms. Reports of different types of alien beings—ranging from the familiar Greys to reptilian and insectoid entities—suggest that if these encounters are real, they might involve multiple species from different parts of the galaxy.

Motivations for Contact: The motivations behind extraterrestrial contact could vary widely, from scientific research and exploration to more complex objectives that we might not fully understand. Some theories suggest that extraterrestrials might be interested in Earth's biodiversity, human culture, or technological development. Others propose that they could be monitoring our planet for potential threats, such as nuclear war or environmental collapse.

The Fermi Paradox: The Fermi Paradox questions why, given the high probability of extraterrestrial civilizations in the universe, we have not yet observed clear evidence of their existence. The UFO phenomenon is sometimes cited as a potential solution to this paradox, suggesting that extraterrestrials have visited Earth but have chosen to remain largely undetected, either to avoid interfering with human development or for reasons related to their own goals and policies.

The Intersection of Time Travel and Extraterrestrial Theories

Some researchers propose a hybrid theory that combines elements of both time travel and extraterrestrial visitation. This theory suggests that advanced civilizations might have mastered both space travel and time travel, allowing them to traverse not only vast distances but also different points in time.

Multi-Dimensional Beings: One possibility is that the beings encountered in UFO sightings are not only from another planet but also from another time or dimension. They might have the ability to move through both space and time, giving them a unique perspective on the universe and enabling them to visit different eras in human history.

The Simulation Hypothesis: Another idea that intersects with both time travel and extraterrestrial theories is the simulation hypothesis—the notion that our reality might be a simulated environment created by an advanced civilization. If this is the case, the beings we perceive as aliens or time travelers might be avatars or observers within the simulation, capable of manipulating its parameters, including time and space.

Temporal Civilizations: Some theorists speculate about the existence of temporal civilizations—societies that exist outside the conventional flow of time. These civilizations might have developed the ability to navigate time as easily as we navigate space, allowing them to observe or interact with different points in history without being bound by the limitations of linear time.

Implications for Our Understanding of Reality

The debate over whether UFOs are piloted by time travelers or extraterrestrials touches on some of the most profound questions about the nature of reality, time, and existence:

The Nature of Time: If time travel is possible, it challenges our understanding of time as a linear progression from past to future. The existence of time travelers would imply that the past, present, and future coexist in some way, and that time might be more like a landscape that can be navigated rather than a one-way journey.

The Limits of Human Knowledge: Both time travel and extraterrestrial theories suggest that there are aspects of reality that are currently beyond human comprehension. Whether it's the ability to traverse vast distances in space or the manipulation of time, these ideas push the boundaries of what we consider possible, highlighting the limitations of our current scientific understanding.

Ethical and Philosophical Questions: The possibility of encountering beings from the future or from other worlds raises significant ethical and philosophical questions. How should we interact with such beings? What rights do they have? How would their existence alter our perception of humanity's place in the universe? These questions challenge us to think deeply about our responsibilities as a species and our role in the broader cosmos.

The question of whether mysterious visitors are time travelers or extraterrestrials presents a fascinating and complex puzzle, one that intersects with cutting-edge science, ancient philosophical questions, and the enduring human fascination with the unknown. Both theories offer intriguing possibilities and challenge our understanding of time, space, and reality.

The time traveler hypothesis suggests that our future descendants may have mastered the ability to move through time, using this technology to visit their past—our present—for reasons we can only speculate about. This theory raises profound questions about the nature of time, causality, and the ethics of interacting with one's own history. The extraterrestrial hypothesis, on the other hand, posits that advanced civilizations from other parts of the universe have developed the technology to traverse the vast distances of space and have chosen to visit or monitor Earth for reasons that may range from scientific curiosity to more complex motivations that we might not fully understand. This theory challenges us to consider the possibility that we are not alone in the universe and that intelligent life exists beyond our planet, potentially in forms that are vastly different from our own.

The Broader Impact of These Theories

Whether one leans towards the time traveler hypothesis, the extraterrestrial hypothesis, or a combination of both, the implications of these ideas are far-reaching and multifaceted, touching on science, philosophy, religion, and the future of humanity.

Scientific Exploration and Innovation: The exploration of these theories encourages advancements in science and technology. For instance, the possibility of time travel, while speculative, drives research in theoretical physics, particularly in areas like quantum mechanics, general relativity, and the study of spacetime. Similarly, the pursuit of interstellar travel has spurred innovations in propulsion technology, materials science, and our understanding of the cosmos. These areas of research, even if they do not lead directly to time travel or extraterrestrial contact, could yield breakthroughs with significant practical applications.

Philosophical and Ethical Considerations: Both theories raise deep philosophical questions about the nature of existence, the ethics of interaction with other beings (whether from another time or another world), and the responsibilities of humanity in the broader context of the universe. If time travel is possible, we must grapple with the potential consequences of altering the past and the ethical implications of such actions. If extraterrestrial civilizations exist and are visiting Earth, we must consider how to engage with them in a way that is respectful, ethical, and mindful of the potential impact on both human society and the alien beings.

Cultural and Religious Responses: The discovery of time travelers or extraterrestrial beings would have profound effects on global culture and religion. Religious institutions might need to reinterpret their teachings in light of such revelations, particularly with regard to the nature of life, the universe, and humanity's place within it. Cultures around the world might experience a paradigm shift as they incorporate the existence of other intelligent beings into their worldviews, leading to new forms of art, literature, and philosophy that reflect these expanded horizons.

The Future of Human Civilization: If either time travel or extraterrestrial contact is possible, it could have significant implications for the future of humanity. Time travel could offer a way to learn from the past and avoid repeating mistakes, potentially guiding us towards a more enlightened and sustainable future. Contact with extraterrestrials could introduce new technologies, ideas, and perspectives that could help humanity solve some of its most pressing challenges, such as climate change, resource scarcity, and global conflict.

Psychological and Sociological Impact: The realization that we are either being visited by beings from the future or by extraterrestrial civilizations could have a profound psychological impact on individuals and societies. For some, this could lead to a sense of awe and wonder, a renewed interest in science and exploration, or a deeper connection to the cosmos. For others, it could cause anxiety, fear, or existential uncertainty as long-held beliefs are challenged.

Sociologists and psychologists would need to study these effects to help societies navigate the potential upheaval that such revelations could bring.

The debate over whether mysterious visitors are time travelers or extraterrestrials is more than just a question of who or what these beings are—it is a gateway to some of the most profound and challenging questions humanity has ever faced. These theories push the boundaries of our understanding of the universe, forcing us to reconsider the nature of time, space, and reality itself. They invite us to explore new possibilities, to imagine futures where humanity is not isolated in time or space, but part of a larger, more complex tapestry of existence.

Whether the ultimate truth lies in one theory, the other, or somewhere in between, the exploration of these ideas has already had a significant impact on science, philosophy, and culture. It has driven innovation, inspired art and literature, and challenged us to think more deeply about our place in the universe. As we continue to explore these mysteries, we may find that the answers not only reshape our understanding of UFOs and other phenomena but also lead to new discoveries about the fundamental nature of reality itself.

In the end, the question of whether these visitors are time travelers or extraterrestrials is less about choosing one explanation over the other and more about embracing the spirit of inquiry and wonder that drives us to explore the unknown. It is a reminder that, despite all our advances, there is still much we do not know—and that the search for knowledge, whether it takes us across the stars or through the corridors of time, is one of humanity's greatest endeavors.

The Galactic Council: A Universal Government?

The concept of a "Galactic Council" or "Galactic Federation" has become a popular idea in UFOlogy, conspiracy theories, and some new age spiritual beliefs. This hypothetical entity is often described as a universal governing body, composed of representatives from various advanced extraterrestrial civilizations, tasked with overseeing the affairs of different planets, including Earth. The Galactic Council is believed by some to be a benevolent force, guiding the evolution of less advanced species and ensuring the peaceful coexistence of civilizations across the galaxy. Others see it as a powerful organization that monitors human activity, intervening only when necessary to prevent catastrophic events or to maintain a cosmic balance. This chapter explores the origins of the Galactic Council concept, the various interpretations and theories surrounding it, and the implications such a universal government would have on humanity and our understanding of the cosmos.

Origins of the Galactic Council Concept

The idea of a Galactic Council or Federation likely has its roots in both science fiction and spiritual movements. In science fiction, the concept of interstellar federations, alliances, and councils is a common theme, with examples found in popular franchises such as *Star Trek* and *Star Wars*. These stories often depict a galaxy populated by diverse civilizations that have come together to form a governing body, usually with the goals of maintaining peace, advancing shared interests, and managing interspecies relations.

On the spiritual side, the concept of a Galactic Council has been embraced by certain new age and metaphysical communities. Channelers, individuals who claim to communicate with extraterrestrial or higher-dimensional beings, often speak of a Galactic Council that is working behind the scenes to guide humanity's evolution and to prepare us for eventual integration into the broader cosmic community. This version of the Galactic Council is typically depicted as a benevolent force, concerned with the spiritual and moral development of humanity.

Key Concepts of the Galactic Council

The idea of a Galactic Council encompasses several key concepts and theories, each of which offers a different perspective on what such an entity might be and how it could operate:

A Cosmic United Nations: The most common interpretation of the Galactic Council is that it functions similarly to the United Nations, but on a galactic scale. This council would be composed of representatives from various extraterrestrial civilizations, each bringing their unique perspectives and concerns to the table. The council's primary objectives would be to promote peace, prevent interstellar conflicts, and foster cooperation among the different species. Decisions made by the council would be aimed at benefiting the galaxy as a whole, ensuring that no single civilization dominates or exploits others.

Guardians of Evolution: In some interpretations, the Galactic Council is seen as a group of highly advanced beings who oversee the evolution of less developed species, including humanity. These beings are thought to possess a deep understanding of the universe and the laws that govern it, and they work to ensure that civilizations evolve in a way that is harmonious with these natural laws. The council might intervene in human affairs to prevent destructive behaviors, such as nuclear war or environmental degradation, that could hinder our spiritual or technological progress.

Non-Interference Policy: Similar to the "prime directive" in *Star Trek*, some theories suggest that the Galactic Council operates under a strict policy of non-interference in the internal affairs of less advanced civilizations. This policy would be based on the idea that each species must be allowed to develop naturally, without external influence that could disrupt their cultural or technological evolution. However, the council might choose to intervene in extreme cases where the survival of a species or the stability of the galaxy is at risk.

Humanity's Role and Integration: A recurring theme in discussions of the Galactic Council is the idea that humanity is on the verge of joining this cosmic community. Proponents of this view argue that Earth is undergoing a period of rapid change, both technologically and spiritually, that will eventually lead to our acceptance into the council. This transition is often depicted as a time of great challenge but also great opportunity, as humanity must prove itself ready to take its place among the stars.

Contact and Disclosure: The question of whether the Galactic Council has already made contact with Earth is a topic of much debate. Some believe that certain world governments, particularly those of major powers like the United States, are aware of the council's existence and may even be in communication with it. This theory ties into broader conspiracy narratives about government secrecy and the potential for future disclosure of extraterrestrial presence on Earth. Others suggest that contact with the council has been made on an individual level, with certain people—such as channelers or mystics—receiving messages or guidance from these advanced beings.

Evidence and Skepticism

The concept of the Galactic Council, like many ideas in UFOlogy and the paranormal, is difficult to substantiate with concrete evidence. Most of the information about the council comes from anecdotal accounts, channeling sessions, and interpretations of various spiritual texts. This lack of empirical evidence has led to skepticism from the scientific community and those who prefer more evidence-based approaches to understanding the universe.

Channeling and Spiritual Messages: Much of the information about the Galactic Council comes from individuals who claim to channel messages from extraterrestrial or higher-dimensional beings. These messages often describe the council as a benevolent force working to guide humanity through a period of transformation. While these accounts are compelling to those who believe in them, they are subjective and difficult to verify. Critics argue that channeling is more likely a psychological phenomenon than actual communication with extraterrestrials.

Government Conspiracies and Secret Knowledge: Some proponents of the Galactic Council theory suggest that governments are hiding evidence of extraterrestrial contact, including interactions with the council. This idea is often linked to broader conspiracy theories about UFOs, secret bases, and advanced technology being kept from the public. While there have been instances of government secrecy surrounding UFOs, such as the U.S. military's recent declassification of certain UFO-related documents, there is no definitive proof that these actions are related to a Galactic Council.

Cultural and Religious Influences: The concept of a Galactic Council may also be influenced by human cultural and religious ideas about governance, authority, and cosmic order. Many human societies have long imagined the existence of divine or cosmic councils—whether in the form of pantheons of gods, celestial bureaucracies, or angelic hierarchies—that oversee the affairs of the universe. The Galactic Council could be seen as a modern reinterpretation of these age-old ideas, adapted to fit contemporary beliefs about extraterrestrial life.

Implications of a Galactic Council

If a Galactic Council does exist, and if humanity were to become aware of or even integrated into such an entity, the implications would be profound:

Global Unity and Cooperation: The existence of a Galactic Council could serve as a catalyst for greater unity and cooperation among human nations. The realization that we are part of a larger cosmic community might encourage Earth's governments to set aside their differences and work together to address global challenges, such as climate change, poverty, and conflict. The council could offer guidance and support to help humanity navigate these challenges and prepare for integration into the interstellar community.

Technological and Spiritual Advancements: Membership in the Galactic Council might grant humanity access to advanced technologies and knowledge that could revolutionize our way of life. This could include new forms of energy, advanced medical treatments, or even technologies that allow for interstellar travel. Additionally, the council's emphasis on spiritual evolution could lead to a global shift in consciousness, with a greater focus on peace, compassion, and understanding.

Redefining Human Identity: The discovery of a Galactic Council would fundamentally change how humanity views itself. We would no longer see ourselves as the dominant species on a single planet but as one of many intelligent civilizations in a vast and interconnected universe. This shift in perspective could lead to a re-evaluation of our values, our goals, and our place in the cosmos.

Ethical and Moral Challenges: Being part of a Galactic Council would also bring new ethical and moral challenges. Humanity would need to consider its responsibilities not just to itself but to other civilizations and species. This could involve making difficult decisions about resource allocation, environmental stewardship, and the use of advanced technology. The council might also impose certain ethical standards that humanity would need to meet in order to be fully integrated into the cosmic community.

Potential Risks and Concerns: While the idea of a Galactic Council is generally presented in a positive light, there are potential risks and concerns associated with it. For example, there is the possibility that humanity could be seen as a threat or as unworthy of membership in the council, leading to isolation or even conflict. Additionally, the existence of such a powerful governing body raises questions about autonomy and freedom—would humanity be able to make its own decisions, or would we be subject to the will of more advanced civilizations?

The concept of a Galactic Council is a compelling and imaginative idea that taps into humanity's long-held fascination with the possibility of extraterrestrial life and our place in the universe. Whether seen as a cosmic United Nations, a group of guardians overseeing evolution, or a spiritual entity guiding humanity's progress, the Galactic Council represents an ideal of universal cooperation and harmony that many find appealing.

However, the lack of empirical evidence and the speculative nature of the concept means that it remains firmly in the realm of theory and belief. For some, the Galactic Council is a symbol of hope—a promise that humanity is not alone and that we are part of a larger, benevolent cosmic order. For others, it is a fascinating but ultimately unprovable idea, rooted more in our cultural and spiritual imaginations than in reality.

Regardless of its actual existence, the Galactic Council challenges us to think about the future of humanity in a broader, more cosmic context. It encourages us to consider the possibilities of interstellar cooperation, the ethical responsibilities of advanced civilizations, and the potential for humanity to evolve into a species capable of joining a universal government.

As we continue to explore the mysteries of the universe and seek answers to the profound questions about our place within it, the concept of a Galactic Council serves as a reminder of the vast possibilities that may lie ahead. Whether as a literal governing body or as a metaphor for the potential future of human civilization, the idea challenges us to expand our thinking beyond the confines of Earth and to consider the broader implications of our actions on a cosmic scale.

The Future of Humanity and the Galactic Council

As humanity advances technologically and explores deeper into space, the possibility of encountering other intelligent civilizations becomes more tangible. Whether through direct contact with extraterrestrial beings or through the discovery of evidence suggesting the existence of a Galactic Council, our understanding of the universe is poised for transformation. The idea of a Galactic Council compels us to prepare for a future where humanity might have to navigate complex interstellar relationships, deal with ethical dilemmas on a galactic scale, and redefine what it means to be human.

Preparation for Interstellar Diplomacy: If a Galactic Council or similar entity exists, it would be prudent for humanity to consider how we would approach interstellar diplomacy. This involves not just technological preparation, such as developing faster-than-light travel or advanced communication systems, but also preparing psychologically and culturally. Understanding the diversity of potential extraterrestrial cultures and value systems would be crucial in avoiding misunderstandings and fostering peaceful relations.

Ethical Frameworks for Intergalactic Interaction: Joining a Galactic Council would require humanity to develop or adopt new ethical frameworks that take into account the well-being of other civilizations and species. This could involve extending concepts like human rights to a broader category of "sentient rights," ensuring that our interactions with other species are guided by principles of respect, fairness, and mutual benefit. It might also mean reassessing our treatment of Earth and its ecosystems, recognizing that our actions could have repercussions that extend far beyond our planet.

Global Governance and Unity: The existence of a Galactic Council could serve as a catalyst for greater unity on Earth. The recognition that we are part of a larger cosmic community might encourage nations to work together more closely, fostering global governance structures that prioritize collaboration over competition. This could lead to the strengthening of international organizations, the establishment of new treaties, and a greater emphasis on solving global challenges that impact all of humanity.

Impact on Religion and Spirituality: The discovery of a Galactic Council would likely have a profound impact on religion and spirituality. Many religious traditions would need to reconcile their teachings with the existence of other intelligent beings and the idea of a universal governing body. Some might see the council as evidence of a divine plan that encompasses all of creation, while others might view it as a challenge to traditional beliefs. This could lead to the emergence of new spiritual movements or the adaptation of existing ones to incorporate these new realities.

The Role of Science and Exploration: Science would play a crucial role in our interactions with a Galactic Council, both in terms of technological advancement and in understanding the nature of the universe. Continued exploration of space, whether through telescopes, probes, or manned missions, would be essential in identifying potential members of the council and learning more about the broader galactic community. Scientific research would also be key in developing the technologies needed for interstellar travel and communication, as well as in addressing the challenges of living in a universe with multiple intelligent species.

The concept of a Galactic Council is both a fascinating and thought-provoking idea that stretches the boundaries of our imagination and our understanding of the universe. Whether it exists as a literal entity or as a symbolic representation of humanity's potential future, the Galactic Council encourages us to think beyond our current limitations and to consider the broader implications of our actions on a cosmic scale.

The notion of joining a universal government composed of diverse extraterrestrial civilizations challenges us to reflect on our own development as a species—technologically, ethically, and spiritually. It invites us to consider what it would mean to be part of a larger galactic community and how we would navigate the complexities of interstellar relations.

While the existence of a Galactic Council remains speculative, the questions it raises are deeply relevant to humanity's future. As we continue to explore space and seek answers to the mysteries of the cosmos, the idea of a Galactic Council serves as a powerful reminder of the possibilities that await us. It encourages us to prepare for a future that may be far more interconnected and expansive than we can currently imagine, and it challenges us to rise to the occasion as responsible and enlightened members of the cosmic community.

The Shadow Government: Who's really in Charge?

The concept of a "Shadow Government" is one of the most pervasive and intriguing ideas in conspiracy theory circles. It suggests that the real power and decision-making authority in a country, particularly in the United States, is not held by elected officials or public institutions but by a hidden network of powerful individuals and groups operating behind the scenes. These entities, often believed to include elements of the intelligence community, military-industrial complex, wealthy elites, and multinational corporations, allegedly exert control over government policies, economic systems, and even public perception. The idea of a Shadow Government intersects with various other conspiracy theories, including those related to UFOs, extraterrestrial contact, and the suppression of advanced technologies. This chapter delves into the origins of the Shadow Government theory, the key players believed to be involved, the evidence supporting or challenging these claims, and the broader implications for democracy and transparency in governance.

Origins of the Shadow Government Concept

The idea of a Shadow Government has its roots in the broader distrust of centralized power and the belief that certain individuals or groups wield disproportionate influence over national and international affairs. The concept gained prominence in the 20th century, particularly during periods of political turmoil and public skepticism about government transparency.

Post-World War II Developments: The end of World War II marked the beginning of the Cold War, a period characterized by secrecy, espionage, and the expansion of the intelligence community. The creation of the Central Intelligence Agency (CIA) in 1947 and the National Security Council (NSC) fueled concerns that these agencies, operating with little public oversight, might be forming a parallel structure of power within the government. The notion that these agencies could operate independently of, or even above, elected officials contributed to the development of the Shadow Government theory.

The Military-Industrial Complex: In his farewell address in 1961, President Dwight D. Eisenhower famously warned of the dangers posed by the "military-industrial complex"—a coalition of the defense industry, the military, and government officials that could exert undue influence over national policy. Eisenhower's warning resonated with those who feared that this complex might prioritize profit and power over the public good, potentially leading to a Shadow Government that served its own interests rather than those of the people.

Watergate and the Era of Distrust: The Watergate scandal in the 1970s, which led to the resignation of President Richard Nixon, further eroded public trust in the government. The revelation that high-ranking officials were involved in illegal activities and cover-ups reinforced the belief that powerful individuals could manipulate the government for their own purposes, operating outside the bounds of democratic accountability. This era of distrust set the stage for the widespread acceptance of Shadow Government theories in the years to come.

UFO Secrecy and Government Cover-ups: The belief that the government is hiding the truth about UFOs and extraterrestrial contact is closely linked to the Shadow Government theory. Many UFO researchers and enthusiasts argue that a secret group within the government, sometimes referred to as "Majestic 12" or "MJ-12," is responsible for managing and concealing information about alien encounters. This alleged group is believed to have access to advanced technologies and knowledge that are kept hidden from the public, furthering the idea that a Shadow Government controls key aspects of national security and scientific research.

Key Players in the Shadow Government

The Shadow Government theory suggests that a variety of entities and individuals, both within and outside of formal government structures, are involved in this hidden network of power. While the specifics vary depending on the theory, several key players are commonly cited:

Intelligence Agencies: The CIA, the National Security Agency (NSA), and other intelligence agencies are often believed to be central components of the Shadow Government. These agencies operate with a high degree of secrecy and autonomy, leading to concerns that they could be engaging in activities that are not subject to oversight by elected officials or the public. The intelligence community's involvement in covert operations, surveillance, and psychological warfare fuels suspicions that it plays a significant role in shaping policy behind the scenes.

The Military-Industrial Complex: Defense contractors, weapons manufacturers, and the military are frequently cited as major players in the Shadow Government. The vast sums of money involved in defense spending, combined with the close relationships between government officials and defense industry executives, have led to concerns that these entities wield significant influence over national security policies. The Shadow Government theory posits that this influence extends to decisions about war, peace, and the allocation of resources.

Wealthy Elites and Secret Societies: The idea that a small group of wealthy individuals and secret societies control global affairs is a common theme in Shadow Government theories. Organizations such as the Bilderberg Group, the Trilateral Commission, and the Council on Foreign Relations are often cited as examples of elite gatherings where decisions are made that impact the world without public input or awareness. These groups are believed to represent the interests of the global elite, who use their wealth and power to manipulate political and economic systems.

Multinational Corporations: Large multinational corporations, particularly those in the finance, technology, and energy sectors, are also seen as key players in the Shadow Government. These corporations are believed to exert influence over government policies through lobbying, campaign contributions, and control of the media. The theory suggests that these corporations prioritize profit over the public good and that their interests often align with those of the Shadow Government.

International Organizations and Global Governance: Some theories extend the concept of the Shadow Government to include international organizations such as the United Nations, the International Monetary Fund (IMF), and the World Bank. These organizations are seen as tools of the global elite, used to implement policies that serve the interests of the few at the expense of the many. The idea of a "New World Order," a global government controlled by a Shadow Government, is a common theme in these theories.

Evidence and Skepticism

The Shadow Government theory is supported by a variety of evidence, much of it circumstantial or anecdotal. While there are documented instances of government secrecy, corruption, and undue influence by powerful entities, the existence of a coordinated Shadow Government remains a matter of debate.

Documented Government Secrecy: There is no shortage of evidence that governments, particularly the U.S. government, engage in secrecy and covert operations. Declassified documents have revealed numerous instances of intelligence agencies conducting illegal or unethical activities, often without the knowledge or consent of elected officials. These revelations lend credence to the idea that certain elements within the government operate independently and with considerable power.

Influence of the Military-Industrial Complex: The influence of the military-industrial complex is well-documented, with defense contractors playing a significant role in shaping U.S. national security policy. The revolving door between government and industry, where officials move between roles in the public and private sectors, has raised concerns about conflicts of interest and the prioritization of corporate profits over public welfare.

Elitist Gatherings and Think Tanks: Organizations like the Bilderberg Group and the Council on Foreign Relations do exist and are known to host meetings attended by influential figures in politics, business, and academia. While these gatherings are often shrouded in secrecy, there is little concrete evidence that they function as a Shadow Government. Critics argue that these organizations are simply forums for discussion and that the decisions made at these meetings are not binding.

Skepticism and Alternative Explanations: Critics of the Shadow Government theory argue that it is based on a misunderstanding of how power operates in a complex, interconnected world. They suggest that what appears to be a coordinated conspiracy is often the result of overlapping interests, bureaucratic inefficiency, and the natural tendency of powerful entities to protect their own interests. Additionally, the lack of direct evidence for a Shadow Government leads many to dismiss the theory as a form of modern mythology, reflecting deep-seated anxieties about authority and control.

Implications of a Shadow Government

If a Shadow Government does exist, the implications for democracy, transparency, and public trust are profound:

Erosion of Democratic Institutions: The existence of a Shadow Government would suggest that democratic institutions are not functioning as intended, with real power concentrated in the hands of a few rather than distributed among the people. This would undermine the principles of representative democracy and raise questions about the legitimacy of elected officials and the policies they implement.

Lack of Accountability and Transparency: A Shadow Government operating behind the scenes would likely be immune to public oversight and accountability. This would allow it to pursue its own agenda without regard for the will of the people, potentially leading to policies that are harmful to the public or that serve the interests of a small elite.

Public Distrust and Disillusionment: The belief in a Shadow Government can contribute to widespread distrust of government and public institutions. When people feel that their voices are not heard and that the real power lies with hidden actors, they may become disillusioned with the political process and less likely to participate in civic life. This can create a cycle of apathy and disengagement, further weakening democratic governance.

Potential for Social Unrest: If the existence of a Shadow Government were to be confirmed, it could lead to significant social unrest. People might demand accountability from those in power, leading to protests, investigations, and potentially even the overthrow of existing political structures. The revelation of a Shadow Government could also exacerbate existing divisions within society, as different groups seek to assert their own vision of governance.

The concept of a Shadow Government taps into deep-seated fears and concerns about power, control, and the true nature of governance. While there is evidence to suggest that powerful individuals and groups exert significant influence over government policy, the existence of a coordinated Shadow Government remains speculative. Whether or not a Shadow Government exists, the theory raises important questions about the state of democracy, transparency, and accountability in modern governance.

The Disclosure Movement: Breaking the Silence

The Disclosure Movement is a global campaign advocating for the release of classified information regarding the existence of unidentified flying objects (UFOs), unidentified aerial phenomena (UAPs), and potential extraterrestrial contact. Proponents of the movement believe that governments, particularly the United States government, have been withholding critical information about UFOs and extraterrestrial encounters for decades. They argue that the public has a right to know the truth about these phenomena and that disclosing this information could have profound implications for science, religion, global politics, and humanity's understanding of its place in the universe. This chapter explores the origins and key figures of the Disclosure Movement, the evidence that has come to light, the challenges it faces, and the potential impact of successful disclosure.

Origins of the Disclosure Movement

The Disclosure Movement traces its roots to the early years of the modern UFO phenomenon, which began in the mid-20th century with high-profile sightings and incidents such as the 1947 Roswell incident and the formation of the U.S. government's Project Blue Book, an official study of UFOs conducted by the U.S. Air Force. Over time, as reports of UFO sightings and alleged encounters with extraterrestrials continued to surface, a growing number of researchers, activists, and former government insiders began to advocate for the release of information they believed was being kept secret.

The Roswell Incident: The 1947 crash of an unidentified object near Roswell, New Mexico, is often cited as a key event that fueled the Disclosure Movement. Initially reported as the recovery of a "flying disc," the U.S. military quickly retracted the statement, claiming the debris was from a weather balloon. This reversal sparked widespread speculation that the government was covering up the recovery of an extraterrestrial craft and possibly alien bodies. The Roswell incident remains one of the most famous and controversial UFO cases, symbolizing the belief that the government is hiding the truth about UFOs.

Project Blue Book and Other Investigations: Project Blue Book, which ran from 1952 to 1969, was the U.S. Air Force's official investigation into UFOs. Although the project concluded that most sightings could be explained by natural phenomena or human-made objects, it left a number of cases unresolved. The closure of Project Blue Book did little to quell public interest, and many researchers felt that the government had not fully disclosed what it knew about UFOs. Other government projects, such as the CIA's Robertson Panel and the U.K.'s Ministry of Defence's UFO desk, have also been criticized for downplaying or dismissing the UFO phenomenon.

The Role of Whistle-blowers: Over the years, several individuals claiming to be former government insiders or military personnel have come forward with stories of secret programs and encounters with extraterrestrial beings. These whistle-blowers have provided compelling, if often unverified, accounts of their experiences, further fueling the belief that the government is hiding information. Notable figures include Bob Lazar, who claimed to have worked on reverse-engineering alien technology at a secretive facility near Area 51, and Philip Corso, who asserted that the U.S. military recovered and studied alien technology following the Roswell crash.

The Emergence of the Disclosure Movement: The modern Disclosure Movement began to take shape in the 1990s, led by figures such as Dr. Steven Greer, a physician and ufologist who founded the Center for the Study of Extraterrestrial Intelligence (CSETI) and later the Disclosure Project. Dr. Greer and his organization aimed to bring together government, military, and intelligence insiders willing to testify about their knowledge of UFOs and extraterrestrial encounters.

In 2001, the Disclosure Project held a press conference at the National Press Club in Washington, D.C., where over 20 witnesses presented their testimonies, calling for the U.S. Congress to hold open hearings on the subject.

Key Figures and Organizations

The Disclosure Movement is supported by a diverse group of individuals and organizations, each contributing to the effort to bring the truth about UFOs and extraterrestrials to light.

Dr. Steven Greer: As the founder of CSETI and the Disclosure Project, Dr. Greer is one of the most prominent figures in the Disclosure Movement. He has dedicated his career to advocating for government transparency on the UFO issue and has produced several documentaries, including *Unacknowledged* and *Close Encounters of the Fifth Kind*, which explore the evidence for extraterrestrial contact and the suppression of this information by government agencies.

The Disclosure Project: Founded by Dr. Greer, the Disclosure Project aims to provide a platform for credible witnesses to share their experiences and knowledge of UFOs and extraterrestrial encounters. The organization has gathered hundreds of testimonies from former military personnel, government officials, and scientists who claim to have firsthand knowledge of secret programs and encounters with extraterrestrial beings.

To The Stars Academy of Arts & Science (TTSA): Co-founded by former Blink-182 musician Tom DeLonge, TTSA has played a significant role in bringing the UFO issue into the mainstream. The organization has focused on researching UAPs, declassifying government documents, and promoting the scientific study of these phenomena. TTSA was instrumental in the release of several Pentagon videos showing UAPs, which have since been confirmed as genuine by the U.S. Department of Defense.

Luis Elizondo: A former U.S. intelligence officer, Elizondo was the director of the Pentagon's Advanced Aerospace Threat Identification Program (AATIP), a secretive program that studied UAPs. After leaving the government, Elizondo became a public advocate for disclosure, working with TTSA and appearing in numerous media interviews to discuss the importance of studying UAPs and the need for greater government transparency.

Other Notable Figures: The Disclosure Movement has been supported by a wide range of individuals, including former Canadian Defense Minister Paul Hellyer, who publicly stated his belief in extraterrestrial visitation, and former Apollo astronaut Edgar Mitchell, who advocated for the release of classified information about UFOs and extraterrestrial encounters.

Evidence and Recent Developments

In recent years, the Disclosure Movement has gained momentum, thanks in part to the release of previously classified documents, high-profile government acknowledgments, and increased media coverage of UAPs.

Declassified Documents and Official Statements: The release of documents through the Freedom of Information Act (FOIA) and other means has provided new insights into government investigations of UFOs. In 2017, The New York Times published an article revealing the existence of AATIP, which reignited public interest in the UFO phenomenon. The Pentagon's subsequent confirmation of the program and the release of UAP videos further validated the concerns raised by the Disclosure Movement.

U.S. Government Acknowledgment of UAPs: In 2020, the U.S. Department of Defense established the Unidentified Aerial Phenomena Task Force (UAPTF) to investigate UAP sightings, marking a significant shift in the government's approach to the issue. In June 2021, the Office of the Director of National Intelligence (ODNI) released a report on UAPs, acknowledging that these phenomena are real and that many sightings remain unexplained. While the report did not confirm the existence of extraterrestrial life, it represented a step toward greater transparency.

Increased Media Coverage: The growing attention to UAPs in mainstream media has helped to legitimize the Disclosure Movement and bring the topic into public discourse. Major news outlets have covered the release of UAP videos, government reports, and statements from credible witnesses, making it more difficult for the government to dismiss or ignore the issue.

Public Perception and Demand for Transparency: As more information about UAPs and the government's investigations comes to light, public interest in the topic has surged. Polls show that a significant portion of the population believes in the existence of UFOs and supports greater transparency on the issue. This growing demand for disclosure puts pressure on governments to release more information and address the public's concerns.

Challenges and Obstacles

Despite the progress made by the Disclosure Movement, significant challenges and obstacles remain:

Government Secrecy and National Security Concerns: Governments, particularly the U.S. government, have long justified the secrecy surrounding UFOs and UAPs on the grounds of national security. They argue that disclosing certain information could reveal sensitive military capabilities, compromise intelligence sources, or create public panic. Overcoming these concerns is one of the biggest obstacles to full disclosure.

Skepticism and Disinformation: The Disclosure Movement faces skepticism from both the scientific community and the public. Many scientists remain cautious about endorsing the idea of extraterrestrial visitation, citing the lack of direct evidence and the potential for alternative explanations. Additionally, disinformation campaigns, whether intentional or not, have muddied the waters, making it difficult to discern fact from fiction.

The Complexity of the Phenomenon: UAPs and UFOs are complex phenomena that may involve a range of explanations, from natural atmospheric events to advanced human technology to extraterrestrial activity. This complexity makes it challenging to reach a consensus on the nature of these phenomena and to develop a coherent strategy for disclosure.

Fear of Social and Religious Disruption: Some argue that revealing the existence of extraterrestrial life could have profound social and religious implications, potentially disrupting established belief systems and causing societal unrest. Governments may be hesitant to disclose information that could lead to such widespread consequences.

The Potential Impact of Disclosure

If the Disclosure Movement achieves its goals and governments release full information about UFOs and potential extraterrestrial contact, the impact on society could be transformative:

Scientific Advancements: Disclosure could lead to breakthroughs in science and technology, particularly if it involves the release of information about advanced propulsion systems, energy sources, or materials science. These advancements could revolutionize various fields, from aerospace engineering to medicine, and could potentially solve some of humanity's most pressing challenges, such as energy scarcity and environmental degradation. If extraterrestrial technologies or knowledge are revealed, they might offer new insights into the nature of the universe, physics, and even the origins of life.

Global Unity and Cooperation: The confirmation of extraterrestrial life and the disclosure of previously hidden information could act as a unifying force for humanity. Faced with the reality that we are not alone in the universe, nations might be more inclined to collaborate on global issues, recognizing that our differences are trivial in comparison to the larger cosmic context. The need to present a united front in potential interstellar relations could drive greater international cooperation and peace efforts.

Religious and Philosophical Reconsideration: The disclosure of extraterrestrial contact would challenge many religious and philosophical beliefs. Religions around the world would need to grapple with the theological implications of intelligent life beyond Earth. Some religious institutions might see extraterrestrial life as part of a divine plan, while others might struggle to reconcile such a discovery with their doctrines. Philosophically, humanity would need to reconsider its place in the universe, potentially leading to new schools of thought and ethical considerations about our responsibilities as a species.

Cultural and Social Transformation: Disclosure could lead to a profound cultural and social transformation. Art, literature, and media would likely be influenced by the new reality of extraterrestrial existence, leading to a renaissance of creativity and exploration. Social structures might shift as people adapt to the knowledge that life exists beyond Earth, possibly leading to changes in how we view ourselves, our history, and our future.

Economic and Technological Impacts: The release of advanced technologies, if they exist, could have significant economic implications. New industries could emerge around these technologies, potentially leading to economic growth and job creation. However, there could also be disruptions, particularly if existing industries are rendered obsolete by new advancements. The transition to a new technological paradigm could be challenging, requiring careful management to ensure that the benefits are widely distributed.

Government Accountability and Transparency: Successful disclosure would likely lead to increased demands for government accountability and transparency, not only regarding UFOs but across a wide range of issues. The public might push for more openness in government operations, reducing the tolerance for secrecy and classified information. This could lead to a shift in how governments interact with their citizens, with greater emphasis on honesty and transparency.

Public Awareness and Education: As part of the disclosure process, there would be a need for public education about the implications of extraterrestrial contact and the scientific, technological, and social changes that might follow. Educational institutions would likely update their curricula to include new information about space, technology, and the broader implications of disclosure. Public discourse would expand to include these topics, leading to a more informed and engaged society.

The Disclosure Movement, with its goal of revealing the truth about UFOs, UAPs, and potential extraterrestrial contact, represents a significant challenge to the status quo of government secrecy and public ignorance. While the movement has made notable strides in recent years, particularly with the release of official documents and the acknowledgment of UAPs by government agencies, the ultimate goal of full disclosure remains elusive.

The potential impact of disclosure on science, religion, global politics, and society is profound. It could lead to unprecedented advancements in technology, a rethinking of humanity's place in the universe, and a new era of global cooperation. However, the movement also faces significant challenges, including government resistance, skepticism, and the complexity of the phenomena involved.

Whether or not the Disclosure Movement succeeds in its mission, it has already sparked a broader conversation about the role of government transparency, the potential for extraterrestrial life, and the future of humanity in a universe that may be far more populated than we have previously imagined. As this conversation continues, it will shape the way we think about our world and our place in the cosmos, pushing us to explore new frontiers of knowledge and understanding.

Cosmic Laws: The Rules of Extraterrestrial Engagement

The concept of "Cosmic Laws" refers to a set of hypothetical universal principles or guidelines that govern the interactions between different intelligent civilizations in the universe, particularly when it comes to contact with less advanced species such as humanity. These laws are often discussed within the context of UFOlogy, the Disclosure Movement, and speculative theories about extraterrestrial diplomacy. The idea is that advanced extraterrestrial civilizations, whether they belong to a Galactic Council or operate independently, adhere to a code of conduct that ensures peaceful coexistence, non-interference, and ethical behavior in their interactions with other species. This chapter explores the origins and interpretations of Cosmic Laws, the possible rules of engagement they might entail, and the implications of such laws for humanity's future encounters with extraterrestrial beings.

Origins of the Concept of Cosmic Laws

The idea of Cosmic Laws likely draws inspiration from both human legal systems and ethical philosophies, as well as from the principles depicted in science fiction and speculative thought. Throughout history, humans have developed codes of conduct to regulate behavior within societies, often extending these principles to international relations and warfare. The notion that similar rules might exist on a cosmic scale is a natural extension of this idea, particularly in the context of a universe that could be teeming with intelligent life.

The Prime Directive in Science Fiction: One of the most well-known examples of a Cosmic Law is the "Prime Directive" from the *Star Trek* franchise. This fictional law prohibits members of the United Federation of Planets from interfering with the natural development of less advanced civilizations. The Prime Directive embodies the principle of non-interference, ensuring that more advanced species do not impose their values, technologies, or social structures on those who are not yet ready for such advancements. This concept has resonated with many and serves as a template for the idea of Cosmic Laws in real-world discussions.

Ethical and Moral Philosophies: The idea of Cosmic Laws also draws from ethical and moral philosophies that emphasize the importance of fairness, justice, and the protection of the vulnerable. Concepts such as Kant's categorical imperative, which suggests that one should act according to principles that could be universally applied, and the Golden Rule, which advocates treating others as one would like to be treated, provide a foundation for thinking about how advanced civilizations might regulate their behavior toward others.

Theosophy and Esoteric Teachings: In theosophical and esoteric teachings, there is often mention of universal laws or cosmic principles that govern the order of the universe. These teachings suggest that the universe operates according to higher laws that reflect the will of a divine or cosmic intelligence. In this context, Cosmic Laws are seen as expressions of a higher moral order, guiding the interactions of all beings in the universe, including extraterrestrial civilizations.

Reports from Contactees and Channelers: Some individuals who claim to have had direct contact with extraterrestrial beings, either through physical encounters or channeling, have reported being told about the existence of Cosmic Laws. These beings allegedly describe these laws as governing the behavior of advanced species, particularly in their interactions with less advanced civilizations like humanity. These accounts often emphasize themes such as non-interference, the importance of free will, and the protection of planetary ecosystems.

Possible Rules of Cosmic Engagement

While the specifics of Cosmic Laws are purely speculative, several key principles are commonly discussed in the context of hypothetical extraterrestrial engagement. These principles reflect the ethical considerations that might govern how advanced civilizations interact with others in the universe.

Non-Interference and the Right to Develop Naturally: One of the most frequently cited Cosmic Laws is the principle of non-interference. This law would prohibit advanced civilizations from directly intervening in the natural development of less advanced species. The idea is that every civilization has the right to evolve at its own pace, without external influence that could disrupt its cultural, social, or technological trajectory. This principle ensures that species are not prematurely exposed to technologies or ideas they are not ready to handle, thereby preserving their autonomy and integrity.

Respect for Free Will: Another key principle often associated with Cosmic Laws is the respect for free will. This law would mandate that advanced civilizations cannot impose their will on others, whether through coercion, manipulation, or direct control. This respect for free will is seen as essential for ensuring that less advanced species have the freedom to make their own choices, learn from their mistakes, and determine their own destinies. Interference would only be permissible if explicitly invited by the species in question or in cases where non-interference would result in catastrophic harm.

Preservation of Life and Ecosystems: Cosmic Laws might also include guidelines for the preservation of life and ecosystems. This principle would recognize the intrinsic value of all life forms and the importance of maintaining the balance of planetary ecosystems. Advanced civilizations would be expected to avoid actions that could harm other species or disrupt their environments. This could involve prohibitions against the exploitation of natural resources, the introduction of invasive species, or the use of weapons of mass destruction.

Peaceful Conflict Resolution: In a universe where multiple intelligent civilizations coexist, conflicts are likely to arise. Cosmic Laws could establish protocols for peaceful conflict resolution, emphasizing diplomacy, negotiation, and mutual respect. The use of force would be restricted to defensive purposes, and efforts would be made to resolve disputes without resorting to violence. This principle would promote harmony and cooperation among different species, reducing the likelihood of interstellar wars.

The Sharing of Knowledge and Technology: While non-interference is a key principle, Cosmic Laws might also include provisions for the sharing of knowledge and technology, but only under specific conditions. Advanced civilizations could be allowed to share information that promotes peace, well-being, and sustainability, as long as it does not disrupt the natural development of the receiving species. This could involve the gradual introduction of new technologies or the sharing of knowledge that helps a species address existential threats, such as climate change or the potential for self-destruction.

Accountability and Cosmic Justice: Cosmic Laws would likely include mechanisms for accountability and justice, ensuring that civilizations adhere to these principles. This could involve a system of cosmic courts or councils where violations of Cosmic Laws are addressed, and appropriate measures are taken to remedy harm. The concept of cosmic justice would ensure that no civilization is above the law and that all actions are judged according to universally accepted principles of fairness and responsibility.

Implications for Humanity

The existence of Cosmic Laws, if real, would have profound implications for humanity and our potential interactions with extraterrestrial civilizations. These implications would influence our understanding of the universe, our ethical frameworks, and our future as a species.

Preparation for Contact: If Cosmic Laws govern the interactions between civilizations, humanity would need to prepare for contact with extraterrestrial beings by understanding and respecting these laws. This preparation would involve developing a more sophisticated ethical framework, improving our capacity for peaceful conflict resolution, and ensuring that our actions align with universal principles of non-interference and respect for life. Such preparation could also involve establishing global institutions dedicated to managing extraterrestrial relations and ensuring compliance with Cosmic Laws.

Re-evaluation of Human Laws and Ethics: The discovery of Cosmic Laws might prompt a re-evaluation of human legal and ethical systems. We would need to consider how our laws align with these universal principles and make adjustments to ensure that we are acting in accordance with the broader cosmic order. This could lead to the development of new international laws that prioritize the protection of the planet, the preservation of biodiversity, and the peaceful resolution of conflicts.

Global Unity and Cooperation: The realization that we are part of a larger cosmic community governed by universal laws could foster greater unity and cooperation among human nations. Recognizing that we are subject to the same Cosmic Laws as other intelligent species might encourage us to transcend our differences and work together to address global challenges. This unity could be essential for ensuring that humanity is seen as a responsible and ethical member of the cosmic community.

Cultural and Spiritual Transformation: The existence of Cosmic Laws might also lead to a cultural and spiritual transformation, as humanity begins to see itself as part of a larger, interconnected universe. This could inspire new forms of art, philosophy, and spirituality that reflect our place in the cosmos and our responsibilities to other forms of life. It could also lead to a shift in values, with greater emphasis on sustainability, harmony, and the pursuit of knowledge for the benefit of all.

Challenges of Compliance and Enforcement: Adhering to Cosmic Laws would likely present significant challenges, particularly in cases where human actions conflict with these principles. For example, practices such as warfare, environmental destruction, and exploitation of resources might need to be re-examined in light of Cosmic Laws. Ensuring compliance with these laws would require strong global governance, effective enforcement mechanisms, and a commitment to ethical behavior that transcends national interests.

The concept of Cosmic Laws offers a compelling vision of how advanced civilizations might regulate their interactions with one another, ensuring that these interactions are guided by principles of non-interference, respect for free will, preservation of life, and peaceful conflict resolution. Whether these laws are real or purely speculative, they challenge us to think deeply about the ethical implications of our actions as we explore the possibility of contact with extraterrestrial beings. For humanity, the existence of Cosmic Laws would represent both an opportunity and a responsibility. It would provide a framework for peaceful and ethical engagement with other civilizations, but it would also demand that we elevate our behavior to meet the standards of a broader cosmic order. As we continue to explore the universe and seek out potential contacts with other forms of intelligent life, the principles embodied in the idea of Cosmic Laws can serve as a guiding light, helping us navigate the complexities of interstellar relations with wisdom, compassion, and integrity.

Alien Agenda: What Do They Want from Us?

The concept of an "Alien Agenda" refers to the theories and speculations about the motives and objectives of extraterrestrial beings that are believed to be interacting with humanity. These theories range from benign to sinister, reflecting humanity's deep-seated fears, hopes, and curiosity about the unknown. If extraterrestrials are visiting Earth, either covertly or openly, what could they possibly want from us? Are they here to help, observe, exploit, or something else entirely? This chapter delves into the various interpretations of the Alien Agenda, the evidence supporting these views, and the broader implications for humanity's future.

Theories about the Alien Agenda

Observation and Research One of the most common theories is that extraterrestrials are observing humanity for scientific research. This view suggests that Earth and its inhabitants are part of a larger cosmic experiment or study. Extraterrestrials might be interested in our biological diversity, our cultural and social structures, or the way we have developed technologically over time. They could be cataloging our species, studying our evolutionary progress, or monitoring our impact on the planet. This perspective often paints extraterrestrials as distant observers, not directly interfering with human affairs but collecting data to enhance their understanding of life across the universe.

Guidance and Protection Another theory posits that extraterrestrials are here to guide or protect humanity. Proponents of this idea believe that advanced civilizations may have taken a benevolent interest in our species, perhaps due to a shared ancestry, a spiritual connection, or a sense of responsibility to help less developed beings. These extraterrestrials could be subtly influencing our development, offering technology or knowledge to help us solve global challenges such as environmental degradation, nuclear proliferation, or societal conflict. This theory often aligns with the idea of a Galactic Council or a higher cosmic order that oversees the welfare of various civilizations.

Resource Extraction Some theories suggest that extraterrestrials may have a more material interest in Earth, specifically its resources. According to this view, aliens might be here to harvest or extract natural resources, such as minerals, water, or even biological materials. This could involve direct extraction, genetic experimentation, or the use of Earth as a biological laboratory.

The idea of resource extraction often carries a more ominous tone, implying that extraterrestrials might see humanity as expendable or merely a means to an end.

Genetic Experimentation and Hybridization A significant portion of UFO and abduction literature centers around the idea that extraterrestrials are conducting genetic experiments on humans. These experiments might involve creating hybrid beings, advancing their own genetic makeup, or even ensuring the survival of their species by integrating human DNA. Accounts from alleged abductees often describe invasive medical procedures, the extraction of genetic material, or the creation of hybrid offspring. This theory raises questions about the purpose of such experiments—whether they are driven by scientific curiosity, a need for genetic diversity, or a more complex agenda involving the manipulation or enhancement of human biology.

Social and Psychological Manipulation Another theory suggests that extraterrestrials might be manipulating human societies and psychology to achieve specific objectives. This could involve influencing political systems, steering technological development, or shaping religious and spiritual beliefs. Some theorists argue that extraterrestrials have been involved in human history for centuries, subtly guiding our evolution and societal structures to suit their needs. This manipulation might be aimed at preparing humanity for eventual open contact, ensuring global stability, or even controlling our species for their benefit.

Preparation for Integration The idea that extraterrestrials are preparing humanity for integration into a broader cosmic community is a popular theory among those who believe in a benevolent Alien Agenda. According to this perspective, extraterrestrials are gradually acclimating humanity to their presence, reducing fear and building understanding so that we can eventually join a galactic federation or similar organization. This process might involve staged encounters, increased UFO sightings, and the slow release of information through government disclosures and public experiences. The ultimate goal would be to prepare humanity for a harmonious coexistence with other intelligent species.

Control and Domination On the more sinister end of the spectrum, some theories propose that extraterrestrials have a hostile agenda aimed at controlling or dominating humanity. This could involve the establishment of a covert influence over world governments, the creation of a global surveillance state, or even the enslavement of humanity through technological or psychological means. Proponents of this theory often point to alleged secret pacts between extraterrestrials and world leaders, the presence of alien bases on Earth, and the use of advanced technologies to manipulate human behavior and consciousness.

Evidence and Interpretations

The idea of an Alien Agenda is largely speculative, but it is supported by a variety of sources, including alleged eyewitness accounts, abduction experiences, and interpretations of ancient texts and artifacts.

Eyewitness Accounts and Abduction Experiences Many theories about the Alien Agenda are based on testimonies from individuals who claim to have had direct contact with extraterrestrials. These accounts often describe encounters with beings who communicate their intentions telepathically or through other means. Abductees frequently report being subjected to medical experiments, shown visions of possible futures, or receiving messages about the state of the planet and humanity's role in the universe. While these accounts are compelling to some, they are also highly subjective and difficult to verify.

Ancient Astronaut Theories Some proponents of the Alien Agenda look to ancient history and mythology for evidence of extraterrestrial influence. The ancient astronaut theory suggests that many of the gods and supernatural beings described in religious texts were actually extraterrestrial visitors. These beings might have played a role in shaping early human civilizations, providing knowledge, technology, or genetic material that influenced the development of humanity. Artifacts such as the Nazca Lines, the pyramids, and ancient carvings depicting beings with advanced technology are often cited as evidence of this influence.

Government Disclosures and Whistle-blowers The Disclosure Movement has brought to light a number of declassified documents and testimonies from former government insiders that suggest an ongoing interest in UFOs and extraterrestrial contact. Some of these whistle-blowers claim that governments have been aware of an Alien Agenda for decades and that they are actively working to manage or suppress public knowledge of this agenda. These claims often involve secret treaties, reverse-engineered alien technology, and the existence of extraterrestrial bases on Earth.

Technological Anomalies The rapid advancement of certain technologies, particularly in the fields of aerospace, communication, and artificial intelligence, has led some to speculate that these breakthroughs may have been influenced by extraterrestrial knowledge. The idea is that extraterrestrials might be sharing or seeding technology to accelerate human development, either to prepare us for future contact or to ensure that we reach a certain level of technological maturity. Skeptics argue that these advancements are the result of human ingenuity, but the idea of alien influence persists in some circles.

Implications of the Alien Agenda

The possibility of an Alien Agenda carries significant implications for humanity, ranging from existential questions about our place in the universe to practical concerns about how we should respond to extraterrestrial presence.

Existential and Philosophical Questions The idea that extraterrestrials might have specific motives for interacting with humanity forces us to confront profound questions about our place in the cosmos. Are we merely one of many species being studied or manipulated by more advanced beings? Or do we have a unique role to play in the larger narrative of the universe? These questions challenge our understanding of life, evolution, and the nature of consciousness.

Global Security and Governance If there is an Alien Agenda, it raises important questions about global security and governance. How should humanity respond to the possibility of extraterrestrial influence, whether benevolent or hostile? Should there be a coordinated global effort to engage with these beings, or should governments work to protect their citizens from potential threats? The existence of an Alien Agenda could necessitate the creation of new international institutions or agreements to manage extraterrestrial relations.

Ethical and Moral Considerations The possibility that extraterrestrials are conducting genetic experiments, manipulating societies, or harvesting resources from Earth poses significant ethical dilemmas. How should humanity respond to such actions? Do we have the right to resist or negotiate with these beings? What are the ethical implications of collaborating with extraterrestrials, particularly if their motives are not fully understood? These questions require a re-examination of our ethical frameworks in light of potential extraterrestrial involvement.

Cultural and Religious Impact The revelation of an Alien Agenda could have a profound impact on human culture and religion. Many religious traditions would need to reconcile their teachings with the existence of intelligent extraterrestrial beings and their motives. Cultural beliefs about humanity's uniqueness and purpose might be challenged, leading to new interpretations of our history and destiny. The integration of extraterrestrial knowledge and influence could also lead to a cultural renaissance or a period of intense societal upheaval.

Preparation for Future Contact Understanding the potential motives of extraterrestrials is crucial for preparing humanity for future contact. Whether their agenda is one of guidance, observation, or control, it is important for humanity to develop strategies for engagement that prioritize our autonomy, security, and ethical standards.

This preparation might involve scientific research, diplomatic initiatives, and public education campaigns aimed at fostering a greater awareness of the possibilities and challenges associated with extraterrestrial contact.

The idea of an Alien Agenda is both captivating and unsettling, reflecting humanity's deepest anxieties and aspirations about our place in the universe. Whether extraterrestrials are here to observe, guide, manipulate, or exploit us, the possibility of an agenda beyond our control forces us to confront complex questions about the nature of life, the ethics of interaction, and the future of our species.

While the evidence for an Alien Agenda is largely speculative, it nevertheless challenges us to think critically about the implications of extraterrestrial contact. It invites us to consider the motivations of beings that may be far more advanced than we are and to consider how we should respond to such potential interactions. Whether these extraterrestrial beings are observers, benefactors, or manipulators, the idea of an Alien Agenda urges us to prepare for a future where humanity is not the only intelligent species we must reckon with.

The Need for Vigilance and Preparedness

Given the diverse and sometimes conflicting theories about what extraterrestrials might want from us, a key takeaway is the need for vigilance and preparedness. Humanity must remain open to the possibility that contact with extraterrestrial beings could happen in various forms—directly, indirectly, or through subtle influences over time. This requires a multi-faceted approach that includes:

Scientific Investigation: Continued scientific investigation into UFOs, UAPs, and potential extraterrestrial technologies is essential. Governments and private organizations alike should invest in research that aims to understand the nature of these phenomena. By developing a rigorous scientific approach, humanity can better discern whether we are dealing with natural phenomena, advanced human technologies, or something truly alien.

Public Awareness and Education: Educating the public about the potential for extraterrestrial contact and the implications of an Alien Agenda is crucial. This includes fostering critical thinking, promoting an understanding of the scientific method, and encouraging open-mindedness without falling prey to fear-mongering or unsubstantiated claims. Public awareness campaigns could help prepare society for the possibility of contact and reduce the likelihood of panic or confusion.

Ethical Frameworks for Interaction: As we speculate about the motives of extraterrestrials, it is important to develop ethical frameworks that guide how humanity should interact with other intelligent species. This might involve creating international guidelines for communication, negotiation, and the sharing of knowledge and technology. These frameworks should emphasize respect for autonomy, the protection of life, and the avoidance of harm.

Diplomatic Initiatives: Just as nations engage in diplomacy to manage their relations with each other, humanity should consider the possibility of interstellar diplomacy. This could involve establishing protocols for first contact, creating international organizations dedicated to managing extraterrestrial relations, and ensuring that any engagement is conducted transparently and with global consensus. Diplomacy could be the key to understanding and navigating an Alien Agenda, whether it is benign or hostile.

Defense and Security Considerations: While the prospect of hostile extraterrestrial intentions is speculative, it cannot be entirely dismissed. Governments should consider the security implications of an Alien Agenda and develop contingency plans to protect humanity in the event of a threat. This includes monitoring potential extraterrestrial activity, safeguarding critical infrastructure, and ensuring that any defensive measures are proportionate and ethical.

The Role of Global Cooperation

The possibility of an Alien Agenda underscores the importance of global cooperation. No single nation or organization can effectively address the challenges posed by potential extraterrestrial contact. Instead, the international community must work together to share information, develop common strategies, and ensure that humanity presents a united front in any interactions with extraterrestrial beings.

Information Sharing: Governments and organizations should collaborate on the collection and analysis of data related to UFOs, UAPs, and extraterrestrial phenomena. By pooling resources and expertise, humanity can gain a clearer understanding of what we are dealing with and how best to respond.

International Treaties and Agreements: The development of international treaties and agreements that govern how humanity engages with extraterrestrial beings is a crucial step. These agreements could establish norms for communication, the sharing of technology, and the protection of Earth's sovereignty. They could also address the ethical considerations of genetic experimentation, resource extraction, and the potential impact on human society.

A Global Approach to Contact: If contact with extraterrestrials does occur, it is important that humanity speaks with one voice. This means developing a global approach to contact, with decisions made through international consensus rather than unilateral actions by individual nations. Such an approach would ensure that the interests of all humanity are represented and that any engagement is conducted in a way that reflects our shared values and aspirations.

The Psychological and Social Impact

The realization that extraterrestrials might have an agenda involving humanity could have profound psychological and social impacts. How we perceive ourselves, our history, and our future could be fundamentally altered by the knowledge that we are not alone in the universe and that other beings might have been influencing us for centuries.

Re-evaluation of Human History: If evidence emerges that extraterrestrials have been interacting with humanity for a long time, it could lead to a re-evaluation of human history. Historical events, religious narratives, and ancient myths might be reinterpreted in light of this new understanding. This could challenge established beliefs and prompt a re-examination of our cultural and spiritual heritage.

Impact on Human Identity: The knowledge that extraterrestrials have their own motives and agendas could affect how we see ourselves as a species. It might lead to a greater sense of unity, as humanity recognizes that we are part of a larger cosmic community. Alternatively, it could provoke fear, uncertainty, or even resistance to the idea of being influenced or controlled by non-human entities.

Cultural and Artistic Expression: The concept of an Alien Agenda could inspire new forms of cultural and artistic expression. Artists, writers, and filmmakers might explore the implications of extraterrestrial motives, creating works that challenge our assumptions and expand our imagination. This could lead to a cultural renaissance, as humanity grapples with the profound questions raised by our place in the universe.

Social Cohesion and Conflict: The revelation of an Alien Agenda could either strengthen social cohesion or exacerbate existing conflicts. On one hand, the knowledge that we are not alone could unite humanity in the face of a common reality. On the other hand, differing interpretations of extraterrestrial motives could lead to divisions, with some groups advocating for cooperation and others fearing or resisting outside influence.

The idea of an Alien Agenda is a complex and multifaceted concept that reflects humanity's deep curiosity about the unknown and our place in the universe. Whether extraterrestrials are here to observe, guide, exploit, or control us, the possibility of such an agenda forces us to confront profound questions about our existence, our values, and our future.

As we continue to explore these possibilities, it is important to approach the idea of an Alien Agenda with a balance of open-mindedness and critical thinking. While the evidence remains speculative, the implications of extraterrestrial contact are significant enough to warrant serious consideration and preparation.

Ultimately, the way humanity responds to the possibility of an Alien Agenda will shape our future in ways we can only begin to imagine. Whether through scientific investigation, ethical reflection, diplomatic initiatives, or global cooperation, our approach to this challenge will determine how we navigate the uncertainties of contact with beings from beyond our world. In doing so, we may discover not only more about the universe but also about ourselves and the true potential of humanity in the cosmic order.

Interstellar War: Are We in the Crossfire?

The concept of an interstellar war—conflicts between advanced extraterrestrial civilizations across the vast expanse of space—is a staple of science fiction. However, some theorists and UFOlogists speculate that such conflicts might not be entirely fictional. Could humanity be caught in the crossfire of a war between alien species? Are the unexplained phenomena we observe, such as UFOs and UAPs, evidence of extraterrestrial battles playing out in or near our solar system? This chapter explores the idea of interstellar war, the potential implications for Earth, the evidence that might suggest such a conflict is occurring, and how humanity could prepare for or protect itself from the consequences.

The Concept of Interstellar War

Interstellar war involves conflicts that span star systems, potentially involving civilizations with technologies far beyond our current understanding. Such wars could be fought over resources, territory, ideological differences, or other reasons that are difficult for humans to comprehend. The idea of interstellar war is often linked to the following theories:

Competing Galactic Powers: One theory suggests that the Milky Way galaxy is home to multiple advanced civilizations, some of which may be in conflict with each other. These conflicts could be driven by competition for habitable planets, strategic locations, or control over advanced technologies. If Earth lies within a contested region, humanity could be at risk of becoming collateral damage in a larger, interstellar conflict.

Defensive Wars: Another possibility is that some extraterrestrial civilizations are engaged in defensive wars to protect their territories or species from hostile invaders. These wars might involve advanced weaponry, space battles, and the use of planetary shields or other defensive technologies. If Earth or our solar system is located near such a conflict zone, we might observe anomalies such as strange energy signatures, sudden disappearances of objects, or unexplained atmospheric disturbances.

Rebellions and Insurgencies: Interstellar wars could also take the form of rebellions or insurgencies, where less powerful civilizations or factions rise up against dominant powers. In this scenario, Earth could be seen as a potential ally, resource, or strategic location by one or more warring factions. The involvement of insurgent groups might manifest in covert activities on Earth, such as influencing human governments, abducting individuals for experimentation, or manipulating technological development to gain an advantage.

Proxy Wars: Much like during the Cold War on Earth, extraterrestrial civilizations could engage in proxy wars, using less advanced species or planets as battlegrounds to avoid direct confrontation. Earth might be a site of such a proxy war, where different alien factions support various human nations, ideologies, or movements as part of a broader interstellar strategy. This theory suggests that some of the geopolitical conflicts we experience on Earth could be influenced by extraterrestrial powers with their own agendas.

Evidence and Speculation

While there is no direct evidence of interstellar war, certain phenomena and reports have fueled speculation that such conflicts might be occurring.

UFO Sightings and UAPs: The high frequency of UFO sightings and UAP reports has led some to speculate that these objects could be extraterrestrial craft involved in interstellar conflicts. Witnesses have reported seeing objects maneuvering at high speeds, engaging in what appears to be evasive actions, or even discharging beams of light or energy. While these sightings are often dismissed as misidentified natural phenomena or human-made technology, some UFOlogists believe they could be evidence of alien battles taking place in Earth's vicinity.

Alleged Military Encounters: There are accounts from military personnel who claim to have witnessed or been involved in encounters with UFOs that exhibited hostile or defensive behavior. Some of these reports suggest that these objects actively evaded capture, engaged in maneuvers that appeared to be tactical, or even disabled human weapons systems. These incidents have led to speculation that Earth's military forces might have inadvertently become involved in extraterrestrial conflicts or that certain UFOs are here on reconnaissance or combat missions related to an interstellar war.

The Moon and Mars Anomalies: Anomalies observed on the Moon and Mars, such as unexplained structures, light flashes, or sudden surface changes, have been interpreted by some as evidence of extraterrestrial bases or the remnants of interstellar battles. These anomalies, though often explainable by natural processes, are sometimes cited as proof that our solar system has been, or is currently, a battleground for alien forces.

Historical and Mythological Accounts: Some researchers look to ancient history and mythology for evidence of interstellar conflicts. They argue that descriptions of battles between gods, celestial beings, or flying chariots in ancient texts could be interpreted as human witnesses describing extraterrestrial warfare. While these interpretations are speculative, they offer a narrative that suggests Earth has long been a site of interest, and possibly conflict, for extraterrestrial civilizations.

Potential Implications for Humanity

If an interstellar war is occurring and humanity is caught in the crossfire, the implications could be profound and far-reaching:

Global Security Risks: The possibility of Earth becoming collateral damage in an interstellar conflict raises significant global security concerns. Advanced alien weaponry could cause catastrophic damage to our planet, disrupt global communications, or even lead to mass casualties. Nations would need to develop strategies for detecting and defending against potential extraterrestrial threats, including monitoring for unusual energy signatures, strengthening satellite networks, and preparing for the possibility of extraterrestrial encounters.

Diplomatic Challenges: If Earth is indeed located in a contested region or is seen as a valuable asset by warring extraterrestrial factions, humanity might face complex diplomatic challenges. We would need to navigate relationships with multiple alien civilizations, each with its own interests, demands, and capabilities. This could involve negotiating alliances, mediating conflicts, or even choosing sides in a war we barely understand. The development of interstellar diplomacy would become a priority, requiring new international institutions and protocols.

Technological Impacts: Exposure to the technologies used in an interstellar war could have significant implications for human development. We might reverse-engineer alien technology, leading to rapid advancements in energy production, space travel, or weapons systems. However, this could also pose ethical dilemmas, particularly if these technologies are destructive or incompatible with our values. The risk of accelerating our technological progress without fully understanding the consequences could lead to unforeseen dangers.

Psychological and Cultural Effects: The revelation that humanity is caught in the crossfire of an interstellar war could have profound psychological and cultural effects. People might experience heightened fear, anxiety, or existential dread, particularly if the nature of the conflict is not fully understood. On the other hand, the knowledge that we are part of a larger cosmic struggle could inspire a sense of unity and purpose, prompting humanity to come together to face this new challenge. Cultural narratives, religious beliefs, and societal values might shift in response to the realization that we are not alone—and that we are vulnerable to forces far beyond our control.

Ethical Considerations: Being drawn into an interstellar conflict raises significant ethical questions. Should humanity take sides in a war between alien civilizations, and if so, on what basis? How do we ensure that our actions align with our moral values and do not result in unnecessary harm to ourselves or others? The ethical implications of developing or using alien technology for warfare, as well as the responsibility to protect our planet from external threats, would need to be carefully considered.

Preparing for the Possibility

While the idea of interstellar war remains speculative, the potential consequences are serious enough that it warrants consideration and preparation. Here are some steps that could be taken to mitigate the risks and prepare for the possibility:

Enhanced Space Surveillance: Expanding and improving space surveillance capabilities would be crucial for detecting potential threats from interstellar conflicts. This includes monitoring for unusual activity around Earth, the Moon, and other celestial bodies, as well as developing systems to track and analyze UAPs and other unidentified objects in space.

International Cooperation: Addressing the potential risks of interstellar war would require unprecedented levels of international cooperation. Nations should work together to share information, develop defensive strategies, and establish protocols for responding to extraterrestrial threats. A global approach would be essential to ensuring that humanity presents a united front and that decisions are made with the collective interest of all people in mind.

Research and Development: Investing in research and development of technologies that could protect Earth from extraterrestrial threats is essential. This might include advancing our understanding of energy shields, propulsion systems, and weaponry that could be used in space combat. However, such developments should be guided by ethical considerations and the desire to avoid unnecessary escalation.

Public Education and Awareness: Educating the public about the possibility of interstellar war and what it might entail is important for reducing fear and panic. Public awareness campaigns could focus on explaining the scientific basis for space surveillance, the potential risks, and the measures being taken to protect humanity. Ensuring that people are informed and prepared can help maintain social cohesion and prevent the spread of misinformation.

Ethical Frameworks and Policies: Developing ethical frameworks and policies to guide humanity's response to interstellar conflicts is crucial. These frameworks should prioritize the protection of life, the preservation of Earth's environment, and the avoidance of unnecessary harm. International agreements on the use of advanced technologies, the treatment of extraterrestrial beings, and the conduct of interstellar diplomacy would help ensure that humanity acts responsibly in the face of such unprecedented challenges.

The idea that humanity might be caught in the crossfire of an interstellar war is both thrilling and terrifying. While the evidence for such a conflict is largely speculative, the potential consequences are significant enough that they cannot be ignored. Whether these conflicts are real or imagined, they challenge us to think deeply about our place in the universe, our responsibilities to one another, and how we would respond to threats that transcend our current understanding.

Preparing for the possibility of interstellar war requires a combination of scientific inquiry and practical measures to ensure humanity's safety and survival. It involves not only advancing our technological capabilities but also fostering international cooperation, ethical considerations, and public preparedness.

The Role of Science and Technology

Science and technology play a crucial role in preparing for the possibility of interstellar conflict. This involves not just enhancing our defense systems, but also developing tools for detection, analysis, and communication that could be vital in such scenarios.

Detection and Surveillance: To detect and monitor potential extraterrestrial conflicts, humanity needs to expand its space surveillance infrastructure. This could include more sophisticated satellites, deep space telescopes, and ground-based observatories that can detect anomalies and unidentified objects at greater distances. Enhancing our ability to detect energy signatures, unusual space debris, and other potential indicators of extraterrestrial activity will be essential.

Defensive Technologies: Should there be any threat of becoming collateral damage in an interstellar war, humanity would need to develop advanced defensive technologies. This might include energy shields, space-based missile defense systems, and EMP-resistant infrastructure. These technologies could protect Earth from both direct attacks and the unintended consequences of extraterrestrial warfare, such as debris or radiation.

Communication Systems: Establishing reliable communication systems that can function over vast interstellar distances would be critical in managing any interactions with extraterrestrial civilizations. These systems would need to be highly secure, resistant to interference, and capable of transmitting and receiving complex data across light years. Understanding how to communicate with extraterrestrial beings—whether through mathematical concepts, symbols, or other means—would also be an important area of research.

Space Exploration and Colonization: Expanding human presence beyond Earth could be a strategic move in case of interstellar conflict. Colonizing the Moon, Mars, and other celestial bodies would not only ensure the survival of humanity in the event of a catastrophic event on Earth but also provide strategic outposts for monitoring and responding to extraterrestrial activities. Developing the technology for sustainable life on other planets would be a significant step in safeguarding the future of our species.

Ethical and Diplomatic Considerations

While technological preparedness is crucial, the ethical and diplomatic dimensions of potential interstellar war cannot be overlooked. How humanity engages with potential extraterrestrial civilizations, especially in the context of conflict, will have far-reaching implications for our moral standing and survival.

Non-Aggression Principles: Humanity should adopt a policy of non-aggression in its interactions with extraterrestrial civilizations. This principle would emphasize peaceful coexistence, respect for autonomy, and the avoidance of unnecessary conflict. By committing to non-aggression, humanity would signal its intent to be a responsible member of the cosmic community, potentially reducing the risk of being drawn into interstellar conflicts.

Diplomatic Protocols: Developing protocols for interstellar diplomacy is essential for managing potential encounters with alien civilizations. These protocols would guide communication, negotiation, and conflict resolution, ensuring that humanity's interactions are conducted in a manner that prioritizes peace and mutual respect. International treaties and agreements could codify these protocols, providing a framework for how to handle disputes, alliances, and other interactions.

Humanitarian Considerations: In the event of interstellar war, there may be opportunities or obligations to provide humanitarian assistance to extraterrestrial beings or other affected civilizations. This could involve offering refuge, medical aid, or other forms of support. Developing policies that outline when and how to offer humanitarian assistance in an interstellar context would reflect our commitment to ethical behavior and the protection of life.

Global Governance Structures: Addressing the complexities of interstellar war would likely require the establishment of new global governance structures. These could include international organizations dedicated to extraterrestrial affairs, space security councils, or even a united planetary defense initiative. Such structures would ensure that decisions about interstellar conflicts are made collaboratively, transparently, and with the interests of all humanity in mind.

The Human Response

The possibility of interstellar war would inevitably provoke a wide range of human responses, from fear and anxiety to curiosity and hope. How humanity collectively responds to such a scenario will shape our future in profound ways.

Public Education and Preparedness: Educating the public about the realities of space exploration, the potential for extraterrestrial contact, and the implications of interstellar conflicts is crucial. Public education campaigns should focus on providing accurate information, dispelling myths, and promoting a sense of preparedness rather than panic. Ensuring that people understand the steps being taken to protect Earth and its inhabitants can help maintain social order and foster resilience.

Cultural and Philosophical Shifts: The realization that humanity could be involved in or affected by interstellar conflicts would likely lead to significant cultural and philosophical shifts. People might begin to see themselves as part of a larger cosmic community, leading to changes in how we view our place in the universe, our relationships with one another, and our responsibilities as a species. This could inspire new forms of art, literature, and philosophy that reflect a broader, more interconnected worldview.

Psychological Resilience: Preparing for the psychological impact of potential interstellar war is as important as preparing for the physical and technological challenges. Governments and organizations should develop programs to help people cope with the stress, uncertainty, and existential questions that might arise from such a scenario. Building psychological resilience will be key to maintaining social cohesion and ensuring that humanity can face these challenges with strength and resolve.

Unity and Cooperation: Finally, the possibility of interstellar war underscores the importance of global unity and cooperation. In the face of such a vast and unknown challenge, humanity must work together, setting aside national, cultural, and ideological differences to protect our shared future. By fostering a sense of global solidarity, we can ensure that we are better prepared to face the challenges of interstellar conflict—should they ever arise.

The idea that humanity could be caught in the crossfire of an interstellar war is both fascinating and daunting. While the evidence for such a scenario remains speculative, the potential consequences are significant enough to warrant serious consideration and preparation. By investing in science and technology, developing ethical frameworks, fostering international cooperation, and building public awareness, humanity can better prepare for the possibility of interstellar conflicts. Ultimately, how we respond to this challenge will define our future as a species. Whether or not we ever find ourselves in the midst of an interstellar war, the process of preparing for such a scenario will help us grow as a global community, advance our understanding of the universe, and reaffirm our commitment to peace, cooperation, and the protection of life—on Earth and beyond.

The Role of the Media: Shaping Public Perception

The media plays a crucial role in shaping public perception of UFOs, extraterrestrial life, and related phenomena. Through television, movies, news outlets, books, and online platforms, the media has the power to influence how people think about the possibility of alien contact, the existence of extraterrestrial civilizations, and the implications of these ideas for humanity. This chapter explores the impact of the media on public perception, how it has evolved over time, and the ways in which it both informs and distorts our understanding of the potential for extraterrestrial life and the mysteries surrounding it.

Historical Context: The Evolution of UFOs in the Media

The portrayal of UFOs and extraterrestrials in the media has evolved significantly over the decades, reflecting changing societal attitudes, technological advancements, and cultural anxieties.

Early 20th Century: Science Fiction and Speculation The early 20th century saw the rise of science fiction as a literary genre, with authors like H.G. Wells and Jules Verne exploring themes of space travel and alien encounters. Radio shows like *War of the Worlds*, famously adapted by Orson Welles in 1938, demonstrated the media's ability to blur the line between fiction and reality, inciting widespread panic by convincing listeners that an alien invasion was occurring. These early depictions laid the groundwork for public fascination with the idea of life beyond Earth, blending scientific curiosity with speculative fiction.

The Post-War Era: The Birth of UFO Culture The period following World War II marked the beginning of the modern UFO phenomenon, with reports of unidentified flying objects capturing public attention. The media played a significant role in popularizing the term "flying saucer" after pilot Kenneth Arnold's 1947 sighting, which he described as objects moving "like a saucer skipping on water." The Roswell incident later that year further cemented the idea of extraterrestrial visitation in the public consciousness, with media coverage fueling speculation about government cover-ups and alien encounters.

The Cold War and Space Race: Heightened Anxieties During the Cold War, the media often portrayed UFOs and extraterrestrials through the lens of fear and suspicion, reflecting broader anxieties about nuclear war, espionage, and the unknown. Films like *The Day the Earth Stood Still* (1951) and *Invasion of the Body Snatchers* (1956) used extraterrestrial themes to comment on the dangers of technological advancement and the threat of ideological infiltration. The Space Race further fueled public interest in the possibility of contact with other civilizations, with media coverage of space missions often hinting at the potential for discovering life beyond Earth.

The 1970s and 1980s: The Era of the Blockbuster The 1970s and 1980s saw the emergence of blockbuster films that shaped the public's perception of extraterrestrials in more complex and varied ways. Films like *Close Encounters of the Third Kind* (1977) and *E.T. the Extra-Terrestrial* (1982) presented aliens as benevolent beings, fostering a sense of wonder and hope about the possibilities of contact. Meanwhile, franchises like *Star Wars* and *Star Trek* depicted a galaxy teeming with diverse civilizations, normalizing the idea of a populated universe and inspiring generations of viewers to imagine what life might be like on other planets.

The 1990s: Conspiracy and Skepticism The 1990s brought a wave of skepticism and conspiracy theories, with shows like *The X-Files* (1993-2002) popularizing the idea that governments were hiding the truth about UFOs and extraterrestrials. This era saw the rise of media that questioned official narratives, portraying extraterrestrials as both real and deeply intertwined with global power structures. The influence of the internet began to grow, allowing for the rapid spread of UFO-related information, speculation, and hoaxes, further complicating the public's understanding of the phenomena.

The 21st Century: A New Era of Disclosure In recent years, the media has played a key role in the increasing public discourse around UFOs, now often referred to as UAPs (Unidentified Aerial Phenomena). The release of previously classified government documents, high-profile news reports, and documentaries have brought renewed legitimacy to the study of UFOs. Major news outlets have covered the topic more seriously, reflecting a shift from the fringe to mainstream acceptance. The media's role in reporting on Pentagon UAP investigations and the 2021 Office of the Director of National Intelligence (ODNI) report has helped to reframe the conversation, making it less about sensationalism and more about national security and scientific inquiry.

The Impact of Media Portrayals

The media's portrayal of UFOs and extraterrestrial life has a profound impact on public perception, shaping everything from individual beliefs to broader cultural attitudes.

Creating and Reinforcing Beliefs The media often serves as the primary source of information about UFOs and extraterrestrial life for the general public. Movies, TV shows, news reports, and documentaries all contribute to the creation and reinforcement of beliefs about these phenomena. For instance, depictions of benevolent or malevolent aliens in popular culture can influence how people perceive the possibility of extraterrestrial contact—whether they view it with hope, fear, or skepticism.

Influencing Public Policy and Government Action Media coverage can also influence public policy and government action. Widespread media interest in UFOs has pressured governments to respond, whether by declassifying documents, acknowledging the existence of investigations, or providing more transparency about what is known. The media's role in highlighting public concerns and demanding answers can lead to increased government accountability and action on these issues.

Shaping the Narrative: From Fringe to Mainstream The media has the power to shape the narrative around UFOs, moving the topic from the fringes of conspiracy theory to the mainstream. This shift has been particularly evident in recent years, as respected news outlets and government officials have begun to take the topic more seriously. By framing UFOs and UAPs as legitimate subjects of investigation, the media has helped to reduce the stigma around discussing and researching these phenomena.

Distortion and Sensationalism However, the media's influence is not always positive. Sensationalism and distortion are common, particularly in entertainment media, where the need for compelling stories can lead to exaggerated or misleading portrayals of extraterrestrial phenomena. These portrayals can contribute to misinformation, fear, and confusion, making it difficult for the public to distinguish between fact and fiction. Sensationalized reports can also undermine serious scientific inquiry by associating legitimate research with fringe or pseudoscientific ideas.

The Role of Social Media and the Internet The rise of social media and online platforms has further complicated the media's role in shaping public perception. On one hand, the internet allows for the rapid dissemination of information, making it easier for people to access diverse perspectives and up-to-date reports on UFOs and extraterrestrial life. On the other hand, it also facilitates the spread of misinformation, hoaxes, and conspiracy theories, which can distort public understanding and fuel unfounded fears. The echo chamber effect of social media can amplify extreme views, making it harder to achieve a balanced and informed public discourse.

The Media's Responsibility

Given the media's powerful influence on public perception, there is a responsibility to report on UFOs, UAPs, and extraterrestrial life in a way that is accurate, balanced, and respectful of the complexities involved.

Accurate Reporting Journalists and media outlets should strive to provide accurate, evidence-based reporting on UFOs and extraterrestrial life. This includes fact-checking sources, avoiding sensationalism, and clearly distinguishing between verified information and speculation. Accurate reporting helps to build public trust and ensures that the conversation around these topics is grounded in reality rather than fear or fantasy.

Context and Nuance The media should provide context and nuance when reporting on UFOs and extraterrestrial life. This means exploring the scientific, historical, and cultural background of these phenomena, rather than simply presenting them as sensational or anomalous events. By providing a deeper understanding of the issues, the media can help the public make informed judgments about the significance of UFO sightings and the possibility of extraterrestrial contact.

Encouraging Critical Thinking Encouraging critical thinking is essential in navigating the complex and often speculative nature of UFO-related topics. The media can play a role in fostering skepticism, not in the sense of outright dismissal, but in encouraging the public to question sources, evaluate evidence, and consider alternative explanations. By promoting critical thinking, the media can help the public engage with these topics in a more thoughtful and discerning way.

Balancing Entertainment and Information While entertainment media often focuses on the dramatic and sensational aspects of extraterrestrial phenomena, it is important to balance this with information that is grounded in science and reality. Documentaries, educational programs, and investigative journalism can provide this balance, offering the public a more comprehensive and accurate understanding of the issues at hand.

Addressing Misinformation The media has a responsibility to address and correct misinformation, particularly in the age of social media where false information can spread rapidly. This includes debunking hoaxes, clarifying misunderstandings, and providing clear explanations of complex topics.

By taking an active role in combating misinformation, the media can help protect the public from being misled and ensure that the conversation around UFOs and extraterrestrial life is based on facts rather than fiction. The media's role in shaping public perception of UFOs and extraterrestrial life is both powerful and complex. Over the decades, media portrayals have influenced how people think about these phenomena, whether through the lens of fear, curiosity, skepticism, or wonder. While the media has the ability to inform and educate, it also has the potential to distort and sensationalize, leading to confusion and misinformation. As interest in UFOs, UAPs, and extraterrestrial life continues to grow, the media's responsibility to report on these topics accurately and responsibly becomes even more critical.

The Future of Media Coverage on UFOs and Extraterrestrial Life

As we move further into the 21st century, the media's role in covering UFOs and extraterrestrial life is likely to evolve in several key ways. These changes will be driven by advances in technology, shifts in public interest, and the increasing complexity of the phenomena being reported.

Integration of Scientific Perspectives With the growing legitimacy of UFOs as a subject of scientific inquiry, the media will likely place greater emphasis on integrating scientific perspectives into their coverage. This could involve collaborating with scientists, astronomers, and other experts to provide more rigorous analyses of sightings and reports. By incorporating scientific methodologies and critical thinking into their reporting, the media can help demystify the phenomena and present them in a more credible light.

Increased Transparency and Government Involvement As governments around the world begin to acknowledge and release more information about UAPs, the media will play a crucial role in interpreting and disseminating this information to the public. The coverage will likely become more focused on transparency, accountability, and the implications of government disclosures. Journalists will need to navigate the complex relationship between governmental secrecy, public demand for information, and the need to avoid unnecessary panic.

Cross-Platform Storytelling The rise of digital media and streaming platforms offers new opportunities for cross-platform storytelling, where narratives about UFOs and extraterrestrial life can be explored across multiple media formats—such as documentaries, podcasts, interactive websites, and virtual reality experiences. This approach allows for more immersive and in-depth exploration of the topics, catering to diverse audiences and providing multiple entry points for engagement.

Audience-Driven Content With the advent of social media and user-generated content, the public now plays a more active role in shaping the media narrative around UFOs and extraterrestrial life. The media is increasingly responsive to audience interests, often sourcing stories from viral videos, social media posts, and crowd-sourced investigations. This shift toward audience-driven content can democratize the flow of information, but it also requires careful curation to ensure that credible information is prioritized over sensationalism or hoaxes.

Ethical Journalism in the Age of Disclosure As more credible information becomes available, ethical journalism will be crucial in guiding public understanding and response. Journalists will need to navigate the fine line between reporting significant developments and respecting the uncertainties and complexities that come with the subject. This includes being transparent about the limitations of current knowledge, avoiding fear-mongering, and acknowledging the broader implications of potential contact with extraterrestrial life.

Educational Initiatives The media could play a more active role in educational initiatives, partnering with schools, universities, and scientific organizations to develop curricula and resources on the topic of extraterrestrial life. By providing students and the public with accurate, well-rounded information, the media can help cultivate a generation that is informed and prepared to engage with the profound questions surrounding life beyond Earth.

Long-Form Investigative Journalism In an age of information overload, there is a growing demand for long-form investigative journalism that can provide deep, nuanced explorations of complex topics like UFOs and extraterrestrial life. By dedicating time and resources to thorough investigations, journalists can uncover new information, challenge prevailing narratives, and offer insights that go beyond the headlines. This approach is particularly important for a subject as multifaceted as extraterrestrial phenomena, where quick sound bites often fail to capture the full scope of the story.

The Impact on Public Perception and Society

The media's evolving role in covering UFOs and extraterrestrial life will continue to shape public perception and have broader societal impacts. As the conversation becomes more mainstream and scientifically grounded, it could lead to significant shifts in how people view the universe and humanity's place within it.

Normalization of the UFO Phenomenon As media coverage becomes more frequent and credible, the idea of UFOs and extraterrestrial life is likely to become more normalized in public discourse. This shift could reduce the stigma associated with discussing and researching these topics, encouraging more open and serious consideration of the implications. Over time, this normalization could lead to greater public interest in space exploration, scientific inquiry, and the search for extraterrestrial intelligence (SETI).

Cultural and Artistic Influences The media's portrayal of extraterrestrial life will continue to inspire cultural and artistic expressions, influencing everything from literature and film to music and visual art. As new narratives and ideas emerge, they will shape how society imagines the possibilities of contact with other civilizations and the ethical, philosophical, and existential questions that come with it. This cultural influence can help society process and understand the potential implications of extraterrestrial life, making the unknown more accessible and less intimidating.

Shifts in Worldview Widespread media coverage of UFOs and extraterrestrial life has the potential to shift worldviews, particularly if credible evidence of extraterrestrial contact is ever confirmed. Such a discovery could challenge existing beliefs about humanity's uniqueness, the nature of life, and the structure of the universe. The media will play a critical role in framing this discovery, influencing whether it is perceived as a threat, an opportunity, or a profound new chapter in human history.

Impact on Religion and Spirituality The media's portrayal of extraterrestrial life could also have significant implications for religion and spirituality. As new information emerges, religious institutions may need to reinterpret their teachings in light of the possibility of other intelligent beings. The media will likely cover these developments, highlighting how different faiths and spiritual traditions respond to the idea of extraterrestrial life. This could lead to a broader conversation about the meaning of life, the nature of the divine, and humanity's place in the cosmos.

Public Engagement with Science The media has the power to engage the public with science in new and exciting ways, particularly through the lens of UFOs and extraterrestrial life. By highlighting the scientific efforts to understand these phenomena, the media can inspire curiosity, critical thinking, and a greater appreciation for the scientific method. This engagement could lead to increased support for space exploration, scientific research, and education, ultimately benefiting society as a whole.

The role of the media in shaping public perception of UFOs and extraterrestrial life is both influential and evolving. As the conversation around these topics moves from the fringes to the mainstream, the media will continue to play a crucial role in informing, educating, and guiding public understanding. With the potential for significant cultural, scientific, and philosophical implications, the media's responsibility to report accurately and ethically has never been more important.

By embracing a balanced approach that integrates scientific rigor, ethical journalism, and a commitment to public education, the media can help society navigate the complexities of extraterrestrial phenomena. Whether humanity eventually makes contact with other civilizations or continues to explore the mysteries of the cosmos from afar, the media will remain a key player in how we understand and respond to the possibility of life beyond Earth.

Skeptics vs. Believers: The Ongoing Debate

The debate between sceptics and believers regarding UFOs, extraterrestrial life, and related phenomena is one of the most enduring and polarizing discussions in the realms of science, culture, and public discourse. Skeptics often demand rigorous scientific evidence and are cautious of accepting extraordinary claims without substantial proof. Believers, on the other hand, argue that the accumulation of eyewitness accounts, unexplained phenomena, and government disclosures points to the reality of extraterrestrial contact. This chapter explores the key arguments from both sides, the impact of this debate on society, and the potential for bridging the gap between these two perspectives.

The Skeptical Perspective

Skeptics approach the topic of UFOs and extraterrestrial life with caution, often emphasizing the need for empirical evidence and scientific validation before accepting extraordinary claims. Their arguments are grounded in the principles of critical thinking, the scientific method, and the understanding of human psychology.

The Burden of Proof A central tenet of the skeptical perspective is that extraordinary claims require extraordinary evidence. Skeptics argue that the existence of extraterrestrial life, particularly in the form of visitors to Earth, is an extraordinary claim that demands robust, verifiable evidence. Anecdotal reports, blurry photographs, and unexplained lights in the sky are often deemed insufficient to meet this standard. Skeptics insist that until such evidence is produced, the most rational stance is to withhold belief.

Psychological and Sociological Explanations Skeptics often point to psychological and sociological factors as explanations for UFO sightings and beliefs in extraterrestrial contact. Cognitive biases, such as pareidolia (seeing patterns in random data) and confirmation bias (favouring information that confirms pre-existing beliefs), are frequently cited as reasons why people might misinterpret natural or man-made phenomena as extraterrestrial. Additionally, sceptics highlight the role of cultural influence, media portrayals, and social dynamics in shaping public beliefs about UFOs and aliens.

Misidentifications and Hoaxes Another argument from the skeptical camp is that many UFO sightings can be explained as misidentifications of conventional objects, such as aircraft, satellites, weather balloons, or celestial bodies. Skeptics also note that hoaxes and deliberate fabrications have historically contributed to the proliferation of UFO reports. They argue that these factors, combined with the occasional lack of rigorous investigation, lead to false conclusions about the nature of the phenomena.

The Lack of Physical Evidence One of the most compelling arguments for skeptics is the absence of physical evidence that can be reliably attributed to extraterrestrial activity. While there are numerous reports of UFO sightings and close encounters, skeptics argue that none have produced tangible artifacts, biological samples, or other physical evidence that can be examined scientifically. Without such evidence, sceptics contend that the case for extraterrestrial visitation remains speculative at best.

Scientific and Technological Challenges Skeptics also point to the immense scientific and technological challenges involved in interstellar travel. Given the vast distances between stars, the energy requirements and technological capabilities needed for extraterrestrial civilizations to reach Earth are mind-boggling. Skeptics argue that these challenges make the likelihood of frequent extraterrestrial visits to Earth extremely low, and they emphasize the need for more plausible explanations that fit within our current understanding of physics and cosmology.

The Believer's Perspective

Believers in UFOs and extraterrestrial life often approach the subject with an openness to the possibility that humanity is not alone in the universe. Their perspective is shaped by a combination of personal experiences, anecdotal evidence, and a sense of curiosity about the unknown.

Accumulation of Eyewitness Accounts Believers argue that the sheer volume of eyewitness accounts and reports of UFO sightings cannot be easily dismissed. They contend that while individual sightings might be explainable, the consistency of certain patterns across different reports suggests something more significant. Believers often emphasize that many witnesses are credible individuals, including pilots, military personnel, and law enforcement officers, whose testimonies deserve serious consideration.

Government Disclosures and Whistle-blower Testimonies In recent years, the release of government documents and the testimonies of whistle-blowers have bolstered the believer's case. For instance, the U.S. government's acknowledgment of UAPs and the existence of programs like the Advanced Aerospace Threat Identification Program (AATIP) have lent credibility to claims that unidentified aerial phenomena warrant further investigation. Believers argue that these disclosures are a step toward uncovering the truth about extraterrestrial visitation and that they validate years of civilian reports.

Historical and Cultural Evidence Believers often point to historical and cultural evidence as support for the idea that extraterrestrial beings have been interacting with humanity for millennia. Ancient texts, religious scriptures, and mythological stories from around the world contain references to beings that some interpret as extraterrestrial visitors. Believers suggest that these accounts, combined with ancient art and architecture that depict otherworldly figures, indicate a long-standing connection between humanity and extraterrestrial civilizations.

Unexplained Phenomena and High-Strangeness Cases While skeptics may attribute many UFO sightings to misidentifications, believers focus on cases that remain unexplained even after thorough investigation. These "high-strangeness" cases often involve multiple witnesses, physical effects (such as radiation or electromagnetic interference), and detailed descriptions of craft and beings that defy conventional explanations. Believers argue that these cases provide compelling evidence of phenomena that cannot be easily dismissed by current scientific understanding.

The Search for Meaning and the Potential for Contact Beyond the evidence, many believers are motivated by a deep-seated curiosity and a search for meaning. The possibility of contact with extraterrestrial civilizations represents a profound and exciting frontier for humanity, offering the potential for new knowledge, cultural exchange, and a greater understanding of our place in the universe. For believers, the pursuit of this possibility is worth the risk of being wrong, as the potential rewards could be transformative for humanity.

The Impact of the Debate

The ongoing debate between sceptics and believers has far-reaching implications, influencing public discourse, scientific research, and cultural attitudes. It also highlights the challenges of reconciling different worldviews and approaches to understanding the unknown.

Encouraging Scientific Inquiry Despite their differences, both skeptics and believers contribute to the advancement of scientific inquiry. Skeptics push for rigorous standards of evidence and critical thinking, ensuring that extraordinary claims are subjected to thorough scrutiny. Believers, on the other hand, often inspire curiosity and drive the search for new discoveries, challenging the scientific community to explore unconventional ideas and expand the boundaries of knowledge.

Polarization and Public Perception The debate can sometimes lead to polarization, with each side viewing the other as closed-minded or irrational. This polarization is often exacerbated by media portrayals that sensationalize the topic or reduce it to a simple binary of "true believers" versus "hard-nosed sceptics." This dynamic can create barriers to productive dialogue and make it difficult for people to engage with the subject in a nuanced way.

The Role of the Media and Popular Culture Media and popular culture play a significant role in shaping the debate, often amplifying the voices of both sceptics and believers. While this can lead to greater public awareness and interest, it can also contribute to the spread of misinformation and the entrenchment of extreme positions. Responsible media coverage is essential for fostering a balanced and informed discussion that respects the complexities of the issue.

Bridging the Gap Bridging the gap between sceptics and believers requires mutual respect and a willingness to engage with different perspectives. Both sides can benefit from recognizing the value in each other's approaches: sceptics can appreciate the curiosity and open-mindedness of believers, while believers can acknowledge the importance of critical thinking and empirical evidence. By fostering a dialogue that emphasizes common goals—such as the pursuit of truth and the exploration of the unknown—sceptics and believers can work together to advance our understanding of UFOs and extraterrestrial life.

The Potential for Consensus As more data and evidence become available, there is potential for a growing consensus on certain aspects of the UFO phenomenon. For example, both skeptics and believers might agree on the need for further investigation of UAPs, particularly in the context of national security. Additionally, the scientific community's increasing interest in the search for extraterrestrial life (through projects like SETI) could provide common ground for skeptics and believers to collaborate on research that benefits both perspectives.

The debate between sceptics and believers is an ongoing and dynamic conversation that reflects broader tensions between science, curiosity, and the human desire for meaning. While the two sides often approach the subject from different angles, their interaction is essential for a balanced exploration of the UFO phenomenon and the possibility of extraterrestrial life.

As the conversation continues to evolve, it is important for both sceptics and believers to remain open to new evidence, to engage in respectful dialogue, and to recognize the shared goal of understanding the mysteries of the universe. Whether or not the truth about UFOs and extraterrestrial life is ultimately revealed, the debate itself is a testament to humanity's enduring fascination with the unknown and our relentless pursuit of knowledge.

Conclusion: Humanity's Place in the Universe

As we reach the conclusion of our exploration into the many facets of extraterrestrial life, UFO phenomena, and the ongoing debates surrounding them, we are left with profound questions about humanity's place in the universe. This journey has taken us through the realms of science, conspiracy, skepticism, and belief, each offering its own perspective on the mysteries that have captivated human imagination for generations. Now, it is time to reflect on what these inquiries and explorations mean for us as a species, and how they shape our understanding of our role in the cosmos.

The Search for Truth

At the heart of humanity's fascination with UFOs and extraterrestrial life is a fundamental quest for truth. This search is driven by our innate curiosity, our desire to understand the world around us, and our need to find meaning in our existence. Whether we are seeking to uncover hidden secrets through rigorous scientific investigation or exploring the possibilities through speculation and belief, the pursuit of truth unites us in our efforts to comprehend the universe. The possibility of extraterrestrial life challenges us to expand our horizons, to question what we know, and to remain open to new discoveries. It invites us to consider the vastness of the cosmos and the myriad forms that life might take. This search for truth is not just about finding answers to specific questions—such as whether we are alone in the universe—but about embracing the journey of exploration itself, with all its uncertainties and surprises.

The Role of Science and Inquiry

Science has always been humanity's most reliable tool for understanding the natural world. Through observation, experimentation, and the application of reason, science has allowed us to make sense of phenomena that were once beyond our grasp. In the context of UFOs and extraterrestrial life, science provides a framework for separating fact from fiction, for testing hypotheses, and for pushing the boundaries of what we know. However, science is not infallible, and it operates within the limits of current knowledge and technology.

The study of UFOs and the search for extraterrestrial life challenge scientists to remain open to possibilities that may lie outside established paradigms. As we continue to develop new tools and technologies, our capacity to explore the cosmos—and to potentially detect signs of other civilizations—will only grow. This interplay between skepticism and open-mindedness is essential for progress. By maintaining a rigorous approach to inquiry while also allowing for the exploration of unconventional ideas, science can help us navigate the complex and often ambiguous territory of extraterrestrial phenomena.

Cultural and Philosophical Implications

The possibility of extraterrestrial life carries profound cultural and philosophical implications. It forces us to reconsider long-held beliefs about our uniqueness, our origins, and our place in the grand scheme of things. The discovery of intelligent life beyond Earth would be one of the most significant events in human history, prompting a re-evaluation of our understanding of life, consciousness, and the nature of the universe. Religions and spiritual traditions would need to grapple with the implications of such a discovery, potentially leading to new interpretations of sacred texts and the development of new theological frameworks.

Philosophers would be challenged to rethink concepts of identity, morality, and the nature of existence in a universe populated by multiple intelligent species. Culturally, the idea of contact with extraterrestrial beings could inspire a renaissance of creativity and innovation. It could lead to new forms of art, literature, and music that explore the possibilities of interstellar communication, coexistence, and the exchange of knowledge. It could also prompt humanity to unite in the face of the unknown, fostering a sense of global solidarity and shared purpose.

Humanity's Responsibility

As we contemplate the potential for contact with extraterrestrial civilizations, we must also consider our responsibilities as stewards of Earth and as potential members of a broader cosmic community. How we conduct ourselves—both in our interactions with each other and with any other species we might encounter—will define our legacy in the universe. This responsibility extends to how we care for our planet, how we manage our technological advancements, and how we approach the ethical challenges of contact. The discovery of extraterrestrial life could serve as a wake-up call, reminding us of the fragility of our existence and the need to preserve the conditions that make life possible. Moreover, if we are to engage with other intelligent beings, we must do so with humility, respect, and a commitment to peaceful coexistence. This means developing diplomatic protocols, ethical guidelines, and a framework for communication that reflects our highest ideals. It also means being prepared to learn from other civilizations, to embrace new perspectives, and to evolve as a species in response to the knowledge we gain.

The Future of Humanity in the Cosmos

The exploration of UFOs and extraterrestrial life is not just about answering specific questions—it is about understanding our place in the cosmos and our potential future as an interstellar species. As we continue to explore space, develop new technologies, and seek out other forms of life, we are laying the groundwork for a future in which humanity may one day reach beyond our solar system and join a broader community of intelligent beings. This vision of the future is both exciting and daunting. It challenges us to think on a grand scale, to consider the long-term trajectory of our species, and to imagine the possibilities that lie ahead. Will we become explorers of the stars, ambassadors of Earth, and contributors to a cosmic civilization? Or will we remain confined to our home planet, isolated and unaware of the life that may exist just beyond our reach?

Conclusion: Embracing the Unknown

As we conclude this exploration, it is clear that humanity's place in the universe is still largely a mystery. We are a young species on a small planet, orbiting a relatively ordinary star in a galaxy full of wonders. The universe is vast, and we have only just begun to scratch the surface of its mysteries.

Yet, it is this very vastness and mystery that drives us to explore, to ask questions, and to seek out the unknown. Whether we ultimately discover that we are alone in the cosmos or that we are part of a rich tapestry of life, our journey of exploration will continue to define us as a species. In the end, it is not just the answers we find that matter, but the pursuit of knowledge, the spirit of inquiry, and the willingness to embrace the unknown. As we look to the stars and contemplate the possibilities, we are reminded that humanity's place in the universe is not fixed—it is something we are still in the process of discovering, shaping, and creating.

Our journey is far from over, and the universe still holds many secrets. As we move forward, let us do so with curiosity, courage, and a deep respect for the mysteries that await us. In this quest, we are not just seeking to understand the universe—we are also seeking to understand ourselves, our potential, and our place in the grand cosmic story.

Don't miss out!

Visit the website below and you can sign up to receive emails whenever Andrew Parry publishes a new book. There's no charge and no obligation.

https://books2read.com/r/B-A-FROLC-EWDCF

BOOKS 2 READ

Connecting independent readers to independent writers.

About the Author

Andrew Parry is a writer whose fascination with the great thinkers, philosophers, and the nature of reality deeply influences his work. His writing is shaped by an enduring curiosity about the fundamental questions of existence—what it means to be human, how we understand the world around us, and the intricate relationships between thought, perception, and reality. Through his exploration of these themes, Andrew seeks to provoke thoughtful reflection and open new pathways of understanding for his readers.

Read more at https://lonetrail.blog.